God, Freedom, and the Body of Christ

God, Freedom, and the Body of Christ

Toward a Theology of the Church

Alexander J. D. Irving

FOREWORD BY
Graham McFarlane

CASCADE *Books* · Eugene, Oregon

GOD, FREEDOM AND THE BODY OF CHRIST
Toward a Theology of the Church

Cascade Books
An Imprint of Wipf and Stock Publishers
199 W. 8th Ave., Suite 3
Eugene, OR 97401

www.wipfandstock.com

PAPERBACK ISBN: 978-1-7252-5855-6
HARDCOVER ISBN: 978-1-7252-5856-3
EBOOK ISBN: 978-1-7252-5857-0

Cataloguing-in-Publication data:

Names: Irving, Alexander J. D., author. | McFarlane, Graham, foreword.

Title: God, freedom and the body of Christ : toward a theology of the church / by Alexander J. D. Irving ; foreword by Graham McFarlane.

Description: Eugene, OR : Cascade Books, 2020 | Includes bibliographical references and index.

Identifiers: ISBN 978-1-7252-5855-6 (paperback) | ISBN 978-1-7252-5856-3 (hardcover) | ISBN 978-1-7252-5857-0 (ebook)

Subjects: LCSH: Church—History of doctrines—20th century. | Church. | Theology, Doctrinal.

Classification: BV600.3 .I78 2020 (print) | BV600.3 .I78 (ebook)

Manufactured in the U.S.A.   10/08/20

To Rachael

Contents

Foreword

In his poem "History Repeats Itself," poet Steve Turner reminds us that

History repeats itself,

it has to,

nobody listens.

There's a Hegelian ring here: Hegel himself held similar sentiments regarding history, namely, that the one thing "we learn from history" is "that we do not learn from history." Indeed! A quick glance over the history of trinitarian theology serves only to evidence the veracity of this point in relation to certain aspects of Christian truth. For over one and a half millennia Christian faith affirmed the triune nature of the God we name "Father" who has been supremely revealed to us through the incarnation, the life, death, resurrection, ascension, and glorification of his Son, Jesus Christ, and by whose Pentecost Spirit we give breath to our own confession of faith, Abba, Father. However, by the nineteenth century the Western Church found its theological voice in the great Schleiermacher who relocated the cornerstone doctrine of the Trinity to the appendix of his *The Christian Faith*. What Schleiermacher could not foresee, however, was the very short time it would take to move from appendix to complete amnesia. No one listened. Nothing was learned.

Or so it was thought. In this postmodern turn where everything once relegated to the margins of modern thought is now centerstage, there were voices—once ignored, volume turned down, forgotten—that fought to be heard above the deconstruction of modernity in the wake of progress. One such voice was Edward Irving, a Scot in London exile, whose biblical theology led him to oppose the Unitarianism he encountered in his Islington-Holborn parish with a robust trinitarian theology that could have been lifted straight from the Cappadocian Fathers, with a dash of Puritan John

Owen as well as Anglican Richard Hooker. His passion for the Kirk along with his own Caledonian spirit drove him to fight the impending trinitarian amnesia he so precociously anticipated.

Once amnesia kicks in, of course, anything goes. For the next century and a half it did so theologically, until another precocious thinker, Karl Barth, began to remember what had been forgotten, what had not been learned. The rest, as it were, is history—history repeating itself. And within this repetition, my own trinitarian enlightenment occurred when, in pursuing my doctoral studies with perhaps the most significant English-speaking trinitarian agitator in the second half of the twentieth century, the late Colin Gunton, I was introduced to this fellow Scot, Edward Irving, who had been fascinated by the relation between Christ and the Spirit. Then, somewhat serendipitously, a descendent of Edward Irving becomes one of my students at the London School of Theology. History may be forgetful, but the God and Father of our Lord Jesus Christ forgets nothing. And so, the trinitarian legacy of Edward Irving is gifted to his own descendent via a fellow Scot. What had been forgotten begins to take root and as a result of his own doctoral studies into another Scot, T. F. Torrance, under the tutelage of Alistair McGrath, another Irving Churchman, Alex Irving, takes up the theological baton, as it were, and addresses the great challenge of his own generation: the trinitarian identity of the Church.

All in all, it is quite delightful to be able to see the creative weaving of the triune God at work in connecting such disparate human threads in what is a much greater kingdom tapestry. It is equally delightful to be given the opportunity to offer some words in this foreword about this book's author, Alex Irving. Clearly, he comes from stubborn Scottish stock, albeit unwittingly given his thoroughly English backdrop. It is a peculiarly *trinitarian* stubbornness, too, one that is unwilling to relinquish the biblical and theological identity of the Church. And like his forefather, Alex does not make reading easy in places, not because the writing is obtuse, but rather due to the rich theological and trinitarian vein he wants his reader to recover from its ecclesial neglect. In particular, I am delighted to read how Alex introduces his reader to a notion very dear to Gunton: the freedom of God to allow creation—and therefore the new creation—to be what it was created to be. Alex is advocating for a robust doctrine of creation in this book—something lacking in contemporary conversation. For Alex it is quite clear: the necessity of a theological understanding of creation will determine the veracity of one's understanding of the Church. Both creation and Church are products of the two hands of God, the Word, and the Spirit. More importantly, the latter—the trinitarian face of creation—is a necessary foundation for what Alex wants to say about the Church. That is, as *Church* we participate in

God's own mission to creation, we do our ecclesiology *missio Dei*. Of course, to understand how this is to happen, Alex moves us to the second key element in his trinitarian understanding of the Church—*participation*. I very much like the way Alex expresses his own thought in describing the Church as *the creature of the Word of God*. And the Church does so by participating in Christ. Here Alex makes very sensitive use of his own doctoral engagement with T. F. Torrance and the rich historical and theological tradition about which Torrance sought to remind the Church. In particular, you will be introduced to two relatively unknown and somewhat complex Greek terms that I shall leave for you, the reader, to discover—the Church's anhypostasic and the enhypostatic states of existence. Interestingly, these were two words his forefather was also comfortable in using in his day, albeit in relation to the head of the Church, Christ, rather than to the Church itself. Both are radically trinitarian terms and both are definitely worth getting your head around conceptually if you are to maximize the benefits you will glean from taking the time to read this book.

I hope that your knowledge of and love for the Church will be energized in reading this book. As Alex says in his opening pages, and I fully agree, there really is nothing within the universe more wonderful, more joyful than the Church of Jesus Christ. Alex wants you, the reader, to see the importance of the Church in knowing this *about* itself in order that it may *be* itself. Alex's aim in writing this book is that each one of us who make up this great creaturely and mystical reality—the Church of Jesus Christ—will know our ecclesial identity better. I most finished the book with a sense that Alex had achieved his goal for me, and I am sure his renowned predecessor would, too. I very much recommend you to read this book so that you might be reminded of what the contemporary Church has forgotten, learn it, and think of ways in which you might earth them in your own Church life and, in doing so, prove the Hegelian maxim wrong!

—Graham McFarlane

Preface

The Church is essentially more than it appears to be.

—Hans Küng, *The Church*

IF WE LOSE SIGHT of the truth that the Church is always more than it appears to be, we run a significant risk. This is the risk of mistaking the human institution that rubs along as part of the fabric of public life of society for only being a human institution. We could come to disconnect it from its actual reality in Jesus Christ. The Church has a theological character that needs to be always kept in view at every level of what we think about it. It is the creature of the Word of God, which has no existence outside of God's act. It is the temple of the Holy Spirit by whom we are incorporated into Jesus Christ and so share in his relation of Sonship to the Father. It is the body of Christ. This invisible union with Jesus Christ by the Spirit is the ground of our visible communion which is organized into a mode of life together (from where comes its character as an institution). The theological character of the Church does not exclude its humanity. Instead, it is the very ground of its full humanity. This strange dynamic in which the Church is both an event of the act of God and yet a fully human reality needs to be established on its proper ground, which is the person of Jesus. The Church has a mode of existence that is characterized by the same logic as the union of the divine nature and human nature in the person of the Son incarnate. The quality of existence of Jesus' human nature is that is dependent on the act of God the Son assuming it into union with himself for personal existence, yet the human nature of Jesus is fully and unqualifiedly human within the person of the Son. Bearing the same logic of existence, the Church must be thought of, at one and the same time, in the aspect of its *dependence* on the act of God as the creature of the Word of God and also in its *freedom* as a human institution, given its own distinct existence not as a response to God's grace but within the distinct reality of Jesus' vicarious humanity.

The body of Christ provides us with a central designation for the Church by which these aspects of the Church can be explored. The Church is what it is by merit of its incorporation into Christ by the Spirit and we share all that Jesus is before the Father. The whole of Jesus now includes his Church, for he is the head of which we are the body. The Church also continues as an earthly-historical reality, awaiting the final and full consummation of its unity with Jesus Christ in the Age to Come. However, the freedom of the Church as a human institution does not exist outside its personal dependence on the act of God, but within it. The Church is not a separate human response to the grace of God but a participation in the humanity of Jesus Christ, who shared our embodied existence so that we might share in his.

—A. J. D. Irving, The Feast of Christ the King, 2019

Acknowledgments

I AM GRATEFUL TO the Reverend Canon Madeline Light and Biddy Collyer. Our conversations were the creative space in which the central idea of this book became sharper in my mind.

This book is indebted to Dr. Graham McFarlane of the London School of Theology, who was the first to introduce me to a dialogical and trinitarian frame for theology.

I am also very thankful to those who read either the whole manuscript or individual chapters at various stages of completion. Particularly, I am grateful to the Reverend Johnny Douglas, Barbara Irving, and Adam Poole who provided insightful and encouraging feedback on the whole text. My thanks also goes to the Reverend Canon Alan Strange, Dr. Ian Fifield, and Bobby Grow who read individual chapters and whose contribution has enhanced the clarity of this work considerably.

I am very grateful to my former student Jacob Hussain for his help with the index.

My thinking in this book has been informed by my experiences of ordained ministry at St Stephen's Church in Norwich. I am immensely grateful to my Church family at St Stephen's for their patience with me as I have learnt and for all they have taught me about openness to God and one other.

Sophia, my wife, remains my most significant partner in every way, including theologically. My gratitude to her and love for her grows every day.

Introduction

BOTH FROM WITHOUT AND from within the Church suffers a range of disturbing influences. It is undermined from the inside by our own failures to conduct ourselves with integrity and lawfulness and its clarity of purpose is eroded by the way we prioritize agendas that are at best tangential (and at worst contradictory) to the mission of Jesus Christ. There is a loss of confidence in what the Church is and a loss of clarity about the gospel of which it is a witness. There is an obsession with removing grounds for disbelief in the place of a positive proclamation of the gospel. Forgetting that "the relevance of the Church can never be easier than the relevance of the Messiah,"[1] we have become more concerned with being acceptable to our culture than with understanding it so that we might best actualize the gospel in its own distinctive concerns and modes of thought. In some quarters, we have become so infatuated with a quest for *personal* experience that we have neglected the *collective* experience of the Church in being united to Jesus Christ in his self-offering to the Father. We have neglected the historic practices instituted by Christ to maintain his Church as his body before his return in a rushed panic that these are no longer effective to the mode of being of modern people, so we must find new ways of invigorating and growing the body of Jesus Christ. In other quarters, we have become defensive of our embattled traditions and sacraments and so we double down upon them, stressing their centrality and efficacy such that we forget that they are miracles of our union with Jesus and so, by definition, come from beyond the Church and are not self-generated tools used for self-perpetuation.

Despite all of this, there is nothing within this universe more wonderful, more joyful than the Church of Jesus Christ. The Church is that in which the dialogue of God and creation in the person of Jesus is celebrated and lived within. The Church is that which knows itself not to be

---

1. Ramsey, *Gospel and the Catholic Church*, 4.

an accident or a chance of fate, but to have actively been called into being by God. The Church is the body of Christ; that which is joined to Jesus Christ in the power of the Holy Spirit through word and sacrament. As the body of Christ, the Church is as one person with Jesus and shares in all he is before the Father. Through this inclusion, the Church is welcomed within the Son into the very life of the triune God. As the body of Christ, the true human, the Church is that in which true humanity can be lived.[2] As such the Church is the most real and the most gloriously human of all things: a loving community of believers released to be orientated to one another in reciprocal love.

The Church's only need is to know and to be itself. We are what we are by sharing in Christ. Jesus is what he is individually and directly. We are what we are corporately and by participating in him. He is the Son of God and we, in him, are the children of God. He is the priest of God and we, in him, are a nation of priests. He is the light of the glory of God and we, in him, are the light of the world. He is the Apostle of the Father who reveals the Father and we, in him, are an apostolic Church sent out into the world. He is the savior of the world who has universal relevance and we, in him, are a catholic Church who cannot fall out of relevance if we hold to the gospel. Our greatest need is not a new strategy or a new religious community. All we need is to understand what we are and to be what we are.[3]

This book sets out to help the Church know itself as the body of Christ. The approach taken is to ground what we think about the Church upon what we think about God made known in Jesus Christ. This, then, is an attempt to think about the Church in a self-consciously *theological* way (as opposed to a more internally focused ecclesiology which is focused on how different elements of the phenomena of the Church relate to one another). For example, what we think about the Church as something that is brought into being by the grace of God through Christ and by the Spirit needs to be understood in relation to what it means for God to be Creator. Similarly, what we think about the Church as that which is brought into communion with God needs to be understood in relation to the way God has his life as communion in his non-transitive relations. This gives our thinking about the Church an objective

2. An engaging study of the Church as the locus of divinely given abundance of life and how this might inform its structures and missional agenda has recently been contributed by Sam Wells. Wells, *Future That's Bigger than the Past*, 2–3 and 38–51. However, the accent of my work falls more firmly on the theological character of the Church as the body of Christ and how that informs its doxology, governance, and corporate life.

3. A similar conviction has been articulated in relation to pastoral ministry by Andrew Root. Root, *Pastor in a Secular Age*.

character, for it establishes meaning not within our own Church traditions but beyond itself upon the grace and being of God.

The Church is brought into existence through being incorporated into Jesus by the Spirit. Such a way of thinking of the Church lends a priority to its designation as the body of Christ. As the body of Christ, the Church is defined by who Jesus is and what he has accomplished both from the side of God and from the side of humanity. The essence of the Church is Jesus Christ. As the body of which Christ is the head, the Church is as one person with Jesus and yet distinct from him. This means that Jesus is our vicarious representative before the Father and we share in his filial relation to the Father in the power of the Holy Spirit. All Jesus is now includes the Church. Therefore, no aspect of the Church's life can be thought of as running in parallel to but not coinciding with Jesus and what he has accomplished as one of us and for all of us. The Church participates in Christ as that which is united to Jesus and shares in his life of obedience, praise, and self-giving to the Father.

The following chapters articulate a theology of the Church as that which participates in all that Jesus is in his vicarious humanity accomplished as one of us and for all of us in the power of the Spirit. This is developed within a dialogical (or covenantal) frame which has its focal point in Christ in whom the faithful love of God toward creation and the faithful love of creation toward God is actualized. The Church as the body of Christ participates in the mediatorial work of Jesus Christ. Each chapter explores a different element of this participatory ecclesiology.

This is not a systematic ecclesiology. It does not intend to say all there is to say about the Church. Nor does it set out to penetrate into the minutiae of technical ecclesiology, although some technical discussion is unavoidable. Instead, this book is a movement toward a theology of the Church which has a pneumatologically enabled union with Jesus Christ and participation in all he is before the Father at its center. It is organized around a range of themes that have their focal point on participation in Jesus. These include (i) a covenantal understanding of creation, centering on Jesus as both the faithful love of God toward creation and the answering faithful obedience of humanity toward God; (ii) the freedom of God and the corresponding freedom of creation with the inner logic of that relationship displayed in the person of Jesus, specifically the unity of two natures in one person without confusion or separation; (iii) the triunity of God and how this shapes the life of the community of the Church through our indwelling in the triune relations through Christ; (iv) the parallel between creation and the Church as creatures of the grace of God which can be delineated through the Christological logic of absolute dependence and real, human existence. The themes of covenant, freedom, and communion coalesce in the designation of the Church as the body of Christ. This designation for the Church causes us to think of it in its absolute dependence on being brought into union with Jesus and also in its distinct existence as a human institution.

Chapter Outline

What we think and say about the Church is dependent upon other areas of theology. The Church is not a source of our knowledge of God. Instead, speaking about the Church is a derivative discipline which takes its lead from the constitutive sources of theology. Even methodologically speaking, Jesus Christ and the Spirit (as the objective and subjective conditions of all theology) condition our thinking about the Church. This basic commitment to the knowledge of God as an event of the grace of God conditions our thinking about the Church from the outset.

In the first chapter, the Church is examined in relation to the dialogical character of God's relation to creation. This chapter functions as a thematic introduction to the central dynamic of the chapters that follow. God is not an arbitrary creator. God created in the freedom of his triune life and in the freedom of his being as the one who loves. There is no rationale for creation aside from the love of God. The mode of existence creation enjoys is the beloved of God. This rooting of creation in the love of God means that there is an inherently *covenantal* structure to creation. Creation, by fact of its existence as the beloved of God, is the covenant partner of God. It bears the responsibility of making a response to the Creator who made it from nothing. This identity and associated responsibility are both focused through humanity as the image of God. Subsequently it is focused through Israel as the nation of priests. Ultimately, however, it is in Jesus Christ who is both Apostle and High Priest, the full and perfect Word of God to humanity in love and mercy and also the full and perfect response of humanity to God in obedience and faith that this covenantal dialogue is perfectly expressed. The Church as a nation of priests is that which participates in Christ and shares in his Sonship. As the body of Christ, the Church is included in the complete dialogue of God and creation. In all the Church does, it joins itself to what Christ has already done as one of us and for all of us.

The second chapter considers the Church in relation to the doctrine of creation. This is the Church established as a creature of the Word of God. This provides the necessary context within which the meaning of the Church as the body of Christ should be understood. Significant differences in the dialects by which different instantiations of the one Church of Jesus Christ speak of the Church can be relativized by recognizing that the Church as a creature of the Word of God is inseparably related to the Church as the body of Christ. Further, this chapter provides the Christological principles to understand the Church as dependent on the act of God and yet still in possession of its own discrete human existence. The heuristic device of *freedom*, parsed in trinitarian terms (as opposed to metaphysical or philosophical terms), is employed here. God, in the infinite perfection of his triune relations, is free from creation. God does not need creation and he is what he is in the fullness of his own triune life. Yet, God chooses to extend beyond himself in a fellowship-making act of creation. On the grounds that God is the Lord of his own existence in his own inner (non-transitive) relations, God's outer (transitive) relations to creation do not constitute who and what he is. A trinitarian account of freedom, therefore, provides a basis upon God is free from creation and free to enter relation with creation, without surrendering his transcendent freedom from creation. Correspondingly, creation is free but not in the same way that God is. God's freedom is absolute, but creation's freedom is *contingent*. God calls creation into being from nothing and gives it its own character and existence quite distinct from his own.

The grammar by which we can understand the relationship between God's absolute freedom and creation's contingent freedom is given to us in the person of Jesus. The humanity of Jesus Christ is utterly dependent upon being assumed into union with God the Son for personal existence (*anhypostasia*). However, the nonexistence of the human person Jesus Christ aside from the hypostatic union does not compromise the full reality of his human nature. Instead, its dependence on the act of God is the very foundation of its personal existence. The human nature of Jesus has a complete and uncompromised existence and historical particularity in the person of the Son (*enhypostasia*). Likewise, creation has the quality that its existence is utterly dependent on the act of God and the non-necessity of creation is the ground of its distinct reality. It has, in short, contingent freedom. The same structure of dependence and freedom is at work in the Church. As a creature of the Word of God, the Church bears a mode of existence which is parallel to creation's mode of existence. The Church does not emerge out from humanity, like any other human option within the freedom of humanity like a cricket match, or a political party. Instead, the Church is a creature of the Word of God, which intersects with creation from beyond it. As a creature of the Word of God, the Church is both absolutely dependent on God in that without God's act it would not exist. Yet, it is also distinct from God in that God gives to it its own distinct reality and historical particularity as the Church. This dynamic is explicated using a Christological grammar in chapters 4 and 5.

The third chapter presents an understanding of the Church as it participates in the communion of the triune God through its incorporation into Jesus. Certainly, the Church is brought into being by the act of the triune God: the Church exists by the will of the Father through the Son in the power of the Spirit. However, the Church is not only brought into being *by* the triune God, it is also brought into being *for relation* with the triune God. By our Spirit-powered incorporation into Christ who has ascended to the Father's right hand, the Church is included in the filial relation of Son to the Father. It has become the common coinage of modern discussion about the Church to say that the Church resembles the life of the triune God in its own relations and structures. This is a dimension of the Church which is riddled with both opportunities and pitfalls. We must not, for example, reverse the movement and begin to think about God in a way that takes its formative movements from the character of the Church. The movement of thought must follow the logic of grace: it must be from God down to us. For this reason, the discussion of this dimension tracks closely to Karl Barth's principle of the analogy of relations. However, there is another pitfall that we need to keep squarely in view when approaching this topic. This is the whole area of *imitation*. It is important to stress that the Church does not resemble the triune communion by imitation alone. If one were to assert that the Church resembles the life of God by imitation, that would be to establish the Church as a parallel human response to God's act. If the Church resembles the divine communion, it is only because it *indwells* the triune communions through its participation in the person of Jesus. Therefore, this chapter gives an account of how the triune communion shapes the ecclesial communion which prioritizes the category of participation.

The fourth and fifth chapters come together as two aspects of the Church's participation in Jesus. Governing this discussion is the designation of the Church as the body of Christ and the themes that have been raised in the previous chapters converge in this designation. The Church is the body of which Jesus Christ is the head such that the whole Christ (*totus Christus*) now includes the Church, while Christ remains distinct from the Church as the head is distinct from body. The very essence of the Church is Jesus Christ. Certainly, we cannot talk about the Church aside from this fundamental relation which has its very foundation stone in the incarnation, where God the Son shared our flesh and bone such that we may share in him as his body. Of course, the vicarious humanity of Jesus is of central importance here. It is because Jesus shared our embodied existence that we may be incorporated into his body. The organizing principle of these chapters is the nature of the relation between the divine nature and the human nature of Jesus Christ. This relationship is again delineated using the

Christological grammar of *anhypostasia* and *enhypostasia*. This refers to the belief that the quality of Jesus' humanity is that it has no independent personal existence and it only exists on account of being assumed into union with the divine Son (*anhypostasia*). However, because of being assumed into personal union with God the Son, Jesus' human nature does have actual existence in the Son (*enhypostasia*). The human nature of Jesus, therefore, does not exist independently from its union with God the Son, but it does exist as human nature within the person of the Son.

The normative significance of Jesus Christ in understanding the relation of God and creation is the foundation of a structural affinity between the Church and creation. Both the Church and creation depend on the act of God for their existence yet have their own distinct existence within that dependence. It is, therefore, not only practically expedient but theologically necessary to discuss the distinct existence of the Church as a human institution. However, any discussion of the Church as an institution must recognize the Church only exists within the person of the Son and it is dependent upon that union for its existence. In this connection, the consideration of the Church in the aspect of human institution must be undertaken with stress laid upon the vicarious humanity of Jesus. To fail to integrate what we think about the Church with the vicarious humanity of Jesus Christ causes significant ecclesiological errors, in which the Church becomes a parallel institution in which we make our own distinct human response to the act of God. If, however, we hold the vicarious humanity of Jesus Christ in the center of our thinking (i.e., that what Jesus did in the flesh he did as one of us and for all of us), then the Church, even in its institutional expression, is more appropriately understood as our participation in what Jesus has already accomplished. This method of approach, I believe, sketches out an important way forward for ecumenical theology, particularly over the question of the relationship between the Church as an event of the grace of God and the Church as an institution which persists through time.

The fourth chapter examines the Church in the aspect of its having no personal existence aside from union with the Son and so in its dependence on being assumed into union with Jesus Christ by the Spirit (the *anhypostatic* aspect). In this discussion, John Calvin's setting of salvation as participation in Jesus is identified as salient in relation to Paul's soteriology, particularly as it relates to Paul's use of the designation "the body of Christ" for the Church. The designation of the body of Christ as the character of our participation in him is discussed in relation to the soteriological arc of the New Testament, in which Jesus shares our embodied existence and our relationship with God so that we may share in his body. Such an association of the core aspect of salvation with the nature of the Church (i.e., participation in Jesus) places

significant, although not exclusive, emphasis on the sacraments. By baptism
we are incorporated into the body of Christ and it is by the Eucharist that
we sustain our unity with him.

The fifth chapter considers the Church in the aspect of its distinct
existence within the person of the Son as a human society and institution
that has a real earthly and particular historical existence (the *enhypostatic*
aspect). This is the way of thinking about the Church which recognizes that
within its dependence on being given life by the direct act of God in Christ
by the Spirit, the Church really does exist as a human reality. In this sense,
there is a strong parallel between the Church and creation itself. The difference, however, is that the Church is *self-conscious* that its discrete existence
is a gift of God. This discrete existence of the Church within its dependence
on the act of God is considered in three areas: order, liturgy, and relationship
to the world. In each of these areas, the Church expresses its distinct reality
as a human institution. Crucially, however, none of these emerge from out
of the common life of the Church in and of itself. Instead, the visible aspects
of the Church's life are themselves directly derived from the Gospel itself.
For example, Church order is not the Church organizing its common life
together in accordance with principles that will facilitate its common life. Instead, Church order is the direct result of the means of Jesus' Lordly presence
with us through Word and sacrament. Faith and order are not in parallel; the
latter grows out from the former because the human reality of the Church is
grounded in the assumption and healing of our humanity by God the Son.
The vicarious humanity of Jesus is central here. In our liturgy, for example,
we do not offer praise and worship that is parallel to and separate from Jesus.
Instead, we offer a common expression of praise as the body of Jesus, joining
in with Jesus' own sacrifice of praise to the Father on the cross. There is one
human praise held in common by the Church and Jesus Christ, Jesus is the
active agent of praise and we, through our liturgy, participate in what he has
achieved as one of us and for all of us.

It will perhaps be clear from this brief summary of the chapters that
lie ahead that this book does not intend to be an exhaustive ecclesiology.
Much remains unsaid, principally about the pneumatological and eschatological character of the Church. This book, therefore, is intended as an
opening volume to at least one other consideration of the theological character of the Church.

1

Dialogue and Participation

THE COINCIDENCE OF INDIVIDUALS brings something new into being. That new thing is the relationship itself, the bond of love between the two. In a relationship each individual retains their own identity and distinct character. Just like two lengths of string that get wrapped up with one another remain two distinct lengths of string, so also individuals coalesce and remain distinct. The emergence of a relationship, then, is not like a chemical reaction. It is not the transformation of two elements into something else by their coming together. Instead, this is something much more like music. When you play several notes at one time, together they form something which none of the notes could be by themselves. They form a different unity, something textured and nuanced which is only possible by the coincidence of those particular notes. The notes that make up that new sound are not lost in that unity. It is just that their own sound is now deposited in the unity of the chord. In the same way, our lives are brought into union with the lives of others. As our lives intertwine a new reality is created, something that one life alone could never be: a relationship, a communion.

Scripture gives witness to the act of God by which creation is established as his corresponding other. In doing so, both God and creation are invested in the new thing that is made: a relationship, a *covenant*. The dialogue within this relationship is the faithful love from the side of God met by the faithful love from the side of creation. However, in the coming to being of something new, God and creation remain what they are in all their radical difference. At the very center of this dialogue is the person of Jesus Christ in whom God and humanity come together without losing their respective integrities and in whom the love of God for creation is fully expressed and in whom the love of creation for God is fully expressed. The Church is that which is introduced into this complete dialogue through participation in Jesus by the power of the Spirit. At every stage, therefore, our thinking about the Church needs to be properly integrated with Jesus and the Spirit. Certainly, this means that the activity of the Church is not a human response to God running parallel, but external, to Christ establishing some new relationship between God and creation. Instead, the Church is one with Jesus, participating in him as the perfect-covenant partner of the Father.

This chapter sets out the broad theological landscape within which this theological consideration of the Church sits. Its purpose is to give some orientation to the themes of covenant and participation which are so central to understanding the Church as the body of Christ. It is intended to be introductory in tone and content. The foundation for ecclesiology that is articulated here is *dialogical*. God made creation to be his dialogue partner, meaning that God made creation in order to share his life with it, to bless it, and to receive the response of creation. The inner rationale of creation, in other words, is covenant relation. Creation is made to be in covenant with God, whereby the actuality of that covenant is not a development of creation to a higher calling than was initially purposed but is inherent within the very rationale of creation's existence. This covenant relationship is focused through humans, the image of God, the meeting point between God and the rest of creation through which God blesses creation and through which creation reciprocally praises God. This vocation of humanity is further concentrated through Israel which is to be a nation of priests, and, ultimately, through Jesus Christ. Jesus is the perfect image of God, the true Israel, in whom this dialogue between God and creation reaches full expression. The Church, as the body of Jesus Christ, participates in all Jesus is and as such the Church is that which is included in the reciprocal love between God the Father and Jesus Christ. In order to illustrate the theme, two aspects of the Church are coordinated to this participatory ecclesiology: worship and mission.

The Dialogue of God and Creation

Creation and Covenant

God does not need. As will be explored much more fully in the next chapter, God is free. God *chose* to make creation in the absolute freedom of what it is to be God. It is not as if God had something lacking in himself and so needed to create something else to answer that need. In bringing something that is not God into being, God is not determined by some other agenda that is external to his own will. It is also not as if God necessarily exists alongside something that is not God. At the very center of the mystery of the existence of creation is the fact that creation does not exist because God needs it. Nor does creation exist because God was compelled to make it, and creation certainly does not exist by sheer necessity of the way things have been, are, and always will be. This is the mystery of our existence: why does creation exist at all? Why, in his utter freedom, did God decide to make something else to exist alongside him? As Jürgen Moltmann has written, "This is the question of a child who is no longer a child."[1] Some light is shed on this mystery by the apostle Paul in the opening of his Letter to the Ephesians.

> Praise be to God the Father of our Lord Jesus Christ, who has blessed us in the heavenly realms with every spiritual blessing in Christ. For he chose us in him before the creation of the world to be holy and blameless in his sight. In love he predestined us to be adopted as his sons through Jesus Christ, in accordance with his pleasure and will—to the praise of his glorious grace, which he has freely given us in the One he loves. (Eph 1:3–6)

The choice of God was to create and adopt what he made into the blessing of his own life. God created so to draw what he created into relationship with himself, as adopted children through the work of the eternal Son Jesus Christ. The will of God in creating is to adopt us into positive relation with him, allowing us to share in a filial relation of sonship. We are created for the purpose of being the dialogue partner of God. We can put this another way: the mystery of our existence is answered only in the love of God. God created us in order to love us. Correspondingly, creation is to reciprocate with praise as the kindness and generosity of God is met by the thankfulness of his creatures.

Jesus Christ stands at the center of this reciprocal relationship between God and his creation. The blessing which we receive from God comes to us "in Christ." The way we are adopted into the family of God is "through Jesus Christ." The glorious grace of God is given us in "the One he loves." The love of God is expressed towards creation through Jesus Christ. On the other hand, it is through Jesus Christ that we creatures respond with praise and thankfulness. As the doxology continues, we find out that God's ultimate purpose is "to bring all things in heaven and on earth together under the one head, even Christ" (Eph 1:10). All things that God has created are to be joined together under the headship of Jesus Christ, through whom "we have access to the Father by one Spirit" (Eph 2:18). This reciprocal relationship, this dialogue of the love of God and the answering love of creation, has its focal point in the person of Jesus Christ who, by the power of the Holy Spirit, reveals and enacts the love of God upon his creation and speaks back with creaturely words and lives of praise to God.

1. Moltmann, *Theology and Joy*, 39.

The phrase "turtles all the way down" has come to express the problem of the absence of foundations. Within the contested field of knowledge claims, it refers to the absence of a necessary truth upon which an argument may be built. What is needed is a statement which verifies itself. A truth which doesn't slip into dependence on another in order to be shown to be true; a still and solid point of rest upon which to build. However, this phrase is not only used with respect to logical argument. The cosmos, it is said, must have a sure foundation which requires no proof from beyond itself. Stephen Hawking made use of the phrase in referring to the mystery of the foundations of the universe.

> A well-known scientist (some say it was Bertrand Russell) once gave a public lecture on astronomy. He described how the earth orbits around the sun and how the sun, in turn, orbits around the centre of a vast collection of stars called our galaxy. At the end of the lecture, a little old lady at the back of the room got up and said: 'What you have told us is rubbish. The world is really a flat plate supported on the back of a giant tortoise.' The scientist gave a superior smile before replying, 'What is the tortoise standing on?' 'You're very clever, young man, very clever,' said the old lady. 'But it's turtles all the way down!'[2]

This exchange raises the question: what is it upon which the vast array we see around us is ultimately established on? Cosmologists can describe the universe in its beauty and power, but this doesn't provide an answer to the question as to what its foundation is. For some, it is arbitrary chance. For others, it is some fundamental coherence, some inner order or principle of constancy, which provides the coherence within which all variety participates without chaos. In Christian theology, *the love of God is its own foundation*. It is the reality of realities, the foundation on which all else must stand. What is it the world is standing on? The love of God. What is it the love of God is standing on? It's the love of God all the way down.

Creation exists because it is the beloved of God. It exists to be blessed by God and to be drawn into relationship with God, and to respond to all God's goodness with an answering love of its own. Henri du Lubac, for so long the *enfant terrible* of Roman Catholic theology but who came to become one of the architects of the theological reenvisioning of the Church in the Second Vatican Council, held that creation is orientated to God, and its purpose was within the fulfillment of that orientation.[3] By his insistence on this point, Lubac reminded the Church that it was created by God for the supernatural

---

2. Hawking, *Brief History of Time*, 1–2.
3. Lubac, *Mystery of the Supernatural*.

end of communion with God. Such a rationale for the existence of creation means that our very existence is tightly connected to the idea of *covenant*. A covenant is a relationship established upon mutual commitments, where these commitments are given formal expression as promises. A marriage, for example, is a form of covenant. It is a bond of love created between two people expressing mutual commitment which is expressed in the making of vows to one another. The relation of God and creation is covenantal in form in that God made creation in order to commit himself to it, to pour his love out upon it and to adopt it into relationship with himself. This love of God for creation calls out the response of creation to God, a reciprocal commitment articulated in praise and thanksgiving.

Karl Barth laid significant stress on the correlation between creation and covenant. First, the existence of creation is for the purpose of covenantal relationship with God: creation is "the external basis of the covenant."[4] Creation is the context for the reciprocal love of God and creation. It is the space in which the love of God is given to creation and in which creation responds with faith and love.[5] Second, the fact of that covenant is not a chance of history, it is the fulfillment of what God always intended for his creation: covenant is the "internal basis of creation."[6]

> The fact that covenant is the goal of creation is not something which is added later to the reality of the creature, as though the history of creation might equally have been succeeded by any other history. It already characterises creation itself and as such, and therefore, the being and existence of the creature.[7]

This means that the very character of created existence is to be in covenantal relationship with God. To be in this relationship of reciprocity with God is the very fabric of what it is to be a created thing. In Barth's theological vision, then, it is impossible to separate creation and covenant because they are bound together from the front and the back. The covenants of Scripture are the expression of this fundamental dialogical structure inherent in the very fact of the existence of creation.[8] For Barth, this meant that the proper way to engage in the Christian doctrine of creation is not to be preoccupied with questions such as how the universe came into being but rather in terms of its *purpose*. For Barth, the purpose of creation is enacted in Jesus Christ

4. Barth, *Church Dogmatics*, 3.1, 43.

5. Barth, *Church Dogmatics*, 3.1, 44.

6. Barth, *Church Dogmatics*, 3.1, 59. For a fuller discussion of this, see Webster, *Barth*, 96–98.

7. Barth, *Church Dogmatics*, 3.1, 231.

8. For more on the relationship between creation and covenant, see Dumbrell, *Faith of Israel*, 26; and Vogel, *God's Universal Covenant*.

in whom both the faithful love of God toward creation and the faithful love of creation to God are fully expressed.[9] In so doing, Barth was looking to integrate the doctrine of creation with other Christian doctrines, especially the doctrine of salvation (instead of the Christian doctrine of creation being more closely associated with the natural sciences or philosophy).[10] Barth's association between creation and covenant provides the foundation upon which to explore the close parallels between creation and the Church, with the latter being understood as creation living its purpose as the covenant partner of God through participating in Jesus Christ.

Humanity: The Covenant-Partner of God

The reciprocal love between God and creation is focused through humanity.[11] Humanity is that part of creation uniquely capable of hearing God's declaration of love *to* creation and responding with an answering love *from* creation. Humanity alone is responsible to receive the word of God and to give the corresponding answer. Within the broader frame of his proposed correlation of creation and covenant, Barth describes humankind's existence-as-answer to the word of God.

> The being of [humankind] is an answer, or more precisely, a being lived in the act of answering the Word of God, a being which in the creaturely sphere and as itself creaturely makes that address and return to God, to the God from whom it flows and in whose Word it is rooted. Called into life by the Word of God, it is not only a reception of His gift, but it fulfils the task of answering Him, and makes that address and return to Him ... To this extent it is an act of responsibility. [Humankind] is, and is human, as he performs this act of responsibility, offering himself as the response to the Word of God, and conducting, shaping and expressing himself as an answer to it. He is, and is [human], as he does this.[12]

For Barth, the locus of the covenant between God and creation is humanity. The human hears God's word and has her existence by way of an answer to that word. This responsibility is constitutive of our very humanity. To be human is to be that part of creation which has its existence as answer. For Barth, then, anthropology is not an independent discipline that can be

---

9. Barth, *Church Dogmatics*, 3.1, 232.

10. Webster, *Barth*, 97–98.

11. For a fuller exploration of this theme, see McFadyen, *Call to Personhood*, 17–44.

12. Barth, *Church Dogmatics*, 3.2, 175.

studied aside from the word of God. For this reason, he was critical of attempts to understand humanity from materialist or naturalist presuppositions alone (i.e., physiology, psychology, economics, sociology, etc.).[13] Ultimately, as will be shown below, for Barth, humanity can only be understood in relation to Christ who has his existence as a being-in-answer-to-God.

In part, this covenantal framing of human nature is to do with structural capacities unique to humanity, which facilitate its position as the focal point of the dialogue between God and creation. For example, one of the most long-standing understandings of the image of God involves human reason. In some ways, this has its roots in Aristotelian categories in which humanity is determined as a species within the genus of animals which is differentiated from the wider genus by its capacity to reason. This identification of reason as that which distinguishes humanity from other creatures is reflected in the Christian tradition. Take, for example, the following statement from Augustine: "God, then, made [humankind] in His own image. For He created [them] a soul endowed with reason and intelligence, so that he might excel all the creatures of earth, air and sea, which were not so gifted."[14]

There is a problem that is inherent to any particular approach to the structuralist understanding of the image of God that needs to be questioned. Why should it be reason that differentiates humankind as the image of God? Unless there is some undergirding principle, an approach to the image of God which focuses on one unique capacity or another runs the risk of allowing the prioritization of any arbitrary quality that a society happens to value. Whatever it means to image God, it must not be shaped by the contingencies of human culture. The greatest horrors of human history have taken place when the Christian Church allows God to become trapped within human self-understanding and the values of any given society. There are examples in living memory, including the Germanism of the Nazi party and the white supremacy of apartheid South Africa.

Underlying the idea that humanity images God by the capacity to reason is not some inherent structural likeness between humanity and God. That is the error that has been responsible for at least one tranche of the unimaginable evil of the twentieth century. Instead, reason as structural capacity is part of humanity's imaging of God because it is a faculty that makes it possible for humanity to be the counterpart of God on creation. Thomas Aquinas explained that reason is so central because it is by reason that *humans may know and love God*. It is a faculty which makes us uniquely capable of being in the distinctive relation to God that we are in as the image of God.

---

13. Barth, *Church Dogmatics*, 3.2, 20–22.

14. Augustine, *Civ.* 12.23.

Since humanity is said to be in the image of God by reason of his intellectual nature, he is most perfectly like God according to that in which he can best imitate God in his intellectual na- ture. Now the intellectual nature imitates God chiefly in this, that God understands and loves himself. Wherefore we see that the image of God is in man in three ways. First, inasmuch as humanity possesses a natural aptitude for understanding and loving God; and this aptitude consists in the very nature of the mind, which is common to all men. Secondly, in asmuch as man actually and habitually knows and loves God, though imperfectly. . . . Thirdly, inasmuch as man knows and loves God perfectly; and this image consists in the likeness of glory.[15]

It is the human capacity to understand which makes us uniquely ca- pable to understand and respond to the word of God. This has the inner structure of a dialogue. God made creation to be his partner in the covenant relationship and to address it as such. As the addressed covenant partner, creation hears and responds. To be a human is to be at the point of intersec- tion between God and his creation. In other words, to be made in the image of God is a *covenantal* reality. It is to be that part of creation in which the mutual commitments of God and creation are lived out. It is to and through humanity that the love of God is spoken to creation. It is by humanity that this word of love is heard and responded to with praise and thankfulness. It is to be that part of creation in which the faithful love of the Creator coincides with the faithful love of creation. The biblical story of the fall is the account of humankind turning from its place in the covenantal structure between God and creation and refusing its place of making a response to the word of the Creator. The corresponding story of redemption is the focusing of that response through Israel and ultimately through Christ.

Israel: The People of God

The people of Israel were chosen to be the counterpart of God on creation. They were to be the people who received the word of God and responded with an answering human word of obedience and love. For this reason, Thomas Torrance has described the story of Israel in their vocation as God's covenant-people as a story of both joy and of suffering.[16] It is a story of joy because Israel knew God and were chosen by God to be his people. However, it is a story of suffering because it is a hard and heavy thing to be the point

15. Aquinas, *Summa Theologica*, 1.93.a4.
16. Torrance, *Mediation of Christ*, 6–22.

at which God and creation coincide. Through the course of its history as the people addressed by the living God and charged with the responsibility to respond, Israel show what it is to be the dialogue partner of God.

Two very important themes that shaped the life of Israel are swirling around here: election and covenant. God elected Israel to be his people, and to give himself to be their God. As with the act of creation before it, the election of Israel has no other foundation than the grace of God (Deut 7:7–8). There is something very important about this. God did not choose Israel because of any particular quality they had. Instead, God chose to give himself to this Israel and call Israel to be his for no other reason beyond the freedom of his will. The implications of this extend further still. Very much like the bond between God and creation on account of the free act of God in creating, the free act of electing Israel to be his establishes a bond between Israel and God. God identifies Israel as the recipients of his kindness who now have a responsibility of making a response to God. This bond that is established between God and Israel by the free choice of God, which is similar to the very bond between God and creation, is given expression in the theme of covenant.

In electing Israel to be his people and drawing them into covenant with himself, God set Israel aside to receive his word and in so doing he laid on them the heavy responsibility of making a response. Another way of putting this is that God set Israel aside to be a "kingdom of priests, a holy nation" (Exod 19:6). Israel's commitments as the covenant partner of God took concrete shape in the form of the law. The law was not the means for Israel to be accepted as God's people. The law was given after God had chosen Israel and after their liberation. Adherence to the law, in other words, is not how Israel became the people of God, it is how Israel were to live as the people of God.[17] For Israel's part, to receive the law meant to receive the word of God in the very fabric of its life. It was to construct a society that was shaped by God's design such that its state organization, its cultic practices, its moral code, its theology, its language, its hopes for the future, the clothes they wore, and even the very buildings they lived in were shaped by the word of God. The word of God was to delve deeply into the heart of Israel and shape the very response of Israel in faithfulness to that divine word.[18] Israel was to embody the word of God in such a way that the very character of its national life was a response of love and trust to the God who had chosen this people and drawn it into covenant partnership with him.

17. This was the epoch-making observation of Sanders, *Paul and Palestinian Judaism*.

18. Torrance, *Mediation of Christ*, 15–17.

Israel were not just the representatives of creation to God; they were also the representatives of God to the rest of creation. Israel had a vocation to the rest of the world. This vocation to the rest of the world is inherent to the parameters of God's call of Abram. From the very beginning, God made promises to Abram, one of which was that the nations of the world would be blessed through him and the nation that would come from his union with Sarah (Gen 12:3; 18:18; 22:18; 26:4; 28:14). Israel was chosen by God from among the nations so to be the means of salvation for the nations.[19] Israel were to be a people through whom the very character of God would be seen by the other nations, who would be drawn by the excellence of Israel's life to share in their relationship with God. As the prophet Isaiah said, Israel was to be the light of the world, "that you may bring my salvation to the ends of the earth" (Isa 49:6). Another way to say this is that Israel was the created counterpart of God through which the rest of creation would be restored as the covenant partner of God.

This raises the question of whether Israel could fulfill this high calling? The history of Israel as it is told in the Hebrew Scriptures is the tortuous realization of humanity's resistance to the word of God.[20] It is as Israel is brought into dialogue with God and made the covenant partner with God that the degree to which humanity is at contradiction with respect to God becomes clear. Israel's repeated idolatry; its refusal to construct a society characterized by tight fists around their identity as God's people and open hands to the poor, the widow, and the outsider; its reluctance to engage with one another on terms shaped by God's very justice was a human response at war with the word of God.[21] The question that lies at the heart of Israel's existence is whether or not the steadfast love of God be met by the steadfast love of humanity? The answer of Israel's history is a shuddering "no." The word of God may course through Israel's veins, but it does so along with the disobedience of humanity.

Jesus Christ: The True Human and Covenant-Partner of God

It is through Jesus Christ, the true Israel, the real image of God, that humankind offers itself as the covenant partner of God. It is in Jesus, the true human, that the covenantal purpose of creation is fulfilled. There is a twofold movement here, as would be expected of a dialogue. There is a movement

19. Jacob, *Theology of the Old Testament*, 209–23.

20. Torrance, *Mediation of Christ*, 10–12, 26–32.

21. Wright, *Old Testament Ethics for the People of God*, 253–80.

from God to creation as Jesus Christ is the movement of God the Father through the Son by the Spirit to his creation. There is also a movement from creation to God in which humanity respond to God the Father through the Son by the Spirit. Jesus Christ is humanity-for-God and he is God-for-humanity.[22] Crucially, though, even though God and creation come together in Jesus, God and creation remain distinct in Jesus. Even in this new unity, God and creation do not become submerged into one another. Instead, in Jesus Christ, the faithful love of God is met by the faithful love of humanity as Jesus is *God* as a human and also God *as a human*.

At one very important level, Jesus' very person accomplishes this unity of God and creation which retains the integrity of both. As God the Son made human, Jesus Christ is fully God and fully human. The divine nature and the human nature are united in the person of Jesus Christ. This personal union of the divine nature and the human nature is, in the language of Chalcedon, without confusion or change and without division or separation. The divine nature and the human nature are personally united in Jesus Christ. This personal unity is such that they will never be separated, and in such a way that they do not collapse into one another. It is here, then, in the very person of Jesus Christ, that God and humanity are brought into a personal unity while retaining their distinct reality. For this reason, we should not think of Jesus as God coming *in* a human. Instead, we should think of Jesus as God the Son *as* a human. God the Son as a human is instantly fully God and fully human, speaking from God to humanity and also from humanity to God. In Christ, there is the full dialogue of God and creation: Jesus is "at once the Word of God to (humanity) and for the first time a real word of (humanity) to God."[23]

It is for this reason that Jesus is the true focal point of the relationship between God and creation. He is fully God and so he makes God known, speaking the love of God to creation. He is fully human, and so he receives the word of God and responds with human love and obedience. As the writer of the Letter to the Hebrews has it, Jesus is the "Apostle and High Priest" (Heb 3:1). He is sent by the Father to us as God's word that is identical with God himself and he is the answering faithfulness of humanity to the divine word. In the designation of Jesus as Apostle, Jesus is God coming from the side of God the Father, making the Father known, laying hold of humanity and not letting go. In the designation of Jesus as High Priest, Jesus is a human from the side of humanity, responding to the Father with faith, laying hold of God and not letting go. Just as humanity as the image of God and then Israel as God's

22. Barth, *Church Dogmatics*, 3.2, 203.
23. Torrance, *Royal Priesthood*, 8.

covenant partner were to be the intermediary between God and creation, Jesus Christ is the one who truly represents God to creation and also creation to God. It is in Jesus that the dialogue between God and creation takes place as it was always supposed to. God speaks out his love to creation and creation responds with its own words of love and praise.

Taking first the God-to-creation side of the conversation: Jesus is the perfect representative of God to creation. Jesus is fully God. John describes Jesus as the Word (who was in the beginning with God and who was God) who became flesh; the one from close to the Father's heart who came among us (John 1:1–18). Jesus Christ as the concrete presence of God among us is a theme picked up by the writer of the Letter to the Hebrews.

> In the past God spoke to our forefathers through the prophets at many times and in various ways, but in these last days he has spoken to us by his Son, whom he appointed heir of all things and through whom he made the universe. The Son is the radiance of God's glory and the exact representation of his being. (Heb 1:1–3)

Glory is a designation of the divine reality. Here it is envisaged in terms of light. Jesus is the brightness of the light of divine glory. He is the light which God is, radiating out to us. An implication which would have been deeply pertinent to the Jewish receivers of this letter is that the presence of God is no longer located in the temple of Israel, but in Jesus Christ. The Son is the exact imprint of God's very being. If we want to know who God is, we look to the incarnate Son.

At the same time as being the perfect representative of God to creation, Jesus is also the perfect representative of creation to God. God the Son became a human and lived out in our humanity a life of perfect obedience to and love of God the Father. In so doing, he took our humanity that had become bent away from God and twisted it back to God. So, in the Gospel of Matthew, buried in a sea of disappointment about humanity's rejection of the word of God and antipathy toward those who carry it, the words of the Son's perfect knowledge of the Father within our humanity shine out.

> At that time Jesus said, "I praise you Father, Lord of heaven and earth, because you have hidden these things from the wise and the learned, and yet revealed them to little children. Yes, Father, for this was your good pleasure. All things have been committed to me by my Father. No-one knows the Son except the Father, and no-one knows the Father except the Son and those to whom the Son chooses to reveal him." (Matt 11:25–27)

The full weight of humanity's hostility to the word of God is in the background here. Suddenly, into that discord comes a new harmony between God and humanity. The Son who has known and been known by the Father in eternity, now lives out that perfect accord as one of us and for all of us. He took on our humanity, including our human mind and will that had become bent away from God in disobedience, and, through the course of his life, bent us back to the Father in obedience and love.

In this, Jesus is the good soil on which the seed fell and produced a return. He is the one who is the true and eternal image of the Father who became a human to recast us according to the image. Jesus took our position upon himself and from within our dislocation from God said "not my will, but your will." In all of this, Jesus' human life is of vicarious significance. He did this as one of us and for all of us. He became just as we are and offered himself as one of us to the Father in obedience and praise.

> We are to think of the whole life and activity of Jesus from the cradle to the grave as constituting the vicarious human response to himself which God has freely and unconditionally provided for us. That is not an answer to God which he has given to us through some kind of transaction external to us or over our heads, as it were, but rather one which has made to issue out of the depths of our human being and life as our own.[24]

Ultimately, it is at the cross that the faithful love of God is finally met with the answering faithfulness of creation. As Jesus hung there and drew into himself the awful reality of humanity's rebellion against God he cried out "My God, My God, why have you forsaken me?" He threw himself into the darkness by his obedience to the Father's will and in faith that beyond the darkness, enveloping the darkness, was the greater light of the loving-kindness of God toward his creation. In faith that through God's shuddering "No!" to creation came bursting out the all-embracing "Yes!" From the darkness the Son spoke to the Father words of human faithfulness and trust, "into your hands I commit my spirit." Human words met by divine faithfulness expressed in the resurrection, the final confirmation that Jesus Christ truly is the one in whom the Father is pleased.

At the heart of the New Testament is the unique relationship between the incarnate Son and the Father in the power of the Spirit. Jesus lives the life of the Son as a human, actualizing the perfect covenant partnership of God in our humanity, presenting himself to the Father on our behalf. In Jesus, God has become one of us and stood in our place to give the response of humanity as the created covenant partner of God. He has come

---

24. Torrance, *Mediation of Christ*, 80.

to do what we could not do, which is to receive the word of God and live a response to the Father characterized by obedience and love. He stands in our place in the presence of the Father, taking what is ours and offering it to the Father in praise and thanksgiving. The Letter to the Hebrews makes this point insistently. Jesus is described as our High Priest. He is in solidarity with all humanity and he offers to the Father a life of obedience and faith and prayer which we could not. Jesus is the one who, by the blood of his own sacrifice, has entered the holy of holies and presents our humanity before the Father in love and praise.

Barth has outlined something very similar in his particular approach to the idea of Jesus as prophet. For Barth, Jesus is not just the announcement of the love and mercy of God which must be answered by some separate and corresponding word of humanity. In Jesus, the human response to the divine word of grace is already given.[25] By this, Barth means that salvation and revelation are inseparably related, not, as Webster rightly notes, as a quasi-gnostic theory of salvation exhausted by the attainment of knowledge,[26] but in Jesus Christ who is God before us acting as a human meeting and overcoming our human opposition to God.[27] God gives himself in love to humanity in a redemptive self-revelation and God the Son incarnate lives as a human to complete for us our part in offering his life as an unbroken act of worship to the Father. Jesus is both perfect Word of God to creation expressing God's self and his compassion and care, and the full and perfect word of creation to God. In this, Jesus fulfilled the covenantal relationship that is intrinsic to the very fact of creation. Jesus is steadfast love from both sides. He is the steadfast love of God for creation and he is the steadfast love of creation for God. This realization of the covenant between God and creation *is* atonement, accomplished by Jesus Christ who acts both from the side of God as God and from the side of humanity as a human.

The Church: Participating in the Covenant Partner

In Jesus Christ there is a double movement of God's grace to humanity and humanity's obedience to and faith in God. The Church is constituted by its participation in this double movement. To be the Church is to be the object of God's gracious actions toward us and it is to be drawn in so to share in the incarnate Son's obedience to and love of the Father by the power of the Spirit. The movement from God to creation and from creation to God has already

---

25. Barth, *Church Dogmatics*, 4.3.1, 11–12.

26. Webster, *Barth*, 133.

27. Barth, *Church Dogmatics*, 4.3.1, 180–87.

taken place and *by the Spirit the Church is caused to participate in it through the Son.* As such, the Church exists as the "amen" to this double-movement of grace, which extends across time and space. The Church is, therefore, included as the covenant partner of God the Father by merit of its Spirit-enabled participation in Jesus Christ, the true covenant partner.

Among the great contributions of the French Reformer John Calvin was the conviction that the essence of salvation is union with Jesus Christ. To be saved is to be incorporated into Christ through his death and resurrection whereby we share in all he is and has received from the Father. As will be developed in chapter 4, what we think about the Church needs to be formulated on the basis of our union with Jesus. The Church is that which has been made one with Christ, who is the perfect covenant partner of God. This is the reason that the designation the body of Christ stands at the center of Paul's thinking about the Church, because it continues so seamlessly from his directive soteriological motif of being transferred from being in Adam to being in Christ. Everything that we can say about the Church from its orders of ministry to its norms of governance derives from this Christ-centered reality.

No more is this the case than in the meaning of the word Church. Lying behind the English word is the term *ekklēsia*, or "called out." Behind the Greek *ekklēsia* is the Hebrew word *qahal*, the principle meaning of which is an assembly. Contained within what is meant by the word Church, therefore, is the *act of God* in calling out a people who he assembles to be his own: "a chosen people, a royal priesthood, a holy nation, a people belonging to God" (1 Pet 2:9). Just as God called out the people of Israel to be his own, the Church is called out to be the temple of the Holy Spirit, the people among whom God dwells (1 Cor 3:17–18). The Church, then, is called into being by God in that it is the assembly of people, both Jew and Gentile, who have been united to Jesus Christ in the power of the Spirit. The Church is, in a manner of speaking, called out of existence in Adam to be the body of Christ.

There will be much more to say on the designation the body of Christ in later chapters. For now, we can make do with a working definition: by the Spirit, the Church participates in all that Jesus is as the Son of the Father such that the whole Jesus (*totus Christus*) now includes the Church. In becoming a human, identifying himself with us and assuming us into union with him through his death and resurrection by the Spirit, Jesus will not have himself without his Church and the Church has no existence aside from Jesus. This means that the Church cannot be separated from Jesus without ceasing to be. The very essence of the Church is Jesus Christ. The Church cannot be separated from Jesus without losing that which makes it what it is. There is a need for caution here. Jesus must not be mistaken for the Church. It is not as if Jesus is constituted by the amalgam of all those that have been incorporated into him. Instead, what is in view is a variegated unity in which Jesus makes room in his very person for his Church, but yet remains distinct. Just as important, the Church must not be thought of as an alternative Christ, acting as Christ on the world after his ascension. The Church does not act *as* Christ, but as the *servant* of Christ. The identification of the Church as the body of Christ is qualified by the distinction made between Christ and his Church because the Church is the body of which Christ is the head. Or, using Jesus' own description, he is the vine and we are the branches.

The identity of the Church as the body of Christ means that the Church has no identity, life, power, or mission outside of Jesus Christ. As we have seen above, the incarnate Son lived a life of obedience and love to the Father and actualized within our humanity a perfect covenant partnership with God. The Church, therefore, has its roots in the incarnation: it is joined to Christ on the strength of the fact that Christ has joined himself to us, enabling us to share his relation of Sonship to the Father. Although the emphasis does not fall here in the current discussion, this participatory account of the gospel does not neglect the sacrificial and penal significance of the cross. Our participation in Christ's perfect fellowship with the Father had to take the form of atonement. The sinful cannot be brought into communion with the holy. Christ loved the Church and gave himself for it, dying in its place that it may be cleansed and reconciled to fellowship with the Father and rising from the dead so that the Church may share in the power of his resurrection.

This is what it means to belong to the New Covenant which is established in Christ's body and blood. Jesus Christ is the perfect covenant partner of God. At the Last Supper and his death and resurrection, Jesus Christ opened up for us a way to participate in that reality through sharing in his body and his blood. Through being united to Christ as the body of which he is the head we share his perfect relationship with the Father: "To be a [human] is to be with God. What a [human] is in this Counterpart is obviously the basic and comprehensive determination of [their] true being. Whatever else [they are], [they are] on the basis of the fact that [they are] with Jesus and therefore with God."[28] We share his perfect obedience, his unbroken life of prayer, his absolute faith in the Father and we take our place in him in his communion with the Father in the power of the Spirit. This book is an elaboration on that theme. It may be helpful to trace out some immediate implications so that by observing some consequences of what is being said the substantive point may become clearer.

---

28. Barth, *Church Dogmatics*, 3.2, 135.

Worship

If the Church is truly included in Christ to share in all Christ is as the covenant partner of God, then what might this mean for the worship of the Church? James Torrance has argued that the worship of the Church is a gift of participating through the Spirit in the incarnate Son's communion with the Father.[29] For Torrance, worship must be understood in a trinitarian way that takes seriously the vicarious humanity of Jesus and our inclusion into him and so into his communion with the Father in the power of the Spirit. In other words, the worship of the Church is worship only as it is joined to the incarnate Son's actualization in our humanity of his perfect love of the Father. In Christ, God has already given to us what he demands from his covenant partner in Jesus' response of love, faith, thanksgiving, and obedience. Jesus has already lived within our humanity the life of perfect and continuous prayer to the Father, actualizing within our human disobedience a new obedience: "not my will but yours be done" (Luke 22:42). It is as the body of Christ that the Church is included within the true covenant partner of God from whom the Church derives its essence and takes its place within the perfect relationship between God and humanity that has been realized for us by Jesus Christ. The human life of Jesus, therefore, is the inner essence of our worship.

In the terminology of the Letter to the Hebrews, Christ is our Great High Priest. He has offered himself once and for all on the cross, a new obedience in the form of a life poured out in worship of God the Father in faith and thankfulness. The worship and prayer of the Church comes to the Father through the Son and it cannot be divorced from that self-offering of Jesus. This, Torrance suggests, undergirds a properly trinitarian account of worship: our participation in the Son's communion with the Father in the power of the Spirit.[30] Worship is not something we offer as a parallel response to God; truly Christian worship is the response to God given in Jesus and our being caught up in that.

Torrance suggests that the explanation as to why the Church has come to see worship as something it does aside from its inclusion into the perfect obedience of Christ is that the focus has been placed on *how* the atonement works rather than on *who* the one that makes atonement is.[31] The Nicene-Constantinopolitan Creed does not advance any particular explanation of how Jesus' death and resurrection is salvific. Instead, it puts all its attention

29. Torrance, *Worship*, 20.
30. Torrance, *Worship*, 20.
31. Torrance, *Worship*, 29.

on *who* the savior is as God the Son as a human. All the attention in the Creed is on God the Son who became a human to live the life of God the Son within our humanity reconciling sinful humanity to God. Certainly, Jesus is clothed in his gospel and cannot be understood outside of the apostolic witness to him, but his person is not just a means to the end of reconciling us to God whereupon we are left to our own devices. The strength of Torrance's point, and why it bears reconsidering today, is that the gospel of salvation is that Jesus has lived our human response to God vicariously for us and we cannot think of our response to God separately from this.

Very often, our understanding of salvation extends only to our forgiveness through Jesus' sacrificial death. This is wonderfully true, but it is not the *whole* truth. If the extent of our thinking about Jesus ends there then the danger is that we begin to see Jesus as the *means* of our worship before God, rather than the very essence of the worship of the Church. Jesus is God the Son among us to live a life of obedience, faith, and worship to the Father. He offers himself as a sacrifice of praise to the Father as one of us and for all of us. In our worship, we do not add anything to what Jesus has done. Instead, we join our voices to the life of Christ. As Torrance points out, this gives us the perspective to understand worship to be "the gift of grace to participate through the Spirit in the incarnate Son's communion with the Father."[32] No more is this so than at the celebration of the Eucharist where we participate in Jesus' sacrifice of thanksgiving and faith to the Father and bind ourselves to him in his life poured out in worship to the Father.

It may be objected that this focusing of our human response to God through Jesus runs the risk of collapsing the Church into Jesus, effectively outsourcing the need for us to *do* anything in response to God. Is this not just making Jesus a receptacle in which to pour our human indifference to God? One way this objection could be met is by following Barth's account of gratitude. For Barth, Jesus may well be the true human whose existence is as an answer to the word of God, however, this does not remove the requirement for our own personal response. The difference, however, is that Jesus' existence-as-answer is *definitive*, while ours is *derivative*. This is the reason that Barth focuses our human response through the category of gratitude.[33] Gratitude does not bring about a new reality but is a response to the divine act of grace.

> When we see [humankind] as the being responsive and comple-
> mentary to the grace of God, as a being in gratitude, we see

32. Torrance, *Worship*, 59.

33. Barth, *Church Dogmatics*, 3.2, 166. See the excellent discussion on this in Webster, *Barth*, 103–4.

[humankind] for the first time. . . . Seen here at its roots, and understood as thanksgiving for the grace of God, this is the act in which he accepts the validity of the act which not he but God has wrought. But in this form, it is his own act. He is the subject of his history. . . . [The grace of God] calls for gratitude. The fact that it finds gratitude, that the God who is gracious to His creatures is honoured in the world of creation, is the being of [humankind], and this being engaged in its characteristic activity.[34]

The worship of the Church, therefore, is participation in the self-offering of Jesus. This does not exclude our individual response and agency. However, it does establish it within definitive limits. Our response to the grace of God is not separate from Christ's. Instead, it is that in which we express our gratitude and love for having been included in Jesus' existence-as-answer. In so doing we have our own true human existence-as-answer to the word of God in giving glory and honor to our Creator and Redeemer and our own personal response within that.

Mission

To take another angle on the point at hand, what does it mean for the *mission* of the Church that the Church derives all it is by its union with Christ by the Spirit? Just as Israel as the covenant partner of God had a vocation to the rest of the world, and God the Son incarnate was sent by the Father into the world, so also the Church as the body of Christ is sent out with a vocation toward the rest of the world: "as the Father has sent me, so I am sending you" (John 20:21). In talking about the mission of the Church, we are talking in terms that are inseparable from the *apostolicity* of the Church as that which is *sent out* into the world (Matt 28:19). To be sent out to the world requires two types of extension. It requires extension across space, certainly as Jesus said his followers were to be his "witnesses in Jerusalem, in all Judea, in Samaria and to the ends of the earth" (Acts 1:8). It also requires extension across time. The apostolicity of the Church also relates to the extension of the Church through history and is the mechanism of the continuity of the gospel. It is an astonishing aspect of the prayer of Christ that he prayed "on behalf of those who will believe in me through their word" (John 17:20). The Church is apostolic in that it is sent out to the ends of the earth and in that belief in Christ is *through* the witness of the apostles for all subsequent generations.

---

34. Barth, *Church Dogmatics*, 3.2, 168.

However, even with this extension geographically and chronologically away from Christ, the center of gravity of the apostolic ministry constantly pulls back to Christ. It would be senseless and self-defeating to try to separate the apostolicity of the Church from Jesus Christ. We must not allow the Church to become so large in our thinking that it takes the place of Jesus and the Spirit. For example, when we say the Church is apostolic, we must not make the mistake of thinking that we are only talking about historical continuity of the apostles succeeded by bishops. Likewise, we must not make the mistake of separating the apostolic mission of the Church from the mission of God in Christ. Certainly, historical succession and evangelistic mission are crucial aspects of the apostolicity of the Church, but they must not obscure the more foundational aspect which is that *apostolicity first belongs to Jesus and the Spirit*.[35] In the most absolute sense, Jesus is the Apostle of the Father. He is the one sent out from the Father to make the Father known. Jesus is sent out from the Father to obey the Father's will and in so doing to draw all people to himself. The Spirit, as the one sent from the Father through Christ, is the Apostle of Jesus Christ. The Spirit is sent to the followers of Christ to "teach you everything and remind you of all that I have said to you" (John 14:26). The Spirit is not a replacement for Christ; he is the personal representative of Christ who does not speak about himself but orientates towards and causes us to see Christ. The Apostolic function of the Spirit, therefore, is to be the light in which we see the light of the Father shining through the face of Christ.

When we describe the Church as apostolic, we are doing so in a way that is derivative from the primary Apostolicity of the Son and the Spirit. The Church's apostolicity is its grounding in the same mission as the Son and the Spirit. However, this does not mean that the Apostolic work of the Son and Spirit can be communicated or delegated to the Church. The way of participating in the mission is different for the Church. For this reason, the apostolicity of the Church does not mean that the Church replaces Christ. Instead, the apostolic mission of the Church is to be a witness to Christ. The whole content of the Church's apostolic ministry is confessional in that it points beyond itself to Christ. Consistent with his sophisticated idea of Jesus as prophet accomplishing realization and response in our humanity, Barth articulates an understanding of the Church as integrated with Christ in its own activity when he says it is "Being called by and to the Christ engaged in the exercise of His prophetic office (the Church has) no option but to attach (itself) to Him with their own action, to tread in His steps, to become with

35. Torrance, *Conflict and Agreement*, 1.23–34.

Him proclaimers of the reconciliation of the world accomplished in Him, heralds of His person and work."[36]

With this in mind, the twelve apostles are those specially commissioned by Christ to be his witnesses and the leaders of the community which he had established. The particular function of the apostles was, by the inspiration of the Spirit, to pattern their minds and their proclamation into accordance with the self-revelation of God through Jesus Christ. It is on account of the fact that the apostolic witness to Christ is the divinely inspired witness to God's self-revelation that the apostles are the foundation upon which the Church is built. In Christ, there is both the Apostle sent by the Father and the High Priest responding to the Father with obedience and love. The apostles witnessed this event and had their own minds conformed to the mind of Christ such that, through the apostles' witness, Christ continued his own work of self-revelation. Accordingly, the apostolic foundation of the Church is not a source of authority *apart* from Jesus. Instead, the apostolic foundation of the Church is the way the Church in its extension throughout time and across space retains its essential grounding in the person of Jesus Christ precisely because the apostles were witnesses to the risen Christ.

The notion of apostolic succession is of especial importance in keeping the Church grounded upon and in the person of Jesus Christ. The Church is sent out by Christ to carry his gospel. For this reason, it extends across space and through time, for if it did not it could not be witness of the good news to all people. Apostolic succession in the form of the episcopacy is how the Church remains anchored upon its apostolic foundation, and through this, how the Church retains its ultimate participation in Jesus Christ. To talk about apostolic succession is to talk about the Church as it extends through history continuing to be built upon the foundation of the apostolic gospel contained in the New Testament. It is not to talk about the transmission of the task of the apostles from one generation to the next. The ministry of the apostles as authoritative witnesses to Jesus is not the beginning of a chain of leaders who exercise the same function. The twelve apostles are utterly unique in that it is only their witness to Jesus that carries authority because it is only they whose words have been shaped by the reality of the person of Jesus by the Spirit such that Jesus uses them today to meet his people and draw them into his own Apostolic and Priestly ministry.

Despite the unique function of the apostles, it is still true to talk of apostolic succession. This apostolic succession is the continuity of the one Church through history which is rooted in the person of Jesus in the power of the Spirit through the apostles. At the heart of this continuity is the episcopacy.

36. Barth, *Church Dogmatics*, 4.3.2, 606.

It is impossible to overestimate how important and precious an office it is that the bishops of the Church inhabit. Just as the apostles did not replace Christ and Christ was not present to the Church through *them*, but through their *witness*, bishops are not a replacement of Jesus Christ. Not only that, the episcopacy is not a replacement of the apostles. Instead, they receive the ministry of the oversight of the Church through which the Church is kept secure on its apostolic foundations. There are two elements to this. The first is a visible, historical chain that connects the Church to the apostles. The Church today bears a historical connection to the apostles through the office of the bishop. It is one and the same Church that has been built upon the foundation of the apostles. The second important aspect is more conceptual. Bishops are the teachers of the Church and guardians of the apostolic faith. It is their task to maintain the Church's teaching and belief in continuity with the apostolic gospel. The Church is apostolic in that its belief is determined by the apostolic tradition and continues to proclaim their gospel as the "pillar and foundation of the truth" (1 Tim 3:15). This is why unity is the central function of the episcopacy. The diocesan bishop manifests the unity of each parish in shared submission to the apostolic gospel and in communion with the Church through the generations. The unity of the bishops themselves manifests the unity of the Church both across the world today and also through time; a common fellowship together with the Church back through the generations to its foundation on the apostles.

Apostolic succession is, therefore, about being hemmed in on the apostolic tradition. Through the apostolic tradition, the Church is kept held tight to the person of Jesus Christ, to whose life and person the apostolic gospel binds us. There is nothing more toxic, more disastrous to the Church than bishops who place any other consideration before maintaining the unity of the Church in its sure grounding upon the apostolic witness. This is not to say that the criterion for episcopacy is theological conservatism. The succession itself contains the power of this generation's unity to the body of Christ diachronically. There must be a balance between the conservative and the progressive. It is in this way that the Church will remain true to its gospel which includes the ever-present necessity to actualize the gospel in the culture of our place and world. So, while the superstructure of the Church may adapt from generation to generation, its establishment on the apostolic foundation remains the same. In this, the apostolic tradition and the Scripture that enshrines it has supremacy over every other concern in the life of the Church. This does not mean the writings of the Church Fathers and the later tradition of the Church are not helpful. Indeed, the very way in which we read and understand Scripture is shaped by those who went before us. It would be irresponsible (and very possibly impossible) for anyone to dispense with the tradition of the Church's interpretation of the apostolic gospel. Instead, our attempt must be to establish ourselves on the word of God through the apostolic witness guided through the teaching of the Church. This is a point which has been effectively made by Stephen Holmes, arguing that the necessity of tradition is a function of the unity of the Church reaching back from today to the apostles.[37]

If the apostolicity of the Church is the being rooted in Christ through the ápostles, then the apostolic ministry of the Church is the mission of the Church sent out to into the world rooted in the mission of Jesus Christ, the Apostle of the Father. The apostolic character of the Church is that it participates in the Apostolic work of the Son and the Spirit through being incorporated into the Son by the Spirit via the witness of the apostles. At the first level, just as Christ was sent by the Father into the world to live the life of the perfect covenant partner of God by the power of the Spirit, so too the Church is sent out by Christ to proclaim the gospel by the power of the Spirit. The very existence of the Church is rooted in the sending out of the Son by the Father and the sending of the Spirit by the Son. In other words, the apostolicity of the Church is first and foremost by our participation in the Apostolic mission of the Son.

It is in this sense that we can talk about the apostolic ministry of the Church, as that which is sent out to be a *witness* to Christ. This means that the apostolic mission of the Church can never be separated from the ministry of word and sacrament, for it is in the proclamation of the gospel and the celebration of baptism and the Eucharist that the Church points to Jesus Christ. As will be developed in chapter 4, through the ministry of word and sacrament the Church participates in the Apostolic mission of Christ in the form of servants and witnesses. For this reason, when we are talking about the mission of the Church and thinking about creative ways in which to actualize the gospel in the communities in which we live and welcome people into the community of the Church (for example, the Fresh Expressions initiative in Great Britain, which are ways of expressing the life of the Church that emerge from within contemporary culture in order to engage with people who are not familiar with the Church), *we can never do so by surrendering the apostolic ministry of word and sacrament.* These activities are not tangential to mission; they are the inner heart of the mission of the Church. It is precisely these activities of the Church that constitute our apostolicity for it is through them that individuals may be incorporated into Christ, the true Apostle of God. It is essential that the Church does not

---

37. Holmes, *Listening to the Past*, 18–36.

neglect these in its efforts to engage the culture, because we have nothing else to engage the world around us with.

This means that the mission of the Church is primarily a matter of our shared participation in the one ministry of Jesus and the Spirit. This does not mean that the ministry of the Church is an extension on earth of the ministry of Christ. The work of the Church is not identical with the work of Christ. However, it also cannot be separated from the work of Christ. The work of the Church is participation in the work of Christ. The Church participates in the ministry of Christ by *serving* Christ. This means that through the ministry of the Church, Christ is at work. Christ is at work through his body in governing it, commanding it, and empowering it through his Spirit. In this, the Church in its preaching and sacraments participates in Christ's ministry of reconciliation. Moreover, while the Church is sent out by Christ, it is not sent out alone. After ascending to universal Lordship, Jesus united himself to his Church through the Spirit. In this way, Jesus remains present with the Church, continuing his own mission of being sent out by the Father through the Church which, in turn, he sends out. As such, the Church is sent out by Christ to be the way Christ communicates himself to the world through the witness of the Church to Christ. In other words, the mission of the Church is not to call attention to itself but, as a servant, it is to point beyond itself to Christ and to call individuals to participate in Christ as the perfect covenant partner of the Father.

2

Freedom

IN HIS 1958 LECTURE "Two Concepts of Liberty" Isaiah Berlin distinguished between positive and negative liberty.[1] Negative liberty is *freedom from* constraints that may be imposed upon an individual by an outside influence. It is the freedom of an individual from a limiting interference from another or an inhibiting set of circumstances. Negative liberty, for example, is freedom from tyranny or war or poverty or hunger. This freedom from coercion, Berlin comments, is characteristic in the English tradition of political philosophy.[2] Positive liberty is the *freedom to* act upon one's will. It is derived from the will "to be a subject, not an object; to be moved by reasons, by conscious purposes, which are my own, not by causes which affect me, as it were, from the outside."[3] This is the freedom to determine one's own life by choices that one makes. Once it has been adapted a bit, Berlin's distinction between positive and negative liberty is a helpful tool through which to explore the theological content of freedom.

Negative liberty as freedom from determination by another provides a reasonable point of access to understand the freedom of God and the freedom of creation as neither has constraints placed upon them by the existence of the other. Creation, for example, is not constrained in what it is and how it has life by its necessary relation to God. However, with respect to God's freedom, we need to develop beyond Berlin's notion of negative freedom and account for the fact that God's freedom is not just liberty from external influence. God's freedom is a *self-grounded* freedom. God's freedom is not the result of the absence of imposition from an external party. Quite the reverse is the case: God is not imposed on by anything

1. Berlin, *Four Essays on Liberty*, 118–72.
2. Berlin, *Four Essays on Liberty*, 123.
3. Berlin, *Four Essays on Liberty*, 131.

else because he is free. God and creation, therefore, are free but they do not have freedom in the same way.

Positive liberty, also, requires a little adaptation for being employed within a theological context. Within a theological frame of thought, positive liberty is not only the freedom to enact our will. Instead, positive liberty is the capacity to be free for one another. Ultimately, this positive liberty as the capacity to be free for another is established upon God's self-grounded freedom. God does not need creation. God creates out of choice and not necessity. This is a free choice made in the intention to be in relation to that which he has made. In his own freedom, God can choose to be free for creation. This has implications for how we think of creation. Creation is not necessary but contingent. As it is not characterized by necessity, creation has a degree of space. Creation is not limited by, or ceaselessly orientated towards, a divine need. Creation is not exhausted of its own life and character by continually fulfilling a requirement that is imposed upon it from without. In the generosity of the fullness of God in his absolute freedom, God gives to creation its own contingent freedom. As such, creation is given its own distinct existence from God. It is from this basis that creation is at liberty to be free for God as his covenant partner.

At the heart of Christian theology is the question of the relationship of God and creation. In the last chapter, this was introduced through the twin notions of dialogue and participation. If, however, a dialogue is to be a true dialogue there must be freedom. A relationship cannot take place properly if either side of that relationship is not free. At all times in thinking about the relationship of God and creation we have got to do our best to resist the seductive pull of un-freedom. For example, the nature of the relationship between God and creation is often approached as if the freedom of God and the freedom of creation are rivals, as if more of one must mean less of the other. For this reason, conceptually speaking, some seek to limit God's power over and contact with creation so to create the space for creatures to exist and act aside from divine interference. Others suggest that divine agency must be supreme over all events within creation and consequently relativize the freedom of the creature as an illusion. Still others might hold that the distinction between divine acts and creaturely acts is superfluous as God and creation are bracketed together within one causal chain of being such that God's power and agency are, in some sense, creation's own. The problem with all such approaches is that they treat God's freedom and creaturely freedom as poles which cannot be reconciled without watering down the content of either side. It is very important to try to think in such a way that does not collapse on either side into un-freedom.

There is a different way forward which does not presuppose that a full-throated affirmation of the freedom of God diminishes the freedom of creation and *vice versa*. If there is to be any progress here it needs to be recognized that God's freedom is not the same as creation's freedom. Both God and creation have freedom, but they do not have freedom in the same way. The freedom of God is *absolute*; it is self-grounded in what it is to be God. The freedom of creation is *contingent*; it is given to creation by God. These two different sorts of freedom are not in competition with one another. God and creation are not in a rivalry for freedom. Instead, the absolute freedom of God is the source and ground of the contingent freedom of creation. If God were not free, creation could not possibly be free. The freedom of creation is not a possibility that lies within the capacities of creation itself; it is a corollary of the way in which God has his life.

God is related to creation by choice not by necessity. This is related to the absolute freedom of God and the corresponding contingent freedom of creation. To say that creation is not necessary to God is to say that creation is not an inevitable outworking of God's creative potential. What it is to be God does not entail the existence of creation in the same way that being a bachelor entails being an unmarried man. Correspondingly, the contingence of creation is a product of divine fullness. God does not create in order to answer some deficiency within himself. Quite the reverse, God chose to create as a free act of grace. By attributing the existence of creation to the will of God, we find a foundation upon which the freedom of God and the freedom of creation can be built together, with absolute freedom the foundation of contingent freedom.

Ultimately, the only way we can have any knowledge of the relationship between God and creation is through Jesus Christ. If the relation of God and creation is one of grace, then theological speculation must be replaced by obedient thinking that struggles to be in accordance with how God has made himself known in the incarnate Son. The relationship between God and creation as it is revealed in Jesus Christ demonstrates what it is for God to be free and for creation to be free. Jesus Christ is the personal union of God and creation. The structure of the relationship between the divinity of Jesus and the humanity of Jesus gives us the basic rules, or the fundamental grammar, by which to understand the relationship of God and creation more generally. In framing the relation of God and creation in a way that is governed by the person of Jesus Christ, a very particular trajectory is set within which to understand the Church as having its existence only by the gracious action of God and yet having its own distinct human existence and agency.

This chapter introduces a broad theological vision of freedom taking as its two vantage points the determinative Christian doctrines of the Trinity and the person of Jesus Christ. Such a foundation affords us with a distinctive view of the Church as the creature of the word of God.

The Freedom of God

Very often when we think of freedom we are thinking of the absence of constraint. The Statue of Liberty in the United States is an icon of freedom positioned to welcome immigrants who travel to America seeking a new life without the restrictions of oppression, famine, or war. A broken shackle and chain lie at Libertas's right foot as she walks forward into the future holding the light of liberty that will enlighten the world. The Statue of Liberty is a representation of what Isaiah Berlin called "negative freedom." As much as this represents a libertarian tradition that is invaluable and requires protection, this is *not* the starting point for the freedom of God. The freedom of God is much more than freedom from external restrictions (although it does include freedom of restrictions). God's freedom is of a different order, and, if we are going to understand it, we need to prepare ourselves to think in different categories.

Barth's doctrine of God is characterized by a joyful affirmation of God's freedom and the corresponding freedom of creation. For Barth, to say "God is free" is identical to saying "God is Lord."[4] First and foremost, Barth argues that God's freedom means that God's life is determined by himself. God's freedom is not constituted by the absence of restrictions, but by the limitless abundance of God's very being. The freedom of God is *absolute*, grounded in the unique Lordship of what it is to be God. The freedom of God is not relative. It is not dependent upon the behavior of another or the correct external conditions. God would not be less God if nothing but God existed. God is that which God is, quite aside from all other considerations.

A consequence of the absolute freedom of God is that God is unrestricted and unconditioned by anything from the outside. God's life is not determined by any other factor precisely because God's life is entirely grounded in God's own self. We have arrived at Berlin's idea of negative liberty, but only as a consequence of an absolute liberty that is exclusively true of God. That this is a consequence is very important. God's freedom is much more than not being constrained or defined by another. If God's freedom were simply the absence of restriction, then entering relation with creation would undermine God's freedom. If God's freedom were constituted by his liberty from the influence

4. Barth, *Church Dogmatics*, 2.1, 297–321.

of creation, then he could not enter relation with creation without undermining his freedom. For this reason, God's freedom *from* creation is the foundation stone upon which God can be free *for* creation.

God's Freedom From Creation and Freedom For Creation

God's self-grounded freedom is the foundation upon which God is free to be in relationship with creation. This is demonstrated through the reciprocity of the theological categories of transcendence and immanence. Transcendence is a way we might speak about the absolute freedom of God. It describes God's infinite otherness to his creation. God is not a comparatively higher being than creation; God is beyond created reality. The transcendence of God was a major theme in the theological mood of the late-medieval period. The architecture of the Gothic Cathedrals with those high ceilings and distinctive arches lifts the worshiper's eyes upward, reminding her of the radical difference of God and creation. Transcendence, though, does not mean that God is somewhere up above us in the highest spheres of the universe. The difference is not quantifiable in terms of distance or altitude. God exists in eternity and infinity and creatures exist in time and in space. God exists in a totally different order of being and in an utterly different way. There is what Søren Kierkegaard called an "infinite qualitative distinction" between God and creation.[5] There can be no innate comparison between God and creation, for the difference, being infinite, is not quantifiable.

It is in this context that we should understand the strong invective against idolatry that runs throughout Israelite theology. It is wholly wrong to apply to created things that which is reserved for God alone (like, for example, worship). Mythology is equally contrary to God's transcendence. While idolatry is the projection of the divine onto the created, mythology is the projection of the created upon the divine. The deities of the Greek pantheon, for example, are described as higher forms of existence within the same reality as mortals. They were distinct from other entities within reality, but they were not separate and beyond mortal reality itself. The gods of Greece coveted the praise of humans and were sensitive to scenarios in which the appropriate praise was not given (as Odysseus found to his cost). They had competing interests to humanity which stretched even to the point of rivalry (as the Titan Prometheus found to his cost). Against idolatry and mythology, the transcendence of God means that God is not bound up with created reality. In this way, transcendence can

5. Kierkegaard, *Training in Christianity*, 139.

be described in terms of God's freedom. God's transcendence is his self-grounded existence (whereas all else derives its existence from him). Unlike the gods of Greece, the Judeo-Christian God does not need humanity and is not submerged in a tug-of-war, desperately trying to maintain his divine freedom against the rising tide of human attainment. God is free because God's existence is a self-grounded existence.

The freedom of God, however, is not exhausted by the category of transcendence. Kathryn Tanner has helpfully shown that transcendence is the ground of God's immanent involvement toward and within creation. God is loving in the exercise of his freedom.[6] Tanner's suggestion that God's transcendent freedom is the presupposition of his immanence has considerable force. Immanence, God's creative involvement with everything that is not him, is God's freedom to be for creation and to be in relation with creation. This freedom to be for creation rests upon God's freedom from creation in his transcendence. Just like an anchor keeps a ship moored in place, the transcendent freedom of God provides the stable foundation from which God is creatively involved with creation without surrendering his own freedom. God's freedom is not defined by liberty from external constraints or interference. God does not need to protect his own frontiers against the creature. God is able to be free for creation on account of the fact that in his absolute, transcendent freedom, he is free from creation. As Albert Heschel observed "God remains transcendent in his immanence and related in his transcendence."[7]

Quite opposed to any idea that creation compromises God's freedom, God's action in creating and his ongoing relationship with what he has made is actually a *function* of his transcendent freedom. God's freedom from creation is the inner possibility of his freedom for creation. God's freedom is exercised in his love for us. It is because God's freedom is self-grounded that he does not need creation and so the decision to create is truly a *choice*. This has been put with clarity by Moltmann:

> If creation is necessary for God himself, then God is not its "free creator." If on the other hand creation is merely a mis-adventure from eternity, then the free creator is not God but a capricious demon. How then can we explain God's freedom relative to creation? The world as free creation cannot be a necessary unfolding of God nor an emanation of his being from his divine fullness. God is free. But he does not act capriciously. When he creates something that is not God but also

6. Tanner, *God and Creation in Christian Theology*, 36–80.
7. Heschel, *Prophets*, 486.

not nothing then this must have its ground not in itself but in God's *good will* or *pleasure*.[8]

It is because God's freedom is self-grounded that he is able to choose to create and so enter a covenantal relationship with that creation and not have this affect his own freedom. Because God is anchored in himself, he is able to enter a relationship in which there are obligations placed upon him as the Creator and not himself be dragged down and constituted by or trapped within his relationship to creation. It is because God's freedom is self-grounded that God can choose to be present with his creation without compromising his transcendent freedom or the distinct existence of creation: God the Son became a human without ceasing to be God and God the Spirit dwells within us without the divine Spirit becoming indistinguishable from some amorphous human spirit. Even in the most intimate of relationship with his creation, God remains who he is in his freedom. God is free in himself. Therefore, God is able to bind himself to creation in love without becoming constituted in his relations to us.

Freedom and Triunity

The theological category through which the freedom of God can be most fruitfully considered is the doctrine of the Trinity.[9] God's self-grounded freedom is the perfect communion of love in which the one God has his life as Father, Son, and Spirit. The freedom of God is not best considered from the perspective of philosophical theism (for example, immutability, eternity, infinity, omnipotence, etc.) because this gives a conception of God that is developed within an impersonal frame. The problem inherent in this classical theism is that God becomes a foundational proposition upon which a system of theology is established. Developing a concept of divine freedom through the triune being of God affirms that God is eternally Father of the Son in the unity of the Spirit and it is out of the fullness of this love that he freely loves us. For this reason, the doctrine of the Trinity ought to come front and center in our understanding of God and his relation to what he has made.

---

8. Moltmann, *Theology and Joy*, 41.

9. There are metaphysical options open to us such as, for example, Aquinas's doctrine of mixed relations. However, such metaphysically driven accounts of divine freedom are both inherently problematic in that they place a human system of thought prior to what is known by revelation and also, in the example of mixed relations, have the consequence of locking God out of any real relation to creation.

In his study on the Trinity, the Roman Catholic theologian Karl Rahner remarked, "Christians are, in their practical life, almost mere 'monotheists'. We must be willing to admit that, should the doctrine of the Trinity be dropped as false, the major part of religious literature could well remain unchanged."[10] It may be thought that the Trinity is perceived to be far too difficult a doctrine to understand and—even if we could understand it—it appears to have little to no direct relevance to human life. However, the doctrine of the Trinity concerns the very heart of the divine life in its limitless abundance, which is the life to which Christian believers are included through our incorporation into Christ. The doctrine of the Trinity has relevance, therefore, inasmuch as we consider it relevant to know the God to whom we stand in relation. As Christoph Schwöbel has written, "the Christian answer to the question 'who is God?' is: the Father, the Son and the Holy Spirit."[11] Moreover, the doctrine of the Trinity describes the way in which God has his life as three-in-one and is the foundation stone upon which we may understand the freedom of God.

It is fundamental to the Judeo-Christian understanding of God that God is one and unique. This is integral to Hebrew theology from the Shema (Deut 6:4). As the nation began to form around the tribes of the land of Canaan, the oneness and uniqueness of God clashed with the corporate divinity of Ba'al, who, by contrast, was a composite of a variety of deities. For Hebrew theology, there is one God who has one will, which is made known in the continuity of his activity toward Israel. This constitutes the theological foundation of the steadfast love of God. The oneness of God's being, will, and power is expressed in the oneness of the work of the Father, Son, and Spirit.

With the coming of Jesus Christ and bestowal of the Spirit, however, something new has been revealed about the way in which God is one. Paul never abandoned his basic Jewish conviction in the oneness and uniqueness of God. However, he had to learn to hold this fundamental pillar of Judeo-Christian theism in a way that included three distinct identities: the Father, the Son, and the Spirit. One of the best examples of this inclusion of Jesus within the one God is Paul's reworking of the Shema in 1 Corinthians 8:6: "There is but one God, the Father, from whom all things came and for whom we live; and there is but one Lord, Jesus Christ, through whom all things came and through whom we live." N. T. Wright has described this as one of the most revolutionary pieces of theology ever written.[12] Paul invoked the

10. Rahner, *Trinity*, 10–11.

11. Schwöbel, "God, Creation and the Christian Community," 155.

12. Wright, *What Saint Paul Really Said*, 66–67.

Shema and included Jesus Christ within the classical Jewish statement of the oneness and the uniqueness of God. The whole logic of the passage pivots on Paul's conventional Jewish beliefs. Paul explains that it is permissible to eat food sacrificed to idols because "we know that an idol is nothing at all in the world and there is no God but one" (1 Cor 8:4). It doesn't matter if you eat food sacrificed to idols precisely because they have been sacrificed to idols which is synonymous with saying they have been sacrificed to nothing. Unlike these idols that do not have existence, God has real existence. Remarkably, Paul proclaims that this real God includes Jesus Christ.

Paul thinks of the Spirit as in inseparable relation to Jesus. The Spirit is the Spirit of Jesus who communicates the presence of Jesus to the believer and enables the believer to share in the Sonship of Christ. This relationship between the Spirit and Jesus is given important expression in Galatians 4:4–6: "When the time had fully come, God sent his Son, born of a woman, born under law, to redeem those under law, that we might receive the full rights of sons. Because you are sons, God sent the Spirit of his Son into our hearts, the Spirit who calls out 'Abba, Father.'" The Son is described as sent out from the Father and this same movement is attributed also to the Spirit. In other words, Paul thinks of the Spirit and Jesus bearing a comparative relationship to God the Father. By extension, if the Son is included within the one divine being, so also must the Spirit be. Consequently, it is by this Spirit that we are enabled to fully realize our adoption through our participation in the divine Son: through Christ we have access to the Father by the Spirit (Eph 2:18).

For Paul, then, there are three distinct identities who belong within the one divine reality. Alongside this, there is the threefold structure of Paul's soteriology. Throughout his letters, the very grammar with which Paul speaks about God's work towards us speaks about the one divine act being undertaken by three distinct agents. In other words, the Jewish theologian Paul, by his experience of Jesus Christ on the road to Damascus in which Jesus spoke to him from the blinding light, undertook the hard task of reworking monotheism in such a way that the Father, Son, and Holy Spirit are internal to what it is to be the one God. Moreover, these personal identities are never presented in isolation. The Son is sent by the Father in the power of the Spirit. The Father is made known through the Son who is the exact representation of the Father's being. The Spirit is the Spirit of the Son, who binds the believer to the Son and through him to the Father. These three identities are not only included within the one God, they are also in reciprocal relationships that intertwine to such a degree that you cannot isolate one from the other.[13]

---

13. For a full discussion on this theme, see Hill, *Paul and the Trinity*.

Crucially, the three identities who are included within the scriptural witness to the one God does not simply refer to modes of God's relation to us. The fundamental doctrine of modalism is that God relates to creation in different modes, but God himself is one. This is a quite unsatisfactory way to think of the scriptural data. The Son and the Spirit through which we know God are God. They are God himself, not modes of God's activity. God has made himself known through himself. This association between God's act and God's being means that the reason God reveals himself as Father, Son, and Spirit is because he *is* Father, Son, and Spirit. The Father, Son, and Spirit are true of the way God has his life quite aside from his relations to creation. A very important corollary of this is that God exists as Father, Son, and Spirit quite independent of his relations to us. God would be Father, Son, and Spirit even if we had never been created.

As is expanded on in the following chapter, in his internal relations, God is simultaneously one and three. God's Threeness is not the division of his oneness, and God's oneness is not the combination of the three. God is one essence which exists in three persons. The three persons are not parts of the divine essence. Instead, the divine persons are ways in which the one divine essence has existence. Each of the divine persons is the fullness of the divine essence existing in a particular and personal way. They are distinct on account of a particular property that differentiates one person from the other two. This particular property is the way they are related to the other persons. The Father alone is the unbegotten source of the Son and the Spirit. The Son alone is eternally begotten from the Father. The Spirit alone proceeds from the Father through the Son. These relations are not voluntarily entered into. God the Father did not choose to generate the Son at some point. Quite the opposite, the Father has never not been the Father of the Son, and the Father and the Son have never not been bound together in the unity of the Holy Spirit. These relations are not something that God became. It is not that behind these relations, there is some other entity who may have become something else. There is no God behind these relations, instead there is God who has his life as these relations.

This is the character of God's absolute freedom, as laid out by Barth. God's triune life as God's life in himself is the perfect and eternal communion of love in which the Father eternally generates the Son and breathes out the Spirit. In his oneness, God is limitlessly abundant in his internal relations. Quite aside from creation, God is eternally perfect love. God's freedom is the freedom of the immanent Trinity. This is God's triune aseity, which is the bedrock of both divine and contingent freedom. The immanent Trinity is the name given to God's internal and non-transitive relations as Father, Son, and Spirit. These are the relations that are necessary to

God in which God has eternally had his life. The immanent Trinity is distinguished from the economic Trinity, which is God's external, transitive relations to us. This does not mean that there are two Trinities, but it means that there is a logical distinction between (i) God's eternal and necessary relations within himself (the immanent Trinity) and (ii) God's temporal and volitional relations to us (the economic Trinity). It is very important to not smudge over this distinction.[14] If there were no difference between the economic Trinity and immanent Trinity then it would be impossible to differentiate between God's voluntary and time-bound relations to us and God's necessary and eternal relations in himself. The cargo being carried by the doctrine of the immanent Trinity is the belief that God has his life as the communion of love of the Father, Son, and Spirit quite apart from and independent of us. This means that God would not be less God if creation had never existed. God is not more or less God by the fact of the existence of creation. God is God in the abundance of the eternal and reciprocal love shared between the Father, Son, and Spirit.

This provides perspective on what it is for God to be love. God's oneness is the oneness of the three persons united in perfect love and God's threeness is the threeness of one essence. The oneness and threeness are utterly inseparable. God is not three in terms of the one divine essence being divided up into three parts. God is not one in terms of the combination of the three persons into a whole as if "God" were the family name of Father, Son, and Spirit. God's oneness is reiterated in three different ways with those three ways being orientated ceaselessly to one another in reciprocal love. The one God exists in a threefold communion of love. By his nature God is a communion in himself; his being is as the one who loves.

God, who has his life in the perfect love of Father, Son, and Holy Spirit, overflows and creates fellowship between himself and creation.

> God is He who, without having to do so, seeks and creates fellow-
> ship between Himself and us. He does not have to do it, because
> in Himself without us, and therefore without this, He has that
> which he seeks and creates between Himself and us. It implies so
> to speak an overflow of His essence that He turns to us.[15]

God, in his perfect abundance, is an ever-living and ever-loving communion in himself and he *chooses* to go beyond the complete perfection in a generous, fellowship-seeking act towards us. The triune creator could have been without the world. God does not need to be Creator. God has his life

14. This is a theme that has been explored at length in the excellent work of Paul Molnar. See Molnar, *Divine Freedom and the Doctrine of the Immanent Trinity*.

15. Barth, *Church Dogmatics*, 2.1, 273.

as the eternal relation of love of Father, Son, and Spirit and so he "does not become relational in the creation of the world, rather his relational being is the ground and end of his relation to what he is not."[16] He is sufficient to himself in that relation of love and in that absolute perfection he extends beyond himself to share his life with something other than him.[17] While God has his life quite aside from creation in perfect completion, he *chooses* to create fellowship with something that is not him. In this way, God is not necessarily related to creation but yet as the one who has his being as communion, it is proper to the being of God that he is creator. It is in this context that we understand what it is to be created. God does not need any being distinct from his own to be the object of his love. He does not need to extend beyond himself to establish something else as the recipient of and respondent to love. God is the one who loves in freedom and this is the foundation of the existence of creation. The question that lies ahead of us is: how do we describe the freedom of creation in its existence and activity? What is it for creation to be free?

The Freedom of Creation

The freedom of creation is built on the foundation of the freedom of God. The freedom of creation is not contrary to its dependence on God. In fact, the freedom of creation is a direct result of it being freely brought into creation by God who himself is free from the creation he has made. This is not something that can be understood on materialistic or naturalistic terms.

Creation as an Article of Faith

The Christian doctrine of creation is not simply about our origins or about the nature of the universe. It is about God's identity as Creator, our identity as creatures, and the sort of relationship that exists between God and his creation. The Christian has something important to say about the created order that is distinct from what the scientist or philosopher has to say about contingent reality. The doctrine of creation is not a human account of our existence, it is not a human attempt at self-explanation and it certainly is not exhausted by what can be said within the well-defined parameters of the natural sciences. The doctrine of creation speaks about creation as exactly that: something that is brought into being by the act of the Creator. What

16. Schwöbel, "God, Creation and the Christian Community," 158.
17. Barth, *Humanity of God*, 50.

can be said about creation is inseparable from what can be said about its Creator. For this reason, a theology of creation is based on what is revealed to us about God. It is, in other words, an article of faith.

As Colin Gunton pointed out, if the doctrine of creation is inseparable from the doctrine of God, then the doctrine of the Trinity is of paramount importance in understanding the nature of creation.

> God is already, "in advance" of creation, a communion of persons existing in loving relations, (therefore) it becomes possible to say that he does not need the world, and so is able to will the existence of something else simply for its own sake. Creation is the outcome of God's love indeed, but of his unconstrained love. It is therefore not a necessary outcome of what God is, but is contingent.[18]

In other words, the character of God's outward relations to creation are understood in relation to God's internal relations as Father, Son, and Spirit. Take away the fact that God is in himself perfect, sufficient communion and you might think that God created in order to overcome some insufficiency in the way he has life, as if God required the act of moving beyond himself. However, when we take as our foundation stone that God in himself is perfect love and is the sufficient ground of his own existence, then we come to understand that God's external relations to us are not necessary but are volitional.

God is not completed or perfected on account of his relationship with creation. Creation does not exist because of something lacking in God. In fact, quite the opposite is the case: creation exists on account of God's fullness. God's freedom is his triune aseity. Out of the fullness of himself, God chose to make something other than himself. This is something that Augustine saw particularly clearly: God does not create out "of the compulsion of his needs," but "out of the abundance of his generosity."[19]

> For from the fullness of thy goodness that thy creation exists at all; to the end that the created good might not fail to be, even though it can profit thee nothing, and is nothing of thee nor equal to thee—since its existence comes from thee.[20]

Creation might never have been, and God would have not been diminished. There would have been no loss of God's perfection. We can put this round the other way: the existence of creation does not mean that God is enhanced or fulfilled. God does not have some latent potential to perfection which requires a relationship with something external to him in order

18. Gunton, *Triune Creator*, 9.
19. Augustine, *Literal Meaning of Genesis*, 1.13.
20. Augustine, *Conf.* 13.2.

to be realized. The inference we can draw from that is that creation is not necessary to God. God chose to bring something into being. This allows us to make a couple of very important statements about creation.

First, *creation is the beloved of God*. To say that God did not need to create is not the same as saying that creation is arbitrary. The opposite of necessity is not chance, but grace. God created out of grace to share his love with something that is not him: "Creation has therefore also to be understood as an expression of the love of God who remains faithful to what he has created in love."[21] Here we need to think about the character of God's freedom. God's freedom is the freedom of the triune God who loves in perfect and limitless reciprocity. Without needing to, God chose for this love to overflow to something that is not him.[22] Creation is the partner made by God to share in the blessing of his love. The purpose of creation, therefore, is to share in the blessing of the divine communion.

Second, *creation is free*. As Rowan Williams has demonstrated, God is wholly sufficient in himself; therefore, creation is free because it has not been created simply to offset some deficiency within the Creator.[23] On account of God's freedom being self-grounded, creation has the room to have its own reality quite aside from God. It is not constantly being drawn into the vortex of divine need wherein it would lose its distinct reality. In the perfection of his being, God is able to grant to creation a reality quite aside from himself. However, creation is not free in the way God is free. The freedom of creation is not grounded in itself. The freedom of creation is grounded in the choice of God to give it its own existence. Dependence, in other words, is a characteristic of the way creation has freedom. Freedom is given to creation by God in his transcendent freedom. Creaturely freedom, in other words, is *never* freedom from the external limit of God. Whatever our freedom as creatures might be, it is a mistake to think freedom is shaking off the shackles of our status as creatures, dependent on our Creator. Any such project is not a pursuit of liberty, but a flight into nonexistence.

Being and Willing

By thinking of creation as the work of the triune Creator, it becomes possible to maintain a clear distinction between God and his creation. Of all the many important distinctions that are made in theology, one of the most important is the distinction between modes of origination from (i)

---

21. Schwöbel, "God, Creation and the Christian Community," 157.

22. On this, see Barth, *Church Dogmatics*, 2.1, 272–97.

23. Williams, "On Being Creatures," 63–78.

the being of the Father and (ii) the will of the Father.[24] The reason that this distinction is so important is because it is the mechanism by which to maintain the difference between God's internal, non-transitive relations as Father, Son, and Spirit and God's external, transitive relations as Creator and Redeemer.[25] This distinction was at work earlier in this chapter in the distinction between the immanent Trinity (God's non-transitive relations as Father, Son, and Spirit) and the economic Trinity (God's transitive relations as Creator and Redeemer). Absolutely central to this distinction is that the immanent Trinity is the way God necessarily has life. There is no choice in this; God eternally has his life as Father, Son, and Spirit. The economic Trinity, however, is God in extension beyond himself, chosen in the freedom of the fullness of his internal relations.

The Nicene-Constantinopolitan Creed operates with a clear and consistent distinction between God's internal relations and God's external relations. The Son is begotten from the being of the Father. The Son is "God from God, light from light." Likewise, the Spirit proceeds out from the Father. These are relations that God does not choose to enter into; they are the way in which God has his life in eternity. The Creed also has a different level of relationships, which are those that God chooses to enter into. These are the relations in which God makes heaven and earth and God the Son becomes part of his creation "for us and for our salvation."

Perhaps the clearest way in which the Creed makes this distinction is in the difference between the begetting of the Son and the making of creation: the Son is "begotten, not made." In doing this, the Fathers of Nicea were responding to a set of theological ideas associated with Arius, the Alexandrian presbyter. Arius taught that the begetting of the Son from the Father was all but synonymous to the making of creation. One of the central ways that this identity of the begetting of the Son and the making of creation was expressed in Arius's thought was that the Father elected to bring the Son into existence. Accordingly, Arius considered begetting and creating as synonymous modes of origination from the Father. This is very well demonstrated in the following extract of a letter he sent to Alexander, the bishop of Alexandria (as it is recorded by Athanasius).

> We acknowledge One God, alone Ingenerate, alone Everlasting, alone Unbegun, alone True, alone having Immortality, alone Wise, alone Good, alone Sovereign; Judge, Governor, and

24. Gunton, *Triune Creator*, 66–68.

25. For an analysis of the development of this distinction in the formative discussions concerning the Christian doctrine of God, see Anatolios, *Retrieving Nicea*, 41–100.

Providence of all, unalterable and unchangeable, just and good, God of Law and Prophets and New Testament; who begat an Only-begotten Son before eternal times, through whom He has made both the ages and the universe; and begat Him, not in semblance, but in truth; and that He made Him subsist at His own will, unalterable and unchangeable; . . . but, as we say, at the will of God, created before times and before ages, and gaining life and being from the Father, who gave subsistence to His glories together with Him. . . . And God, being the cause of all things, is Unbegun and altogether Sole, but the Son being begotten apart from time by the Father, and being created and founded before ages, was not before His generation, but being begotten apart from time before all things, alone was made to subsist by the Father. For He is not eternal or co-eternal or co-unoriginate with the Father, nor has He His being together with the Father, as some speak of relations, introducing two ingenerate beginnings, but God is before all things as being Monad and Beginning of all. Wherefore also He is before the Son.[26]

For Arius, the Father alone is God, whereas the Son is a creature that is brought into being by the will of the Father in some antecedent period before time. For Arius, then, the Son is not necessary but is a contingent reality.

In the most explicit of ways the Nicene-Constantinopolitan Creed rejected Arius's theology by insisting upon the Son's unity of nature with the Father. But, as well as rejecting the headline of Arian Christology, the Nicene Creed also dismantles the inner workings of Arius's system of thought. This is where the utility of the distinction between the making of creation and the begetting of the Son is seen. The earlier Nicene Creed does this by making a specific claim about what is meant by begotten. In a parenthetic elaboration on what begotten means, the Creed says "the only begotten, that is of the essence of the Father, God of God." To be begotten, in other words, is to come out from God the Father in a way that only God can. The Son is "light of light, very God of very God." The Son, in other words is God in the mode of existence of being begotten from the Father. This specification of what is intended by begotten establishes the relation of the Son and the Father as necessary to the way in which God has his life. It is not a relation God chose to enter into; it is the way in which God has his life.

This settlement was defended by the pro-Nicene theologian Athanasius of Alexandria. Athanasius argued that the relationship between the Son and the Father is not a relation of will because they are necessarily related to one another. The Father has never not been the Father because he is in

26. Athanasius, *Syn.* 16.

an eternal relationship with the Son.[27] On the other hand, creation is made, a product of the will of God. More recently, the centrality of the distinction between the necessary relation of Father and Son and the relationship between God and creation was stressed by the Georges Florovsky. Florovsky asserted the heterogeneity of God and created reality through a posited contradistinction between the relation of God and creation and the unity of nature of the Son and the Father in the generation of the Son *from the being* of the Father.[28] Unlike the Son, creation is made from nothing *in accordance with the will* of the Creator.[29] Florovsky maintained a careful difference between divine generation as true of the nature of God, and creation as an act external to the nature of God, but in accordance with God's will. Crucially, Florovsky understood this to not be a merely *logical* distinction, but rather an *ontological* distinction.[30] Florovsky argued that God is eternally Father as the "Son's existence flows eternally from the very essence of the Father."[31] On these grounds, the trinitarian names of Father and Son do more than denote logical order; rather they are "ontological names," which pertain to the being of God.[32] By contrasting the generation of the Son from the creation of the world, Florovsky ensured that creation must not be introduced into the intra-Trinitarian life, as a coeternal reality: "The idea of the world has its basis *not in the essence, but in the will* of God."[33] Creation is determined as a heterogeneous something, given its own extra-divine reality through the volitional act of God.[34] Very significantly, in attributing creation to the will of God, Florovsky emphasized that creation is not necessary to God, but is a supererogatory work of the sheer goodness of God.[35]

The distinction between (i) the non-transitive relations (those that are internal to the life of God, specifically the begetting of the Son and the procession of the Spirit) and (ii) the transitive relations (those that are external to the necessary way in which God has his life, specifically the making and sustaining of creation) makes it possible to affirm that the Son and the Spirit come out from the Father in their respective ways, but

27. Athanasius, *C. Ar.* 3.23.6.

28. Florovsky, "Creation and Creaturehood," 47. For a fuller discussion of Florovsky's doctrine of creation, see Irving, "Florovsky and T. F. Torrance on the Doctrine of Creation," 301–22.

29. Florovsky, "Creation and Creaturehood," 47–48.

30. Florovsky, "Concept of Creation," 61–62.

31. Florovsky, "Concept of Creation," 53.

32. Florovsky, "Concept of Creation," 52.

33. Florovsky, "Creation and Creaturehood," 56.

34. Florovsky, "Creation and Creaturehood," 46–47.

35. Florovsky, "Creation and Creaturehood," 57.

do *not* do so by the will of God. Creation, on the other hand, comes out from God as a product of the will of God. This has two major applications. First, it is the very lifeblood of trinitarian doctrine because it enabled theologians to recognize difference between Father, Son, and Spirit without dividing them at the level of what they are. Second, it is integral to our understanding of God's freedom from creation because it enables us to say that God chose to create, and he is not in a necessary relation to creation. This becomes the foundation of the distinctive freedom of creation.[36] However, as Gunton points out, this emphasis on the sheer will of God in creating must be balanced by a recognition of why God should want to create.[37] In part, this has to do with God's inherently relational being whereby it is proper to what he is to stand in relation to creation. However, this needs to be complemented by a Christological starting point in which we see the orientation of God toward creation revealed. From this basis, the naked will of God to create becomes clothed with love. This will-of-God-to-communion is explored in the next chapter.

The Contingent Freedom of Creation

The character of creation's freedom is not absolute, but contingent. Creation is given its own free existence by the direct and gracious act of God. Frances Young superbly captures the spirit of Basil of Caesarea's sermons on the biblical account of creation by describing it as "a summary of the sheer gift of finite existence, a doxological invitation rather than a philosophical or scientific exposition of origins."[38] Basil's sermons have the constant theme that the world did not come into being by chance but by the will of God. One of the bluntest expressions of this is the idea of creation from nothing. To say God created from nothing is not to say that God created out of a material called nothing. Instead, it is to say that aside from God there was nothing else and God brought something that isn't God into being.

The Judeo-Christian notion that God created from nothing was very distinctive in the ancient world. The surrounding cultures tended to ascribe to God some sort of initiative as the head of a chain of being in which creation flowed inevitably from the creative potential of God, or to think of God as imposing some order upon some eternally existing matter that was in a state of chaos and non-life. The problem with these ideas is that they make the

36. For a systematic discussion of this theme, see Webster, "Trinity and Creation," 4–19.

37. Gunton, *Triune Creator*, 76–77.

38. Young, *God's Presence*, 47.

relationship between God and something-that-isn't-God a necessary relationship, and thereby undermine the freedom of God. Without the doctrine of creation from nothing, we would be left with two eternal realities: God and the non-divine entity that became creation.[39] By contrast, creation from nothing asserts an absolute beginning to creation. There was nothing other than God and God brought something other than him into existence in an utterly free choice. Creation from nothing states in the clearest possible terms that creation is not necessary. The world might not have existed and might have been other than it is. In other words, creation is *contingent*.

The meaning of contingence is well explained by Georges Florovsky.

> The world exists. But it *began* to exist. And that means: *the world could have not existed*. There is no necessity whatsoever for the existence of the world. Creaturely existence is not self-sufficient and is not independent. In the created world itself there is no foundation, no basis for genesis and being. Creation by its very existence witnesses to and proclaims its creaturehood, it proclaims that it has been produced.[40]

As contingent, creation does not contain within itself the reason or the possibility for its own existence. In being brought to existence by the will of God, creation might not have been. As such, creation has no internal reason in itself for it to be or to be the way that it is. It exists because it has been brought into being. The existence of creation comes from outside of creation, given to it as a gift. In the generosity of his own freedom, God gives to creation a distinct existence alongside himself. Creation from nothing means that God is absolutely free from creation and that creation is utterly dependent on God for its existence. This means that the fact of creation is the gift of God. God has given existence to something which would not otherwise have been.

Contingence means that any necessity in relation is not reversible. God is not in a necessary relation to creation but creation is in a necessary relation to God. It is an important characteristic of creation's freedom that it is not mutually exclusive with necessity. The freedom of creation is a *contingent* freedom. As contingent, creation is dependent upon God for being brought into being. As creation is freely brought into being by the will of God it is clearly distinct from God. Creation has its own free existence as creation. This is what T. F. Torrance has called the "peculiar interlocking of dependence and independence" that characterizes contingence.[41] Although

39. Young, *God's Presence*, 53-55.
40. Florovsky, "Creation and Creaturehood," 45.
41. Torrance, *Divine and Contingent Order*, 35.

creation is entirely dependent on God for its existence, it is independent in
that it is given an existence that is distinct from God. The independence, or
freedom, of creation is that God, in his divine freedom, gives to it an existence wholly differentiated from his own. In other words, that creation is
made by the will of God in accordance with the freedom of God, creation is
characterized by its own contingent freedom. The freedom of God from creation is the foundation upon which creation can be given its own freedom.
The freedom of creation is not like the freedom of God. God has an absolute
freedom and creation has a contingent freedom, which is grounded in the
absolute freedom of God. It is precisely because God is free from creation in
the sufficiency of his triune aseity that he is able to give to creation its own
existence wholly differentiated from himself.

It is not only that creation is free in that it has its own differentiated
existence. In his freedom, God also gives to creation its own free agency.
On account of the fact that creation is not made to mechanistically address
some divine need, God gives to creation the liberty to develop and to act
quite independently from any divine coercion. The freedom of creation is
not a rival to the freedom of God. The more one may stress the freedom of
creation does not diminish the freedom of God: "(God) is not exalted in the
suppression of the creature. He does not find his triumph in the creature's
lack of freedom or power compared with His own unconditional and irre-
sistible Lordship."[42] In his freedom, God gives agency over to that which has
made to freely choose and act within creation. Terrence Fretheim points out
that the creation narratives do not present creation as an inertial system,
but rather something that can be developed through the creative agency of
creation itself.[43] As Fretheim says, "God is a power-sharing God."[44] Creation
is given agency to bring forward new creatures according to their kind (Gen
1:24). Humans as the image of God are given a special share in God's do-
minion over creation and are endowed with the task of subduing creation
and enable it to flourish (Gen 1:28). The necessity of humanity as a creative
agent facilitating the realization of all creation's potential is continued in
the second creation narrative: no plant had yet appeared on earth because
there was no human to work the ground (Gen 2:5). God's response to the
loneliness of the man is to involve him in determining what will be a suitable partner for him (Gen 2:20). Remarkably, in his providential care and
governance of creation, God makes space for human choice and activity to
determine the development of the created order. All of this demonstrates

42. Barth, *Church Dogmatics*, 3.1, 130.
43. Fretheim, *God and World*, 48–61.
44. Fretheim, *God and World*, 49.

that "God so values human freedom that God will take into account the free human response from within the creative process in shaping the future."[45] Created things have the freedom to affect creation because God gives that agency over to what he has made. Creation has responsibility for the way in which it exercises the agency God has given it. God has placed enormous value in human choice and agency. We must never downplay the significance of this because, if we do, we may lose sight of the fact that we are responsible for how we live as God's creatures.

God gives over to his creation the freedom to act and respond, which in no way compromises God's transcendent freedom. As the image of God, this is focused specifically through humanity. As Alistair McFadyen has rightly said "in the provision of space for free human response to the divine address, the divine-human relationship is structured from God's side as a dialogue."[46] God's respect for creation's freedom means that humanity is addressed as God's dialogue partner and it must make its response. Humanity is free to reject God consciously or unconsciously. In other words, because humanity's freedom is a contingent freedom (as opposed to an absolute freedom) and because God created something to be his beloved, the freedom of creation has built into its very structure the responsibility of response to the one who created us. However, while our specific freedom as human creatures contains the responsibility of being God's covenant partner (a being who has existence-as-answer to God), God does not determine the content of our response. In our freedom, we are constantly before God and we live as those who carry within our very distinct existence the burden or the joy of responding to the overflowing love of God. The end of this is for God's creation to be drawn into communion with the triune God, to the glory of its Creator. This is too great a thing to lay at the feet of humanity in our current fragility. The burden of it would be overwhelming if we did not turn immediately to Jesus Christ, God as human for humanity.

The Person of Jesus Christ: The Freedom of God and the Freedom of Creation

The relationship between God and creation is established on the act of God, which, while it is consistent with his triune being, is not a necessary act. Devoid of necessity, the relationship of God and creation is not one of ontic continuity, but of grace. Therefore, all elements of Christian theology must not start with innate human ideas about God, as if there were some

---

45. Fretheim, *God and World*, 59.

46. McFadyen, *Call of Personhood*, 19.

bond of being between us and God. Instead, Christian theology begins and ends with what we learn about how God acts towards us through Christ and what he reveals to us by the Spirit. This is the matter at hand in Paul's opening two chapters of 1 Corinthians where the wisdom of humanity is exposed by the apparent foolishness of the cross and the necessity that the Spirit makes known to us the things of God. Any proportionality between God and creation is not innate but is established by the purposive act of God in his self-revelation.

For this reason, the person of Jesus Christ is utterly fundamental to any description of the relationship between God and creation. This point has been made with considerable clarity by Torrance.

> The analogy of proportionality grounded upon the Word and grace of God will be set forth in this fashion; [humanity] and God are related in the mutual relation of faith and grace *proportionaliter* to the relation of [humanity] and God in the hypostatic union in Christ Jesus. That means that a Christian doctrine of the Word of God and human decision, of election and human faith, of the Divine Presence and the worldly element in the sacrament, etc., will be grounded entirely upon the hypostatic union as its true and only valid analogy; that is, upon the central relation and union of God and [humanity] of which every other relation must partake.[47]

Torrance's point is that the relation of the divine nature and human nature within the person of Jesus Christ is the normative basis upon which to understand the relationship between God and creation more broadly.[48] The dynamic between divine grace and human faith and dependence is set out in Christ. Accordingly, Torrance argued that Christian theology as it pertains to the divine-human relation takes the hypostatic union as its governing structure. As God among us, Jesus Christ brings to focus what the relationship between God and creation is. Therefore, the person of Jesus Christ provides us with the fundamental grammar of the broader relationship of God and creation. This does not undermine the particularity and the unique reality of Jesus. Instead, Jesus reveals the truth of God and of his relationship to creation.

In Jesus Christ, divine nature and human nature are in personal union without any confusion or change and without being divided or separated. The possibility of positive union between the divine and the human is not earthed in anything other than actuality. In contrast to this Ebionitism and

---

47. Torrance, *Reconstruction*, 114.

48. See also Irving, "Person of Jesus Christ," 349–66.

Docetism neglect the actuality of personal union of God and humanity and construct different accounts of the person of Christ which are inconsistent with him being both fully God and fully human. Ebionite Christology (believed among a community of Jewish converts to Christianity) held Jesus to be a human who was later elevated to the status of the son of God. Within Ebionitism, Christ does not have existence as God the Son prior to the incarnation. Instead, it understands the human Jesus Christ to come before his elevation to become the son of God. This form of Christology describes Jesus Christ as God's agent on creation in such a way that attempted to protect both the unique transcendence of God and the distinct reality of creation. Docetic Christology, on the other hand, emerged from a Greek framework of thought which prioritized the purity of the ideal and the non-material existence and held this in a sharp distinction from the mundane and corrupting influence of the material world. Unlike Ebionite Christology, Docetism accepted that Jesus was God but rejected the actuality of his humanity. Instead, Docetic Christology asserted that the divine only seemed to become human, an illusion which was unreal.

Ebionite and Docetic Christologies have one thing in common: they envisage a gulf between God and creation which cannot be traversed without compromising the transcendent freedom of God or the contingent freedom of creation. The misapprehension that the divinity of Jesus must compromise the integrity of his humanity and *vice versa* continued into the more formalized Christologies of subsequent centuries. Within the Alexandrian tradition, Apollinarianism operates with the assumption that the full integrity of human existence needs to be compromised in order to bring about a personal union with the divine. Apollinarius held that God the Son took humanity into a real union with himself but that the humanity which the Son assumed was not complete. In becoming united with humanity, the divine *Logos* displaced the human mind and spirit such that the *Logos* became the directive center of intelligence and action within the person of Jesus Christ. Apollinarianism offers a view of the relation of God and creation which involves compromising the full integrity of creation in order to accommodate the real presence of the divine.

Within the Antiochene tradition, the difficulty fell on the question of the authenticity of the personal union of divinity and humanity. Theodore of Mopsuestia affirmed the full reality of the humanity of Jesus Christ alongside the full divinity existing in one person. If Christ were to overcome human sin, Theodore believed, then Jesus must assume the source of sin in the human mind and soul. In this, Theodore insisted that the human nature which was assumed by God the Son was complete and remained its integrity. In this way, Theodore held that the two natures remain unaltered despite being united in one person. Nestorius was deeply influenced by Theodore in that he insisted that the two natures of Jesus remain unaltered in their union. However, it is the way in which he argued this point that demonstrates uncertainty about the capacity for the divine and the created to be in personal union without being in rivalry. Nestorius equated any idea of a personal union of God and humanity in the person of Jesus with a threat to the distinct integrity of both. He was concerned with preserving the integrity of the divine nature from such human things as birth, deterioration, and death. Likewise, he was concerned to preserve the integrity of humanity by protecting a full human existence and agency being displaced by the presence of the divine nature. In view of this uncertainty concerning the possibility of the divine and human natures to be in personal union without rivalry, Nestorius reasoned that the two natures must have existed side by side each retaining their own respective properties and fields of activity. For this reason, the traditional picture of Nestorianism is that Jesus Christ is divided into two persons, one divine and one human, with separate wills and works.[49]

The underlying theological currents of Apollinarian and Nestorian Christology presuppose that God and creation are rivals and that the more stress is laid upon the presence and agency of one must necessarily mean a reduction for the other (unless, of course, some way is found to account for their isolation from one another). Against both of these trends the Chalcedonian Settlement affirms that, in the personal union, the divine and human natures are unconfused and unchanged. They retain their respective integrity despite being brought into an inseparable and indivisible union. The divine nature and the human are in a personal union without loss of freedom to either side.

> Following, then, the holy Fathers, we all unanimously teach that our Lord Jesus Christ is to us One and the same Son, the Self-same Perfect in Godhead, the Self-same Perfect in Manhood; *truly God and truly Man*; the Self-same of a rational soul and body; co-essential with the Father according to the Godhead, the Self-same co-essential with us according to the Manhood; like us in all things, sin apart; before the ages begotten of the Father as to the Godhead, but in the last days, the Self-same, for us and for our salvation (born) of Mary the Virgin *Theotokos* (Mother of God) as to the Manhood; One and the Same Christ, Son, Lord, Only-begotten acknowledged in Two Natures unconfusedly, unchangeably, indivisibly, inseparably; the difference of the Natures being in no way removed because of the

49. See Kelly, *Early Christian Doctrines*, 289–317.

> Union, but rather the properties of each Nature being preserved, and (both) concurring into One Person and One Hypostasis; not as though He were parted or divided into Two Persons, but One and the Self-same Son and Only-begotten God, Word, Lord, Jesus Christ.

Jesus Christ is fully God and fully human. The two natures retain complete integrity in their union in the one person of Jesus Christ. There is one person, Jesus Christ, who is both God and human. While the two natures may not be confused with one another they also must not be separated from one another. In the person of God the Son incarnate, the divine nature of the eternal Son and the human nature have their subsistence together such that they cannot be divided from one another or separated from one another.[50] The Chalcedonian definition, therefore, presents an understanding of Jesus in which the divine nature and the human nature are united in one person without the full reality of one compromising the full reality of the either. This is a noncompetitive account of the relationship between God and creation within which God the Son opens himself to receive description in human terms (i.e., born of a woman) without experiencing any change or confusion with created reality.

The personal union of divine nature and human nature in the person of Jesus Christ is an act of grace.[51] God the Son chose to become a human by the power of the Spirit in accordance with the will of the Father. The mutuality of the divine nature and the human nature in the person of Jesus Christ does not undermine the priority of divine action and grace. The humanity of Jesus Christ only has personal existence by the act of God the Son to assume it into personal union with himself. There was no independent human person who existed prior to being assumed into union with God the Son. For example, it is not the case that the human person Jesus Christ was adopted as the Son of God at some point.[52] Instead, Jesus Christ's humanity was brought into existence through the free act of God the Son assuming human nature into union with himself. This secures the priority of the grace of God and the dependence of the human nature on its being assumed into union with God the Son. This point is categorized as *anhypostasia*.

Crucially, the priority of God the Son's assumption of human nature over the independent personal existence of the human Jesus Christ does not compromise the freedom of Jesus' humanity. The human nature of Jesus

---

50. To subsist is to exist as a concrete and particular reality. It is close to the meaning of exist, meaning to actually *stand out* as a real thing with an actual presence.

51. Torrance, *Incarnation*, 229.

52. For a superb study on this theme, see Bird, *Jesus the Eternal Son.*

Christ only has existence from the very beginning within the person of God the Son and has no independent personal existence (*anhypostasia*). However, having been assumed and so brought into being, the human nature of Christ has a real and true subsistence within the person of the Son. This means that the human nature of Jesus is given existence in union with God the Son but remains fully human.

> Although there was no independent personal being called Jesus apart from the incarnation, that does not mean that in the incarnation there was no particular individual called Jesus existing as a particular human being, with a rational human mind and will and soul and therefore it does not mean that he did not completely possess human nature. Jesus had a fully human mind and human soul and human will; he lived a fully human life in hypostatic union with his divine life, and in that union with his divine life, his human life had manifested the most singular and unique personality as a man.[53]

This point is categorized as *enhypostasia*: the human nature of Jesus only has existence within the person of God the Son, but it does have a real and true existence as human nature. As Gunton has argued, it is necessary to undergird this affirmation of the true humanity of Jesus Christ with the recognition of the centrality of the Spirit in the conception and enabling Jesus to live the life of God the Son within the fragilities and limitations of our humanity.[54] It is this that preserves the historical particularity of the Son's real human activity.

Anhypostasia and *enhypostasia* are in complementary and should not be separated. On one hand, the dependence of the personal existence of the human nature of Jesus needs to be held in relation to the real historical particularity of the existence of the human nature of Jesus within the person of the Son. On the other hand, the real historical particularity of the existence of Jesus' human nature in the Son needs to be held in relation to the primacy of the act of God the Son. Without balance on this point, there is every possibility of toppling either into Docetism or Ebionitism. That Jesus Christ's humanity has existence only from its personal union with God the Son (*anhypostasia*) is the presupposition of the real existence of the human nature in the person of the Son (*enhypostasia*). This means that the existence of the human nature is entirely by the grace of God *and* that the human nature that is brought into being by God's gracious action has a fully human existence. In this way, *anhypostasia* and *enhypostasia* together give formal expression to

---

53. Torrance, *Incarnation*, 230.
54. Gunton, "Two Dogmas Revisited," 359–76.

the priority of grace, the nonnecessity of the existence of the human nature of Jesus alongside its actual, full existence in union with God the Son.

There are two very important points to draw from this which address the extremes of Nestorianism and Apollinarianism. First, against Apollinarianism, the human nature of Jesus Christ exists only in union with the divine Son, but it is given a real and discrete existence. The human nature of Jesus may be dependent upon the divine act of grace, but this does not diminish the integrity of that human nature. God's freedom does not undermine the freedom of creation but is its very condition. Second, against Nestorianism, it is only within the person of God the Son that the human nature exists. There is no separate personal existence of the human nature of Jesus. There is only existence as God the Son incarnate.

The hypostatic union is the normative expression of the relationship between God and creation. This can only be said with the immediate qualifier that the personal union of God and creation is utterly unique in the person of Jesus Christ and we cannot extend it beyond the person of Jesus. However, the inner logic of the doctrine of the hypostatic union as it is expressed in the theological grammar of the *anhypostasia-enhypostasia* couplet does demonstrate a relation of God to his creation in which God's freedom in his grace takes priority (there is no created thing outside of God's grace, but God exists in freedom from his creation), but far from obscuring the discrete reality of creation, this is actually the basis on which creation has its distinct and free existence. God and creation are in a personal relationship of love without the freedom of either side being compromised. The relationship of God and creation needs to be refracted through this Christological lens, without taking the extra step of saying that all creation participates in the incarnation. What we are interested in is the inner logic of the relation of God and creation which is set forward in Jesus Christ. The independent existence of God the Son aside from the union. The dependence of the human nature in being assumed into personal union for its existence. The actual discrete and full existence of the human nature as human within the person of the Son. This provides the basic structure and grammar for our understanding of the relationship between God and creation. God is free from creation existing in the self-sufficiency of his own triune life. Creation is not necessary to God and is created by the free act of God's grace. In creating, God truly gives to creation its own existence which may depend on the act of God but is still gifted its own distinct existence. Creation has its own contingent freedom but its life is within the personal will of God for it. In other words, the very pattern of God's absolute freedom from creation and creation's contingent independence is grounded upon the person of Jesus Christ.[55]

This discussion has centered on the static categories of the discrete divine and human natures. However, there is the equally important area of agency, in terms of the relationship between God's activity as Creator and ours as creature. The same Christological principles apply here, too. If God is the source of created reality, then every action and every agent is derived from God. God is the supreme actor who makes everything else active. If God did not create, there would be nothing that could be active. This does not make the agency of created reality any less free. God's activity in creation does not remove the integrity or limit the agency of that which he created. Instead, it means that creatures have received their freedom to act from God's freedom to create. God's action is not in competition with the activity of creatures. The more there is of God's activity on creation does not diminish creaturely freedom. The more there is of creaturely freedom does not diminish divine freedom. This is not a "God of the gaps" scenario in which God is used as an explanatory hypothesis to cover over gaps in our understanding of how the finite universe functions. God's action as Creator does not overwhelm activity in the created realm. Rather, God's activity *causes* the activity of creation.[56] This means that God's agency as Creator is different order to our agency as creatures and the freedom of both is uncompromised by their interaction.

Even so, the gospel refers to God's interaction in creation in such a way that affects and transforms his creation. God accomplishes something in creation which does not arise naturally from within the scope of created agency itself: God reveals himself, God saves sinners and pours his Spirit out upon human flesh. God the Son draws humanity into personal union with himself by assuming human nature. The way in which we might coordinate the way we talk of the relationship between God and creation such that it is comprehensible and objectively governed is to say that what we understand about Jesus is key to understanding what we can say about the relationship between God and creation overall. Once again, Jesus Christ provides us with the basic *grammar* by which to understand how God and creation relate.

This is a theme that has recently been explored by Rowan Williams in his magisterial study *Christ: The Heart of Creation*. In the opening pages of this work, Williams lays out the fundamental point that the study of the

---

55. For a more detailed exposition of this point, please see Irving, "Person of Jesus Christ," 349–66.

56. McSwain, *Scripture, Metaphysics and Poetry*, 22–27.

person and work of Jesus Christ provides the model by which to understand the relation of God and creation more generally.

> God makes the world to be *itself*, to have an integrity and good-ness that is—by God's gift—its own. At the same time, God makes the world to be open to a relation with God's own infinite life that can enlarge and transfigure the created order without destroying it. The model developed in Christology is the model that clarifies all we say about God's relation with the world, the relation between the infinite and the finite, Creator and creation. The fullness and the flourishing of creation is not something that has to be won at the Creator's expense; the outpouring of God's life into the world to fulfil the world's potential for joy and reconciliation does not entail an amputation of the full reality of the world's life. And all this is summed up in our belief in a Christ who is uninterruptedly living a creaturely, finite life on earth and at the same time living out depths of divine life and uninterruptedly enjoying the relation that enterally subsists be-tween the divine Source or Father and the divine Word or Son.[57]

The divine interruption of God's gracious activity toward us does not replace creaturely activity precisely because in Jesus Christ *God acted as a human*. The distinct reality of the divine act is not compromised by its personal union in Jesus Christ with human act, and nor is the integrity of human act compromised by that union. We must now ask the question: what does all of this mean for the Church?

The Freedom and Catholicity of the Church

To begin to think about the Church from the basis of God's relation to creation requires a little bit of conceptual shift for many of us. Just as we may find it difficult to think of the doctrine of redemption in stereo with the doctrine of creation, we have grown accustomed to thinking of the doctrine of the Church in isolation. Christoph Schwöbel has observed that this conceptual isolation of ecclesiology takes the form of the division of the work of the persons of the Trinity, with creation thought of as the act of the Father and the bringing into being of the Church thought of as the act of the Son or the Spirit.[58] However, the work of God is indivisible. Like creation, the Church is the work of the triune God and needs to be thought

57. Williams, *Christ*, xiii.

58. Schwöbel, "God, Creation and the Christian Community," 171. See also Schwö-bel, "Creature of the Word," 110–45.

of in its appropriate network of relations. The Church has its origin in the threefold act of God as by the will of the Father we are united to the incarnate Son in the power of the Spirit. The Church is brought into existence by our being drawn to participate in the glory of the triune God through Jesus Christ who assumed our humanity and ascended to the Father's side. As a creature brought into being by the act of the triune God, the Church stands in the same relation as creation to the absolute freedom of God: it is contingent and characterized by a contingent freedom. This should not be understood in the same way as John Macquarrie's suggestion that the fact of creation contains within itself the Church.[59] The Church is not a necessary act of the being of creation in seeking self-transcendence. The Church is an act of God. It is in the act of God, not in the being of creation, that there is correspondence between creation and the Church.

The Church as a Creature of the Word of God

The Church is that which is called into being by the Word of God and the Spirit of God. This is a point that was insisted upon by the theologians of the Reformation. Both the nature and the mission of the Church were given to it from the outside and it was not a self-perpetuating or self-sustaining institution. Of course, this insight is not unique to the Protestant tradition. However, it has been expressed with particular urgency in the Protestant tradition as a reaction to the heightened clericalism and institutional abuses of the late-medieval Catholic Church. Like creation, the Church is a creature of God's grace. The Church does not exist in and of itself. The Church is not brought into being by the immanent processes of creation. The Church does not exist as the intensification of admirable human desires for self-transcendence, communion, and altruism which have coalesced into an institutional expression. This means that there is something the Church and creation have in common: both have been brought into existence through the Word of God and in the power of the Spirit: "the Church is thus the creature of God's Word and of the Holy Spirit. It belongs to God, is God's gift and cannot exist by itself and for itself."[60]

From the beginning, the people of God have always been assembled by the word and act of God calling them into existence. Abram was called out from Ur and was made the father of a nation covenanted to God. God chose Israel to be his people and called them out of Egypt and established them as his people. Jesus established a messianic community around

59. Macquarrie, *Principles of Christian Theology*, 347.
60. *Nature and Mission of the Church*, 4, para. 9.

himself through calling people to follow him to take part in his messianic mission. Through the death and resurrection of Christ we are called out of the power of sin and death through into new life. The Holy Spirit is poured out through which believers are incorporated into Christ and receive the gifts required for the existence and flourishing of the Church. The Church is established by the redemptive work of God in which "those who were far off have been brought near by the blood of Christ" (Eph 2:13), establishing the people of God "a chosen race, a royal priesthood, a holy nation, God's own people, in order that you may proclaim the mighty acts of him who called you out of darkness and into his wonderful light" (2 Pet 2:9). The Church is brought into existence by the act of God by which "he has made known to us the mystery of his will, according to his good pleasure that he set forth in Christ, as a plan for the fullness of time to gather up all things in him" (Eph 1:9–10). In other words, the Church has its origin in the act of God. For this reason, it has the same fundamental structure as creation as a whole: the Church is called into existence by God's creative action.[61] This has been well explained by P. T. Forsyth.

> The Church rests on the grace of God, the judging, atoning, regenerating grace of God which is his holy love in the form it must take with human sin. Wherever that is heartily confessed and goes on to rule we have the true Church. Insofar as the Church is a creature, it is the creature of the preached gospel of God's grace, forgiving, redeeming and creating us anew by Christ's cross. The Church was created by the preaching of that solitary gospel and fortified by the sacraments of it which are, indeed, but other ways of receiving, confessing and preaching it. The Church is the social and practical response to that grace.[62]

In being brought into being by the call of God, the Church has the word of God as the center and the ground of its existence. The Church is brought into existence by participation in Christ, the incarnate Word, which is the Word of God that is witnessed to in the Scriptures and the faithful exposition of the Scriptures in preaching. As such the Church is the "creature of God's Word (*creatura Verbi*)."[63]

Something very similar is expressed by Calvin in a section outlining the grounds for separation from the Roman Catholic Church. For Calvin, the Church is "Christ's Kingdom, and he reigns by his Word alone."[64] The

---

61. Schwöbel, "Creature of the Word," 110–45.

62. Forsyth, *Church and the Sacraments*, 31.

63. *Nature and Mission of the Church*, 4, para. 10.

64. Calvin, *Inst.* 4.2.4.

reality of the Church as the Church is contingent upon its remaining established on the "teaching of the apostles and prophets, with Christ himself the chief cornerstone."[65] The reality of the Church, therefore, is not in a necessary relationship to the institutional entity that persists through time (instead, the visibility of the Church, Calvin argues, is in the teaching of Scripture and the celebration of the sacraments[66]). As the Church is contingent upon the word which calls it into being, to depart from the Lordship of Christ exercised through Scripture, for Calvin, is to remove the core criterion which makes the Church truly the Church.[67] The Lordship of Christ manifested through the gathered assembly ordering its life under his word is the ground of the unity of Church,[68] and so to no longer coordinate the corporate life of the Church under that criterion is the same as revoking true ecclesial identity and unity.

The Church, as brought into being by the act of God in his work of new creation, is constituted by a structure that corresponds to the structure of creation. Just as creation is made from nothing, so God establishes for himself a holy community from an unholy group of strangers. Just as creation was not necessitated by some deficiency in the life of God, so the Church is not necessitated by any such deficiency. The Church is a creation of God in his sovereign freedom and kindness. Like creation, the Church is brought into being by the sheer grace of God, whereby its entire existence depends upon the generosity of God. Within this absolute dependence on the grace of God, the Church is given its own distinct reality, its own contingent freedom. Like creation, the structure of the Church is patterned in accordance with the person of Jesus Christ. That is to say, the divine acts which gives it life are not discontinuous with, but constitute the foundation of, its actual existence as a human reality. In this, the Church corresponds to the relationship between God and creation set forward in the person of Jesus. The act of grace which brought about the union of God and humanity in God the Son assuming humanity into union with himself is the basis of the existence of the human nature of Jesus. Without this, there would have been no Jesus. Jesus was not a human being who was living and then, at some point in his life, became adopted as the Son of God. Likewise, the Church exists because it has been brought into being by the act of God in which we are adopted as his children. The Church, therefore, has a pronounced *anhypostatic*

---

65. Calvin, *Inst.* 4.2.1.
66. Calvin, *Inst.* 4.1.9.
67. Calvin, *Inst.* 4.2.9–12.
68. Calvin, *Inst.* 4.2.6.

character: it depends from first to last on the grace of God to bring it into being by assuming it into personal union with Jesus Christ.

Just as with creation, in bringing the Church into being, God gives his Church a real human existence that is distinct from himself. The Church is not God and should never be mistaken for God, or even for an extension of the incarnation. If it were then its institutional structures would be given a level of divine authority that would compromise the Church's dependence upon the word of God. God gives his people an existence that is distinct from his own. The Church is entirely dependent on God's action in being brought into existence. The Church does not emerge from humanity as one of the possibilities of human existence. Though, having been brought into existence by the act of God, the Church does have a humanity that retains its integrity. The Church, therefore, has a contingent freedom which is like the freedom of creation. As such, the Church has a clear historical particularity and belonging within human history at certain points. It has its life in a specific generation and must take this historical particularity as part of its essential nature. This is the Church's *enhypostatic* aspect: the Church has its life as a really human institution within the person of Jesus Christ. The dependence and freedom of the Church is the organizing principle for the last two chapters of the book, which considers the Church as the body of Christ in both its *anhypostatic* and *enhypostatic* aspects. Before this, we can draw some implications from the structural similarities between the Church and the whole of creation for the *catholicity* of the Church.

The Catholicity of the Church

The third of the credal marks of the Church is that the Church is catholic. *Kataholos* means (i) according to (or directed to) the whole, or (ii) complete, depending on how the term is being used. These two meanings are undergirded by the idea of *universality*. The Church has an influence and a relevance that extends to all, irrespective of how this relevance and influence is acknowledged. Cyril of Jerusalem outlines two senses in which the Church is described as catholic.

> The Church is thus called "catholic" because it is spread through the entire inhabited world, from one end to the other, and because it teaches in its totality and without leaving anything out every doctrine which people need to know. . . . It is rightly called the Church, because it calls forth and assembles together all humanity.[69]

69. Cyril, *Catechetical Lectures of St. Cyril of Jerusalem*, 18.23.

Here, the catholicity of the Church has two dimensions. First, the Church is catholic in that it teaches the whole gospel. Second, it is catholic in that it extends across the whole world, calling all people, irrespective of age, race, gender, socioeconomic group, to be gathered as the people of God. These aspects of the catholicity of the Church receive their full evangelical content when we view them from the view of the Church as a creature of the grace of God, corresponding to the whole of creation.

The Whole Gospel

Just as Paul did not shrink back from teaching the whole counsel of God to the Ephesians (Acts 20:27), the catholic Church, as the pillar and bulwark of the truth, is not to be intimidated in its proclamation of the whole gospel of Jesus Christ. The Church does not depend on approval from the state, the culture, or the population in general in order for its existence. In its proclamation of the gospel the Church should not take the attitude of the world toward it as an impediment. Public disapproval does not touch the fact of the Church. The Church is free from the world around it because it exists by an act of God, not by an act of the world. The Church does not exist by the affirmation of the world as if its existence were in its perceived relevance or the degree to which it can be tolerated by whatever paradigm that the world might be operating with at any given time or place. The Church does not exist as an act of the world, but as an act of God. It is only from this foundation that the Church will be able to proclaim the whole gospel, irrespective of the hatred poured upon it for doing so.

This element of catholicity provides a foundation upon which the gospel the Church proclaims does not need to be diluted to try to make it more palatable to the surrounding community. Certainly, this does not mean that the Church can talk past the world or over and above the world. As Helmut Thielicke has appositely said, "the history of theology is fundamentally no other than the history of its various attempts at address,"[70] with the variety of attempts of address being sequential adjustment to the changing circumstances and ways of thinking of each generation. The way the Church expresses the gospel must relate to the contemporary world. One age may be troubled by questions of security, another by shame, another by identity, another by anxiety and the accent by which we announce the gospel of Christ must change so that we are speaking to and not beyond our contemporaries.

---

70. Thielicke, *Evangelical Faith*, 1:25.

However, in this task, Thielicke presents a very important distinction between actualization and accommodation.[71] The accommodation of the gospel is the taming of it to any particular cultural set of norms and expectations, such that sociological or economic contingencies of any day dominate the fundamental essence of the message that we proclaim to the world. Actualization, likewise, acknowledges that, in order that the gospel may be responded to, it must first be *heard*. However, it must be the gospel itself that is heard. For the gospel to be actualized in a culture it needs to be interpreted appropriately such that it is heard by the generation to whom we are speaking. Thielicke writes that "actualization always consists in a new interpretation of the truth, in its readdressing, as it were. The truth itself remains intact. It means that the hearer is summoned and called 'under the truth' in his own name and situation."[72] To actualize the gospel in a culture, therefore, involves drawing a connection between the hearer and the gospel; to announce the good news in such a way that it is perceived to be good news *to a particular generation*.

The temptation facing the Church is to accommodate the gospel such that it does not strike the ears of the culture to whom it is addressed for good or for bad. It is to domesticate the word of God as if it were a well-behaved house cat. This is precisely what happened to the Jesus produced by the biblical scholarship of figures such as David Friedrich Strauss: a Jesus divested of the miraculous and a pillar of morality, fully acceptable and not at all challenging to the comfortable settlement of nineteenth-century Europe. The gospel must strike the ears of those who hear it and it is the Church who must proclaim it such that it does. Such a preaching of the whole gospel will be offensive to our cultures today, but that is of little consequence. It is only preaching of the whole gospel that will bring about the obedience of faith. Ultimately, it is understanding the Church as a creature of God, not of the world, that frees us to this expression of our catholicity.

The Relevance of Jesus Christ

Connected with the struggle to actualize but not accommodate the gospel within a particular culture is the perceived struggle for the Church to remain relevant. If the Church knew better what it is in its connection to Christ, it would not have such an anxiety about its relevance. The relevance of the Church is not primarily about anything we do at all. First and foremost, the relevance of the Church is established by the act of God. This aspect of

71. Thielicke, *Evangelical Faith*, 1:27.
72. Thielicke, *Evangelical Faith*, 1:27.

catholicity, like all the other marks of the Church, is a divinely established reality. The Church is that which is united to Jesus and shares in his mission as witnesses to him in the power of the Spirit. As Jesus Christ is the one through whom all things were made, by whom all things hold together, through whom all things must be saved and to whom all things will be gathered together, he is inescapably relevant. As the body of Christ and that which points to Christ, the relevance of the Church is the relevance of Jesus Christ.

The Christocentric relevance of the Church includes the Church's capacity to uncover society's creaturehood. In Jesus Christ, the true relationship between God and creation is revealed, characterized by God's absolute freedom and gracious interaction alongside an interlocking structure of the dependence and independence of creation. The Church as that which is established by the act of God and yet having its own distinct existence embodies this same structure in its own way of being. The Church, therefore, embodies in its own structures, language, and attitudes the essence of creaturehood. In its sacraments the Church acknowledges that its life and essence is not derived from within itself, but from God. The Church is that which knows that it has been brought into being from nothing by the gracious act of God. In other words, in the whole universe, the Church is unique in that it understands and proclaims the grace of God behind its very existence. This is the Church's relevance to the world. As is developed in chapter 5, the Church is a visible reminder to creation of its own contingence. It is for this reason that the Church is hated. However, it is for this reason that the Church can address the whole of creation and proclaim our shared provenance in the gracious decision of God and call humanity to the stuttering response of faith, heard by God through Jesus Christ.

Open without Conflation

As the Church is universally relevant to all people, it must also be universally open to all people. Clubs, societies, and political parties tend to coalesce around particular interests or shared values which tends to lend a homogeneity to any particular gathering of people. Human civilizations have tended to work in this way. They function through some shared narrative or value system that perpetuates some human characteristic or another. Even the well-intentioned clubs, societies, or nations that try to be as inclusive as possible have a tendency to drift into the shadow side of community which is to strengthen the bond of the *us* by having a very definitive *them*. The proclivity to identify with one's group is disturbing today. One need only look at the totalitarianism of social collectivism (also called "intersectionality") to see how a movement of inclusion becomes an orthodoxy that outlaws the heterodox and encourages individuals to see themselves only in terms of their demographic components and the wider collective that this associates them with. On the other side of the political spectrum, there is the proclivity for nations to identify the parameters of their group by race, with the viscerally evil potential to descend into claims of national (and so racial) superiority.

The Church is not immune from this. The Church has its own language and ways of being that definitively mark the *us* from the *them*. In part, this is unavoidable if we are to continue to be grounded on the tradition that constitutes the very identity of the apostolic Church. We need to be aware of the darker elements of our humanity that can manipulate this. The tradition of the Church (of any branch of the Church) must not become the boundary line of an internally focused and defensive collective. This would not be the Church as God established it to be; it would be the Church having drifted away from its essence by the fact of human weakness. The essence of the Church does not emerge from within itself or the qualities of its members, but from Jesus Christ through the power of the Spirit. The Church is not trying to perpetuate any human ideology or culture. This is why any established Church needs to be very careful to not be co-opted into becoming the guardians of a particular nation's traditions or a particular ideology's account of suffering and its solutions. That the Church should be a bulwark in the defense of British values, or an advocate of the neo-Marxist vision of eutopia (as two examples), is irreconcilable with the reality of the Church. Even though it may be tempting to seek support of any potential ally, it would be an alliance built on the Church surrendering its divine origins. For this reason, the Church can be open to all people without the fear that its core character will be diluted by the presence of such diversity. The Church is able to be utterly open to the world without being conflated with the world.

For the Good of All Creation

The Church is catholic in that it is for the good of the whole of creation. Just as God promised to Abraham that his people would be a blessing to the nations, so also the Church is free to be a blessing to the world. That the Church is a creature of the action of God gives the Church a freedom from which it can pour itself out to the world in love. In a lot of political discourse, a nation's freedom is correlated to its capacity to defend itself. Having the power to hold off enemies is crucial to freedom from being subjected to power from without and is viewed as a deterrent to maintain a nation's freedom from the limitations of war. Freedom, in this sense, is intimately tied together with the capacity to protect our boundaries. In this aspect, freedom does not spring out from our inner being as is the case with divine freedom. Our being is not the source of our freedom. This is why in a world of competing interests we battle for freedom. Freedom and the maintenance of our borders from an external limit encroaching upon them are inseparable. By contrast, the command of Christ is to love God and love neighbor. To pour ourselves out in gratitude, praise, and obedience to God and to be ceaselessly orientated to the good of others. Jesus understood his mission in the following way: "The Spirit of the Lord is upon me, because he has anointed me to bring good news to the poor. He has sent me to proclaim release to the captives and recovery of sight to the blind, to let the oppressed go free, to proclaim the year of the Lord's favor" (Luke 4:18–19). This ceaseless pouring-out for the good of the world would culminate the pouring out of his very life as a sacrifice for the sins of humanity. The Church is included in this mission by the commission of Christ and by the empowering of the Holy Spirit. The Church is called to love as Christ loved. How can it be possible to be characterized by such a borderless existence in a world like this?

On one level, the ground on which we can build is theological. God's immanence, his free involvement in creation, has its ground in the sure anchor of God's freedom in himself. God's extension beyond himself, his relation to something that is not him, is a product of his freedom. On the grounds that God's freedom is self-grounded in the perfect completion of his triune life, God is free to wholly give himself in his relation to creation in the freedom that he will not become subsumed into that relationship. Now, the freedom of the Church is not self-grounded, but, very importantly, its existence is not rooted in the world which it is trying to reach with the hope of the gospel. Instead, the existence and the essence of the Church is derived from the existence God gives it by its inclusion into Christ by the Spirit. In this way the Church's relationship to the world has something in common with God's relation to the world: *the ground of its existence is not its relation to the world.* The Church shares something of God's freedom from the world inasmuch as the Church is not constituted by its relation to the world, but rather has the ground of its existence in the work of God. In just the same way that God's absolute freedom in his triune aseity is the ground of his free involvement in his creation, the freedom of the Church from the world is the foundation upon which it can be free for the world.

In the same way that God's life is self-grounded and so not constituted by his outward relations to what he has made and so God is free to pour himself out in love to his creation, the Church's life is not constituted by its outward relation to the world, but by an internal relationship of its inclusion into Jesus Christ. The essence and life of the Church is Jesus Christ in the power of the Spirit. Because of this, the Church is at liberty to pour itself out in love to the world, fearlessly proclaiming the kingdom of God and binding up the brokenhearted and serving the needs of all without being constituted or consumed by this limitless self-giving. The Church can be orientated in utter generosity, pouring itself out in love to the world because it can never exhaust itself from its essence. In its proclamation of the gospel, its social action, its ecological advocacy, its political engagement, the Church can pour itself out in serving the needs of the world in the confidence that, in so doing, it does not empty itself of its evangelical content. Provided, that is, the Church in its open hands to the world does not cease to be tightfisted around the source of its existence, which is the grace of God in Christ by the Spirit.

3

Communion

THE RELATIONSHIP BETWEEN TRINITARIAN theology and the Church has been in vogue in recent decades. There has been a concerted effort to form an understanding of the Church shaped by the triune being of God. There are many reasons for this, but two are particularly significant. First, there has been a spectacular renewal of interest in trinitarian theology in Protestant and Roman Catholic theology due to the influence of, among others, the work of Karl Barth and Karl Rahner. Second, the twentieth century was characterized by intense ecumenical efforts and the doctrine of Trinity offered a stretch of common ground upon which compatible conceptions of the Church could be established. This is closely related to the broader ecumenical movement that ran through the latter half of the twentieth century. There has been a significant rethinking of the doctrine of the Church, expressed in corporate forums such as the Faith and Order statements of the World Council of Churches and the Second Vatican Council as well as in the dialogue between specific theologians including (among others) the Orthodox John Zizioulas, the Protestant Miroslav Volf, and the Roman Catholic Joseph Ratzinger. As a result of these developments it has become very common to read about the communion (or *koinōnia*) of the three persons of the Trinity being treated as the model of the communion (or *koinōnia*) of the Church. One example of just how far-reaching this approach has become is the 1998 World Council of Churches Faith and Order Paper *The Nature and Purpose of the Church*, which is organized around headings such as "The Church of the Triune God," "Church as *Koinonia*," and "Life in Communion."[1] The upshot of all this is that current thinking about the Church has the benefit of being able to establish itself upon the underlying and weighty agreement that the fundamental character of the Church bears a positive relation to the very life of God. For example,

---

1. *The Nature and Purpose of the Church.*

Zizioulas has said that the "the Church as a communion reflects God's be-ing as communion,"[2] a sentiment which is shared by Volf, who has said that "the [idea] that ecclesial communion should correspond to trinitar-ian communion enjoys the status of an almost self-evident proposition."[3] Clearly for an Orthodox theologian and a Protestant theologian to share such common ground is not insignificant.

Our concern in this chapter is not to pick through the dense and complex differences between how Roman Catholic, Protestant, and Ortho-dox theologians establish an understanding of the Church in correlation to God's triune being. Instead, this chapter looks to give an account of the ecclesial communion within the dialogical frame set out in the first chapter. The Church as communion reflects the divine communion not by bare imi-tation but by participation. It is as the Church is incorporated into the Son and shares in his relation of Sonship to the Father that the Church indwells the reality of triune communion and comes to reflect this in its own struc-ture of being. As will be expanded below, the likeness that exists between God and the Church is a result of God's grace. As Paul Fiddes has rightly said, the correlation between the Church and the triune life of God is "not to provide us an example to copy, but to draw us into participation in God, out of which our human life can be transformed."[4]

This does *not* mean that the mystery of the Trinity can be distilled from the Church. Even if we look at it very hard, we can't study the Church and draw conclusions about what God must be like. However, to say that the Church corresponds to the communion of the triune God means that as God has his life as a communion of love of the Father, Son, and Spirit and welcomes the Church into relationship with himself, through which some likeness is established in the Church in its own communion.

This chapter explores the relationship between the communion of the triune being of God and the communion of the Church. However, the job of understanding the Church based upon the triune God certainly does not start here. The two previous chapters have already been establishing an understanding of the Church on trinitarian theology and we are now just coming to the third stage of this. The first chapter presented the Church as that which is drawn into the dialogue of God and creation as the Father sends the Son to live the life of the perfect covenant partner on our be-half, a state of Sonship into which we are adopted through the Holy Spirit. The second chapter established some lines of analysis of the Church as it

2. Zizioulas, "Church as Communion," 8.

3. Volf, *After Our Likeness*, 191.

4. Fiddes, *Participating in God*, 66.

emerges from a trinitarian theology of creation as brought into existence by God but yet still having its own integrity. If we were to miss out these first two steps and jump straight in at how the communion of the Church reflects the communion of God then, as John Behr points out, God and the Church become thought of as two parallel communions with it not being entirely clear how they connect.[5]

If the Church is a communion that in some way corresponds to the life of the triune God, it is because the Father has bound his people to the Son by the Spirit and given them their own life which is entirely dependent upon his act and under the authority of his word. It is because the Father has called the Church into being through uniting it to Jesus, and as the body of Christ the Church receives the gift of the Holy Spirit and is transformed such that it may come to reflect the love of God in its own fellowship and structures. To put the case more boldly: the Church derives its existence and essence by its inclusion in the person of Jesus Christ through whom the Church takes part in the eternal communion of the triune God, and it is for this reason that it receives a pattern of being to which its entire life conforms. This pattern of being is both structural (as it pertains to Church governance) and ethical (as it pertains to the way we love one another). One way into this participatory account of ecclesial communion is through the notion of the Church as visible and invisible.

The Visible and Invisible Church

The Church is very often described as a communion. Andrei Rublev's fifteenth-century icon *The Hospitality of Abraham* depicts the three angels for whom Abraham prepared a meal. Rublev's work has been interpreted as an icon of the triune life of God. The three figures are curved towards one another such that the lines of their bodies form a circle. The perspective of the work is front-on, such that, as we look at it, the table is open to us as if we are being invited in. At the center of the circle is a table upon which there is a cup. The implication is that through the Eucharist, that is (perhaps more accurately) through the new covenant established in the incarnate life, death, and resurrection of Jesus, we, humans though we are, are drawn into that divine communion. The icon suggests that at the heart of what it is to be the Church is to be communion and that this communion has got two dimensions: communion within God and communion with one another. In other words, to be drawn into God's triune communion is to be established

5. Behr, "Trinitarian Being of the Church," 166.

in communion with one another: "As you, Father, are in me and I am in you, may they also be in us" (John 17:21).

The Church as communion has got two dimensions. It has a vertical dimension in that the Church is constituted by its being gathered into communion with God. As a consequence of this vertical dimension, the Church also has a horizontal dimension which is communion with one another. These two dimensions intersect because our participation in the communion of the triune God is the foundation of the Church's own nature and calling as a living fellowship of human persons: "they form one interlocked reality which is comprised of a divine and a human element."[6] Another way to describe the vertical and horizontal dimensions of the Church is to say that *the Church is at one and the same time visible and invisible.*[7] The Church is invisible in that it is the spiritual communion of human beings with God the Father by our inclusion into the Son in the power of the Spirit. This invisible communion corresponds to the vertical dimension. On the other hand, the Church is visible in that there is an observable communion of human beings who meet as a community in fellowship. Just as important as this visible community is the visibility of the Church in its more institutional forms. That is, in its reading and proclamation of the gospel, in its sacraments, its liturgy and orders of ministry, and the confession of the faith passed on through its credal formulas: "the visible Church of Christ is a congregation of believers in which the pure Word of God is preached and in which the sacraments are rightly administered" (Article IXX). This visible fellowship is the Church's horizontal dimension of communion.

On occasions the visible and invisible dimensions of the Church have been treated as if they were in opposition. Just as the freedom of God and the freedom of creation can be misunderstood as rivals in which more of one must mean less than the other, so also with the Church in its visible and invisible aspects. It may be the case that someone may stress either the visible or the invisible aspect of the Church and reduce the other. For example, it could be held that what really matters is membership of the invisible Church and the visible Church is a human interference that gets in the way of our actual and spiritual communion with God and so requires rethinking from the ground up, such as Brian McClaren has recently suggested.[8] On the other hand, the visible aspect of the Church can receive such an accent as a religious and political institution which just exists to perpetuate itself

---

6. Paul VI, "Dogmatic Constitution on the Church (*Lumen Gentium*)," 22.

7. Ratzinger, "Letter to the Bishops of the Catholic Church."

8. McLaren, *Great Spiritual Migration.*

that it neglects that it is simply the visible consequence of our gathering together in communion with God through Christ.

Depending on the Church tradition with which we are most familiar we will find ourselves with the proclivity to stress one dimension of the Church over another. Those for whom the visibility of the Church is a dominant dimension must remember that the Church in its visible aspect derives its existence and character from the Church in its invisible aspect. The Church is a community of human people, but a community in which we share a common inclusion into Christ and are bound together in the unity of the Spirit. The Church initiates new members by baptism because baptism is the means through which the Spirit incorporates us into the body of Christ. The unity of the Church is visible at Eucharist because this is the means by which our corporate participation in Jesus Christ is confirmed and strengthened. The Church worships in song and prayer, but this worship proceeds through the eternal words of love from the Son to the Father into which we have been joined. The Church is always more than it appears to be.

On the other hand, those for whom the invisibility of the Church is the dominant expression should be careful to not go too far in denying the visibility of the Church. As will be developed in chapter 5, to undermine the visibility of the Church is illegitimate on Christological grounds. Even before we get to that, it is not immediately obvious that it is even possible to relativize the centrality of the visible Church. The Church has its existence in history and it is made up of real people who are in a real fellowship which expresses itself in real organizational structures (formal or otherwise), an audible confession of faith, sacramental acts, and discernible forms of worship. You cannot separate the visibility from the Church without removing the people who make up its community and the way in which they are organized. However, it is not simply practically impossible to neglect the visibility of the Church, it is also irreconcilable with the mission of the Church. The Church must be visible and present to the world, because how else could it fulfill its task of being sent out to the world to proclaim the gospel and welcome people in?[9] In being visible, the Church is not betraying its spiritual reality. In being visible, the Church is true to what God has made: a communion of real people, believers united in Jesus Christ by faith in the power of the Spirit, actualized in the sacraments of baptism and Eucharist who reach out to the world, proclaiming Christ as Lord.

A middle route is required through the various extremes. There are not two Churches, a visible and an invisible, vying for attention and priority. There is one Church which has two aspects. There is one Church which is, at

9. Küng, Church, 34–39.

one and the same time, visible and invisible. What is really interesting about
the visible and the invisible aspects of the Church as communion is that *they
provide a foundation for one another*. One does not exist without the other
one. They are necessary correlates of one another.

On the one hand, the vertical communion between the Church and
God is the basis of the horizontal communion between one another. The
invisible communion is the ground of the visible communion; the horizontal dimension emerges out from the vertical dimension like light refracting
through glass. As Barth has put it, "By belonging to Christ we belong to
all who belong to Him—not secondarily but *a priori*, not by the exercise
of Christian virtue, but according to our nature, i.e., for Christ's sake, and
therefore not by accident or disposition or choice, but in the strictest possible sense, by necessity."[10] On account of the fact that we are welcomed into
relationship with God as his children, we also receive a new relationship
to one another. Our participation in the communion of the triune God is
the foundation of the Church's own nature and calling as a communion of
believers. It is because the Church is united inseparably to Jesus as the body
of Christ that the Church enjoys the vertical dimension of participating in
the triune communion. However, to be the body of Christ is a communal
identity and so carries along with it the horizontal dimension of our new
communion with one another.

On the other hand, the functions of the visible Church in the proclamation of the word of God in the Scriptures and the sermon and by the reception of the sacraments of baptism and Eucharist, are the means by which
human believers are in communion with the Father through incorporation
into Jesus Christ in the power of the Holy Spirit. The visible dimension
of the Church as communion is also *the means of entrance and continuation in the invisible communion*. As Cyprian of Carthage said, "you cannot
have God for your Father unless you have the Church as your mother."[11]
As we read the apostolic witness to Jesus Christ and are actually addressed
by Christ himself through their witness as it is preserved in Scripture, we
see the light of the glory of the Father radiating out in the person of Jesus
and we recognize this divine light for what it is in the light of the Holy
Spirit. In baptism "we have been united with him in a death like his [and]
will certainly be united with him in a resurrection like his" (Rom 6:5). We
are transferred into the person of the Son through baptism and are bound
to him such that his life becomes our life, "for in the one Spirit we were
all baptized into one body" (1 Cor 12:13). In the Eucharist, we sustain our

10. Barth, *Church Dogmatics*, 2.1, 217.
11. Cyprian, "Unity of the Church," 6.

inclusion in the body of Jesus Christ as we incorporate his sacramental body into our physical bodies. In this way, the visible aspect of the Church is the means God has given us to enter and sustain our belonging in the invisible communion. Clearly there is a particular understanding of the sacraments at work here, which will be developed in chapter 4.

The visibility and the invisibility of the Church are both integral to what the Church is and are not in competition with one another. The more we think of the Church as the invisible communion of believers with God does not require us to think less of the Church as a visible fellowship and institution with regulations for worship, a framework for liturgy, orders of ministry, established sacraments and *vice versa*. This reciprocity between the visible and invisible dimensions of the Church introduces us to something very important: *the existence of the Church as communion is a gift from God.* It is God who draws us into invisible communion with him and it is God who gives us Scripture, faith, the bond of love, and the sacraments through which we both enter and express that communion. This means that to think of the ecclesial communion in relation to the divine communion is a function of our participation in (not bare imitation of) the divine communion.

This is made clearer considered in relation to the first of the credal marks of the Church: that the Church is one. That the communion of the Church in both its visible and invisible dimensions is a gift of God means that the oneness of the Church is a divinely established oneness. In other words, the statement that the Church is one is an expression of faith, not an observation of the way the Church appears. Certainly, the Church does not appear to be one with the fundamental division between the Roman Catholic and the Eastern Orthodox and the subsequent divisions between the Roman Catholic and Protestant Church and the ever-increasing divisions within the Protestant tradition. Here we deal with what Hans Küng has called the "un-nature" of the Church; the Church as it departs from its core essence by the failings of the humans who make up the Church.[12] In appearance, the Church is divided. In truth, the Church is one and it can never be divided because its oneness is an act of God the Father through the one Lord Jesus Christ, actualized in the power of the Spirit by the concrete means of the sacraments.

Paul's exhortation to the Ephesian Church is to respond to the great act of God in establishing them as one by living like it: "Making every effort to maintain the unity of the Spirit in the bond of peace. There is one body and one Spirit, just as you were called to the one hope of your calling, one Lord, one faith, one baptism, one God and Father of all, who is above all and

12. Küng, *Church*, 28.

through all and in all" (Eph 4:3–5). The oneness of the Church is described in unmistakably *theological* terms. There is one Church because there is one Jesus in whom we are united by the Spirit through baptism and the Eucharist. The Church is indivisibly one because it is the body of Christ and the body of Christ cannot be divided into disconnected parts. The Church is one because it has been established in unity by the work of the Holy Spirit and the Spirit is eternally the bond of love between the Father and the Son who now mediates the relationship between believers. The Church is one because there is one apostolic faith by which we are saved. Ultimately, the oneness of the Church has its source in the oneness of God. Just as God is indivisibly one, so the Church is indivisibly one.

Therefore, as we express our belief in the oneness of the Church, we are not expressing an aspiration, a shared goal to which we orientate ourselves. It is not the task of the Church to *establish* oneness, it is the task of the Church to *live* oneness. It is the task of the Church to live as the communion of believers who are united in Christ and participate in the triune life on account of the fact that this is what God has established us as. The vocation of the Church is to be what we are. The challenge of the Church is that its oneness is a multifaceted oneness. The Church is one by the act of God whereby it is united to Christ and so participates in the triune life and has a oneness that takes the divine triunity as its normative pattern. The one God exists as three persons in a communion of love; likewise, the Church exists as diverse human persons in a communion of love. If we are to understand what it is for the one Church to exist as a communion of believers, then our primary paradigm is not anthropological or sociological. We are not talking about a group gathered around a common aim or identity. Instead, our primary paradigm for understanding the multifaceted oneness of the Church is *theological*. It is for this reason that it is must be understood in terms of the triune God.

Divine Communion

In the last chapter, the theme of God's life as Trinity was introduced in connection to the self-sufficient perfection of God in his freedom from creation. God's triune aseity is the ground on which to establish both the freedom of God and the contingent freedom of creation. That creation is not characterized by necessity does not mean it is arbitrary, instead it means that creation is chosen by God in love. Creation is given its own distinct existence, its own contingent freedom, in the generosity of God. The current chapter considers what it is for the one God to have his life in the eternal and perfect communion of Father, Son, and Spirit and on what terms and in what ways this can inform our understanding of the Church.

Finishing with Starting Points

In some quarters through the twentieth century it became very popular to account for differences in ways of thinking about the doctrine of the Trinity by appealing to different starting points. The story goes that theologians from one theological tradition begin their discussion of God's life as Trinity with an account of the one divine essence and only then consider the three persons and theologians from another theological tradition do the reverse. On one level, this is fully understandable. It is impossible for humans to think two things at once. So, when it comes to thinking of God who is three and one, we are inclined to start with either the oneness or the threeness.

However, thinking two things at once is precisely what we have got to try and do. It is something very special about the character of God's unity that it, as the Athanasian Creed has it, is a unity in Trinity. The one divine essence has life as three persons. This is what is intended by the word *triunity*, a neologism to conceptualize the fact that God is one and three simultaneously. The unity of God is not an aggregate of parts. The one God is not a combination of the three persons. Neither is the unity of God the unity of a higher genus like the one humanity which has many individual human persons who belong to that genus. God is not the designation for a class of being to which the Father, Son, and Spirit belong. Instead, the one God exists simultaneously in three personal modes as Father, Son, and Spirit. This does not mean that there are three gods. The simultaneous, eternal existence as Father, Son, and Spirit is the life of the one God. The Father is holy, the Son is holy, and the Spirit is holy, but there are not three holies, but one holy. God is one essence existing in a threefold personal modification through the respective modes of origin: the unbegotten (the Father); the eternally begotten of the Father (the Son); the eternally proceeding from the Father through the Son (the Spirit). The three personal modes in which God has his life are inseparable from the divine essence. The divine persons are not portions of God; they are personal modes in which that one divine essence exists in its fullness. The personal existence of the divine essence, therefore, is not something secondary to it because the one God has his life eternally in threefold personal modification all of whom are orientated to one another in love.

With this in mind, the attempt to think of God's unity and trinity indivisibly can operate through the application of two principles.

1. The persons cannot be separated from the essence because a divine person is the one essence of God having its life in a particular, personal, and concrete way.

2. The essence cannot be separated from the persons because the divine essence subsists as and in the three persons.[13]

Because of the reciprocity of the unity of the divine essence and the threeness of the divine persons we have to be disciplined in our thinking and resist any notion of starting points when we think about God's triunity. We don't start with God's oneness and then move on to his three persons and we don't start with the three persons and then move on to the oneness. As Karl Rahner has demonstrated in his critique of the Western tradition of trinitarian theology, thought about God which prioritizes the unity of the divine essence, leads to an overly philosophical and abstract idea of God. The dominant key of our theology is the divine but impersonal essence. Such a starting point is not easily grounded in the personal categories of love or action.[14] If, on the other hand, the three persons are prioritized over the one divine essence, it is correspondingly difficult to affirm God's unity without appealing to unsatisfactory metaphors common among social trinitarians such as the family of God or the divine society. Or, it will lead to the misapprehension that the oneness of God imposes its unifying force upon the three persons in a manner that shares characteristics with tyranny.[15] By contrast, Gregory of Nazianzus stated that "I cannot think of the One without immediately being surrounded by the radiance of the Three; nor can I discern the Three without at once being carried back to the One."[16] For Nazianzus the reality of the one divine essence is inconceivable without the personal mode of its life as Father,

---

13. "Subsistence" is intended to communicate that the divine essence has actual, substantial existence in the divine persons. It is connected to the Greek term *hypostasis*, which we refer to as "person." *Hypostasis* means that which stands underneath and gives concrete extension to something. For the divine essence to have subsistence in the *hypostasis* (person) of Father, Son, and Spirit means that the divine persons are the concrete individuals in which the divine essence has actual existence. For the sake of clarity, some technical language is inescapable. I consider the relationship between essence and person in this connection to track closely to the Aristotelian notion of immanent-universals in which the universal only has existence within a concrete particular (*universalia in re*). Obviously, this needs some adaptation to be suitable in a trinitarian context because the divine essence is not an abstract genre with various instantiations, but the one God subsisting in three personal modes.

14. Rahner, *Trinity*, 17. See also Gunton, "Trinity, Augustine and the Theological Crisis of the West," 33–58.

15. See Moltmann, *Trinity and the Kingdom of God*, 129–50.

16. Gregory of Nazianzus, *Or. Bas.* 40.31.

Son, and Spirit. Likewise, the plurality of the distinct personal modes is the variegated life of the one divine essence.

The three persons are the one divine essence having its life in a particular, personal, and concrete way: the divine essence in unbegotten mode of existence, in begotten mode of existence, and in spirated mode of existence. These different modes of God's existence are actively orientated to one another in a unity of reciprocal love. The Father is the Father of *that* Son, for example. The one God exists in three eternally differentiated and personal modes, which return to one another in mutuality and self-giving love. This takes us to the heart of the problem of thinking-two-things-at-once: God, in his very being, is *personal*.

The Personal Being of God

T. F. Torrance has argued that the innermost nature of what it is to be God is that God is "essentially personal, dynamic and relational being."[17] The one God has his life as the *communion* of the three persons. Integral to Torrance's way of parsing the doctrine of the Trinity is God's act of self-naming as "I am" (Exod 3:13–14). First, Torrance argues that the identity "I am" means that God's name and very self are identical. Accordingly, the people of Israel refuse to use the name of God, because this personal name is inseparable from the divine reality itself. This association between the divine reality and his personal name is important because it means that God reveals himself as one who must be known personally.[18] This means that the way we think of God cannot be separated from the personal categories of act and speech by which God makes himself known. God is not abstract and cannot be thought of in impersonal terms. This means that the knowledge of God is not primarily analytical, as is the case with concepts. God's very being is personal and so cannot be abstracted from his personal actions. We don't think of God by starting with the concept of God and then loosen away everything nascent within the concept. Quite the opposite, we look to where God gives himself to be known through his personal actions.

The second aspect of this self-naming is an identity between the reality of God and his actions toward us. Torrance argues that the divine self-naming has a dynamic sense in which God is who he will be in his relations to Israel; that God's "Being and Act are not separable from one another."[19] In taking this approach, Torrance is following closely in the footsteps of

17. Torrance, *Christian Doctrine of God*, 124.

18. Torrance, *Christian Doctrine of God*, 121.

19. Torrance, *Christian Doctrine of God*, 119–20.

Barth who said that "God is who He is in His works . . . in His works He is Himself revealed as the One He is."[20] This does not mean that Barth thought it theologically inappropriate to talk about God's being. Instead, our knowledge of the reality of God is shaped by the acts in which his being is communicated to us. Central here is the category of self-revelation in which God reveals himself through himself. In Jesus Christ and the Spirit God's action toward us and his very reality are one and the same thing.[21] This is why, for Barth and for Torrance, the doctrine of the Trinity is inseparable from the category of revelation.

If this is the case, if God really does make himself known to us through his actions toward us, then what is the God who makes himself known in his acts like? What do his actions tell us about him and how he has his life? We are given some insight into this a little later in the Exodus narrative: "I am the Lord and will bring you out from the burdens of the Egyptians and deliver you from slavery to them. I will redeem you with an outstretched arm and with mighty acts of judgement. I will take you as my people and I will be your God" (Exod 6:7–8). The acts of God are to redeem Israel and establish it in covenant relationship with himself. God is known in his communion-creating acts through redeeming Israel, giving himself to be their God and taking Israel to be his covenant partner. If it is through these acts that God makes himself known, then God reveals himself to be a personal being who creates communion.[22] The act which is so tightly related to God's being is an act which is all about creating relationship. With respect to the making of creation, God's communion-making acts to creation are the overflow of what he is eternally and independently in himself. God has his life as an ever-loving communion of Father, Son, and Spirit and this is the source of his communion-making acts to creation.[23]

> In himself, God does not will to exist for Himself, to exist alone. On the contrary, He is Father, Son and Holy Spirit and therefore alive in His unique nature with and for and in another. The unbroken unity of his [nature], knowledge and will is at the same time an act of deliberation, decision and intercourse. He does not exist in solitude but in fellowship. . . . That he is God—the Godhead of God—consists in the fact that He loves and it is the expression of His loving that He seeks and creates fellowship with us.[24]

20. Barth, *Church Dogmatics*, 2.1, 260.

21. Barth, *Church Dogmatics*, 2.1, 257.

22. Torrance, *Christian Doctrine of God*, 122.

23. Torrance, *Christian Doctrine of God*, 112–35.

24. Barth, *Church Dogmatics*, 2.1, 275.

God acts toward creation as a covenant-making, communion-building God because God in himself is perfect communion. The freedom of God in his internal and eternal relations as Father, Son, and Holy Spirit do not isolate God from creation, but actually are the foundation of God's communion-creating acts toward creation.[25]

Person and Relationship

The one God exists in the reciprocal love, the perfect communion, of Father, Son, and Holy Spirit. One strategy for describing this has been to say that the one God is the community of the three persons, as if God's unity were like the unity of a family or society. Leonardo Boff, for example, described the triune God as "God the Family," a divine society of mutuality and equality that can serve as a paradigm for the ideal human community.[26] Problematically, such a social analogy of the Trinity operates with the assumption that the three divine persons are logically (and ontically) prior to the one divine essence, because the latter is the aggregate of the former. Beyond this, as Sarah Coakley has argued, social analogies of the Trinity are unable to give a satisfactory account of divine personhood. According to Coakley, social trinitarianism has intruded modern notions of personhood as an individual center of activity on top of classical theological ideas of personhood. In other words, social trinitarians tend to envisage the Father, Son, and Spirit as if they were independent centers of activity which possess relationship to one another.[27] Certainly, there appears to be some truth to this criticism when one considers the way Cornelius Plantinga parses his own understanding of divine personhood within a social analogy.

> Father, Son and Spirit are conceived as persons in a full sense of "person," i.e. as distinct centres of love, will, knowledge and personal action . . . related to each other in some central ways analogous to, if sublimely passing, relations among the members of a society of three human persons.[28]

The concern is that all such presentations of divine personhood have been shaped by modern psychology, with its emphasis on a person as a center of consciousness capable of individual thought and will. Such an idea of personhood is not exhaustive of trinitarian personhood, nor is it a

---

25. Webster, *Barth*, 85.

26. Boff, *Faith on the Edge*, 98.

27. Coakley, "'Persons' in the 'Social' Doctrine of the Trinity," 123–44.

28. Plantinga, "Gregory of Nyssa and the Social Analogy of the Trinity," 325–52.

particularly suitable way to speak of the divine persons if we are to think of person and essence at the same time (without, that is, separating into three gods all as their own distinct center of consciousness). The unity of God is not simply the unity of three individuals orientated to one another in love but is the unity of the one divine essence which subsists as three distinct personal modes of being. Certainly, these personal modes of being are orientated to one another in self-giving love but this is not the ultimate ground of the unity of the divine essence.

To understand what it means for the one God to exist in the communion of Father, Son, and Spirit, we need to think in more detail about the relationships between the divine persons and how these relationships correlate to the divine persons themselves. In what follows, it is argued that the divine persons are the ways in which the one God has life, personally differentiated through relationships and these relationships not only differentiate but also unite in love. Moreover, it is argued that these relations are not possessed by the persons but *are* the persons themselves.

The thing that makes the divine persons distinct from one another is their relations to the other persons. The Father alone is not derived from any other (the Father is unbegotten) and the Father is the fount from which the Son and the Spirit come in their particular ways. The Son is begotten from the Father and the Spirit proceeds from the Father. Exactly what constitutes the content of begotten and procession and how they are different is undetermined. However, there are two things we do know about these modes of coming out from the Father.

First, *they are ways of coming out from the Father that only God can.* The Nicene-Constantinopolitan Creed describes the Son as begotten by clarifying that the Son is "God from God, Light from Light." The Son is God in a personal mode of existence that comes out of God. The Spirit who proceeds from the Father is to be worshiped and glorified with the Father and the Son. This means that to be begotten and to proceed from the Father is not inconsistent with being God. Here we need to remind ourselves of the difference between God's internal and external relations which was introduced in the last chapter. The begetting of the Son and the procession of the Spirit are internal to the divine life. However, the making of creation is external to the life of God. As the Nicene Creed makes explicit the divinity of the Son is demonstrated in that he is "begotten, not made" in opposition to Arian views on Christ in which begetting and making were all but synonymous.

The second thing we know about begetting and proceeding is that *they are not the same as one another.* These terms refer to distinct ways of coming out from the Father. While the exact content of this difference is unknown to us, the fact of difference is itself crucial as it is the means by which the Son and the Spirit are distinct from one another. The Son is distinct from the Father and the Spirit because the Son alone is begotten. The Spirit is distinct from the Son and the Father because the Spirit alone proceeds. These different relations differentiate one person from the other two. Human persons have a variety of characteristics that make us distinct from one another; we have different locations in space and time, faces, personalities, sizes, and so on. The divine persons only have one characteristic that distinguishes them from one another. The Father is the Father because he is the unbegotten fount of the Son and the Spirit. The Son is the Son because he is the eternally begotten out from the Father. The Spirit is the Spirit because he eternally proceeds from the Father through the Son.

The Father, Son, and Spirit are names which signify the distinct divine persons, who are differentiated by their particular property which derives from their particular relation to one another (the unbegotten source, the begotten, the one who proceeds). This means that there is a cast-iron connection between relationship and personhood. Each divine person is, and is who he is, because of his relation to the other two. The Father is the Father precisely because of his relation to the Son and the Spirit. The Son and the Spirit are who they are precisely because of their respective relations to the Father.

So far, one might have the impression that the Father, Son, and Spirit are all individuals that possess a relation to the others as though they had an existence aside from the relations. But, how can the divine persons have distinct existence aside from the relations which they are? The Son is the one who is begotten from the Father; the Son is not a distinct individual at one end of a Father-Son relation. Instead, the Son *is* the relation of Sonship. There is no other basis for the distinct personhood of the Son other than the relationship Son-of-the-Father. This is the notion of subsistent relations: the persons are the relations and these relations actually exist in and of themselves. The relations of unbegotten, begotten, and spirated don't need to be instantiated within, what is perceived to be, a more metaphysically concrete notion of individual, such as within some idea of person as a center of consciousness.

This connection between person and relation is not one that is immediately obvious in the context of contemporary Anglo-European culture. We are more attuned to thinking of a person as an individual, normally with a strong focus on the inward life leading to a prioritization of the category of self-consciousness. The self-conscious individual may stand in a series of relations to others but is not circumscribed by those relations. We have become used to thinking of the person as an individual characterized by the possession of self-consciousness. Consciousness is a deeply complex area, but at its root it includes capability for sensation, being aware of being impacted by and responding to stimulus. *Self*-consciousness is the capacity to be aware of and respond to the self. The English philosopher John Locke, for example, defined a person as a "thinking intelligent being, that has reason and reflection, and can consider itself as itself, the same thinking thing at different times and places."[29] Integral to personhood, Locke suggests, is the ability to reflect upon one's own existence. A person, according to Locke's definition, must be able to be aware of one's self through time. Memory, as consciousness of ourselves extending through time, Locke reasons, is the necessary condition of personhood. For example, I recall that, as a seventeen-year-old boy sitting in a Classics class, I made a resolution to remember that moment, what I was doing, what I was seeing, what I was feeling and thinking. It was my intention to establish some continuity between myself at that moment and who I would be in the future. This is a view of personhood that is entirely locked into the self, an introverted corruption of what a person is, which, I suspect, we all have to separate ourselves from.

Through the course of the twentieth century and carrying forward into the twenty-first, this idea of the person has been contested. Martin Buber argued that a person cannot be defined by internal characteristics alone but is a function of relationship. It is as we encounter another (a "Thou" in Buber's language) and experience the material of that relationship that we are a person.[30] Likewise, John Macmurray rejected the idea of personhood as the thinking agent, and advanced instead the idea that the person is an active agent. The key difference is that thought drives us into ourselves and action drives us beyond ourselves. If personhood is associated with action then we are necessarily characterized by readiness for engagement with the world beyond ourselves; the person becomes defined by the relations in which she stands to others.[31] Such an understanding of personhood as socially determined has proved to be deeply attractive to theological discussion. An important representative of this tradition is Alister McFadyen, who argues from a theological perspective that persons have to be understood in social terms: "individuality, personhood and selfhood do not, I shall argue, refer to some internal and independent source of identity, but to the way one is and has been in relation."[32]

---

29. Locke, *Essay Concerning Human Understanding*, 2.27.9.

30. Buber, *I and Thou*.

31. These theories have been advanced in Macmurray's two seminal works: Macmurray, *Self as Agent*, and Macmurray, *Persons in Relation*.

32. McFadyen, *Call to Personhood*, 18.

This is now standard fare in some contemporary trinitarian theology. Divine persons are who they are on account of their relationship to the others, not on account of their relationship to themselves. However, the relations between the divine persons do not only distinguish between them, they also rebound back upon the unity of the one divine essence. One of the most fundamental things about these three personal modes in which the one God exists is that they are meaningless without the others. For example, the Son does not mean anything on its own, because it is a name signifying a relationship. By its very internal meaning, it necessitates a correlate other. The three persons can only be thought of in reciprocity to one another. This introduces us to a very important point: relationship is both the mechanism of differentiation and also a force of unity. In their very difference from one another the three persons carry us back to their differentiated communion. We cannot think of the one God without knowing God as the three persons and we cannot think of the three persons without being confronted by the one God. Once again, we follow in the footsteps of Gregory Nazianzus: "No sooner do I consider the One than I am enlightened by the radiance of the Three; no sooner do I distinguish between them than I am carried back to the One."[33] This means that relationship is absolutely fundamental in describing the character of God's oneness. In other words, the one God has his life in the communion of the three. The triunity of God is a unity of communion. The unity is not a product of the communion (that would be social trinitarianism). Instead, the communion is the communion of the one God who has his life as three persons who are orientated to one another in love. It is with this that we turn to consider the theme of God's perichoretic unity.

Perichoresis: The Unity of Love

The theological term for the reciprocal relationships which return the distinct divine persons to one another in self-giving love is *perichoretic* relations. This term describes how each of the divine persons is permeated by the others. The Father, Son, and Spirit interpenetrate one another such that their personal identity is inseparable from their unity as the one God. One important foundation of the doctrine of perichoresis is Jesus' statement "I am in the Father and the Father is in me" (John 14:10–11). This is part of a narrative arc of the deep intimacy of work and nature between the Father and the Son that runs through the whole gospel. As John's Gospel develops, the Spirit is revealed to belong to this unity of work and nature, for as the Son was sent by the Father, so the Spirit is sent by the Father (John 14:16,

33. Gregory of Nazianzus, *Or. Bas.* 40.41.

26) and the Son (John 16:7) to continue the work of Christ among the apostles (John 16:12–13) and engage in the reciprocal glorification of the Father and the Son (John 16:14–15). The relationship between the divine persons is one of mutual encircling of one another in which the identity and agency of one coexists and is bound up together with the identity and agency of another. The relationship is so tight that each of the divine persons is said to contain the others without any confusion of their distinct identity. This intertwining of existence is spoken of as a mutual indwelling. This indwelling is what *perichoresis* describes.

When we were waiting for the birth of our daughter, my wife and I had to make room in our house for her. We had to clear out a room and make it ready for her, which involved both of us clearing out books and clothes which had not seen use in quite a number of years! Much more wonderfully, the new existence of our daughter established within us new identities as mum and dad. In this, both my wife and I made room in our personal identities to incorporate our daughter into ourselves. Our personal identities changed because we are the parents of that daughter. Perichoresis conveys the idea that the divine persons each make room for the other two in their own personhood. The Father, the Son, and the Spirit contain one another. This containing of one another does not mean that they lose their own personal distinction, but rather stresses that they are so interconnected in their relations that they can never be divided from one another. In one sense, this tracks quite closely to the example of family relations, in that the person of the Father contains in his personal identity the Son and *vice versa*. However, it also goes far beyond this idea. In a mysterious way that exceeds our family relations, the divine persons are actually in one another and interpenetrate one another. Each of the divine persons contains the other two and is contained within the other two. The Father is in the Son and the Spirit; the Son is in the Father and the Spirit and the Spirit is in the Father and the Son. It is in this way that the relations of the persons do not only differentiate but actually return back to the unity of the one God.

However, the doctrine of *perichoresis* is not exhausted by static terms. Perichoretic unity is not exclusively a product of the structure of the relations. We need to also think in the more dynamic terms of communion. Sometimes, *perichoresis* is described as if God's life were a divine dance of the persons circling around one another.[34] This is a very attractive image and does have some positive associations with the dynamism of the divine life. The persons are the divine essence subsisting in particular ways which are orientated to one another in reciprocal love. As we have seen above, the very differentiation

---

34. For example, Rohr, *Divine Dance*.

of the persons contains an orientation to one another: The Father is the Father of the Son; the Spirit is the Spirit of Jesus Christ who proceeds from the Father. These are correlate, relational terms in which the distinct names actively move beyond themselves to find complete identification only in relation to one another. The reciprocity of these relations is the movement of love from one to the other. Each is ceaselessly and wholly orientated to the other. The relations of Father, Son, and Spirit demonstrate that the one God has his life as an eternal movement of loving communion. The Son is eternally the beloved of the Father who eternally comes out from the Father and eternally returns to the Father in the unity of the Holy Spirit.

In this way, the perichoretic relations of the Father, Son, and Spirit undergird and enlighten the fundamental principles of trinitarian theology. God is one essence existing in a threefold communion of love. It is impossible to speak of the one God without also the three persons in whom the one divine essence has its subsistence. Likewise, it is impossible to speak of the three divine persons without being returned to the unity of the divine essence on account of which they are united in nature, action, and reciprocal.

An Ordered Communion

The divine communion is an ordered communion. The perichoretic relations of the divine three do not only underscore their unity, but also their personal distinction from one another. The Father is not the Son, the Son is not the Father, and the Spirit is not the Father or the Son. The distinction between the divine persons is preserved by the fact that in there is a definitive order to their relations. Now, we need to tread very carefully here to not insert a distinction in divinity between the divine persons. Each of the divine persons is the one divine essence subsisting in a particular way. However, the three personal ways in which the divine essence subsists are differentiated and constituted by relations. These relations are characterized by a definitive order. It is essential that this relational order is affirmed, because without it the distinctions between the persons becomes blurry. Although they are coequal, coeternal as the divine essence subsisting in a particular way, the divine persons are relationally differentiated in such a way that there is personal priority. The Father is the source of the Son and the Spirit, each of whom come from the Father in their own particular way.

The priority of the Father (*monarchia*) is not one of superiority but of *relational specificity*. The Son is begotten of the Father in eternity. The Son is God from God and not the other way around. The Spirit proceeds out from the Father, not the Father from the Spirit. The Father is first, not in time or in quality of being, but in the relationship of the three. This eternal relational order constitutes a pattern which is discernible in God's outward relations in history. It is the Father who sends the Son, and the Son does the will of the Father. It is the Father who sends the Spirit (through the Son) and the Spirit is the divine light in which we are enabled to see the light of the glory of the Father shining in the face of Jesus Christ. These outward relations in history are controlled by the eternal order of the divine life in which the Father is the fount of the Son and the Spirit, who each come out from the Father in their respective ways that only God can. In other words, the communion in which the one God has his life is one of ordered relations.

The Analogy of Relation

Method is very important in coming to draw some implications from the character of the divine life for the Church. The analogy of relation asserts that there is a correspondence between the way in which God exists in relationship and the way God has created humanity to exist in relationship. It is important to be careful with this idea because it can elide very easily with the idea that there is an inherent correspondence between God and creation, which is exactly what good chunks of chapters 1 and 2 were spent resisting. The crucial difference is that the analogy of relation lays great stress on the centrality of God's grace in establishing the correspondence between the way God has his life as communion and the way human beings can have their life in communion.

One aspect of the analogy of relation has already been at work in the grounding the understanding of God's external, transitive relations to us upon God's internal, nontransitive relations as Father, Son, and Spirit. The fact that God exists in an eternal relationship of love as Father, Son, and Spirit was deployed as the basis from which to understand his outward relations to us as our free Creator. Here, our concern is with a second aspect of the analogy of relation: the correlation between the way God has his life in communion and the way humanity can have their life in communion through grace.

> God created [humanity] in his own image in the fact that He did not create [humans] alone but in this connection and fellowship. . . . God exists in relationship and fellowship. As the Father of the Son and the Son of the Father He is Himself I and Thou, confronting Himself and yet always one and the same in the Holy Ghost. God created [humans] in His own image, in correspondence with His own being and essence. He created

[humans] in the image which emerges even in His work as the Creator and Lord of the covenant. Because He is not solitary in Himself, and therefore does not will to be so [in his outward relations], it is not good for [humans] to be alone, and God created [humans] in his own image, as male and female . . . there can be no question of an analogy of being, but of relationship. God is in relationship, and so too is the [humanity] created by Him. This is his divine likeness.[35]

This is a relatively complicated passage, not least for the tightrope that Barth is trying to walk between affirming that humanity correspond to God in the fact that we have our existence in communion with one another while trying to resist the gravitational pull toward affirming that humanity are like God quite independent from God's gracious act to establish that likeness. The point is that God exists eternally in reciprocal relations, and God has created humanity to correspond to that reciprocal relationality in its own existence. Obviously, there is dissimilarity within this correspondence. God has his existence-in-reciprocal-relations within the unity of the triune God, whereas a reciprocal relationship takes place across two or more distinct human beings. Even so, the ultimate source of every relationship of reciprocal love is patterned in accordance to the mutual self-giving and loving of the Father, Son, and Spirit.

What is crucial is that this likeness is given in the gracious action of God and is received by humanity through faith. It is axiomatic for Barth that any correspondence between God and creation is the result of grace and not nature. This is the reason why, at the very center of the correspondence between the divine communion and human communion, is the person of Jesus Christ. In Jesus Christ two things happen. First, the reciprocal relations of love between the Father, Son, and Spirit are revealed such that they are opened up to us for our participation through our inclusion into Jesus. Second, the possibility for a corresponding human communion is received and lived as Jesus lives the life of the perfect covenant partner of God in giving himself for the sins of the world in his love for the Father and his love for humanity. It is here then, in the person of Jesus Christ, that some correspondence between the divine communion and human communion is lived out as Christ displays the self-giving love of the divine communion and actualizes it in human history in his self-giving love for his brothers and sisters.

Through the incarnation of the Son and the sending of the Spirit, God reveals that he exists in a communion of love. The Church is that which is joined to Christ by the Holy Spirit through the concrete means of baptism

35. Barth, *Church Dogmatics*, 3.2, 323–24.

and the Eucharist. In this way, the Church is drawn in to participate in the divine communion. In this way, the Church are exposed to the love of the triune God and are to reflect this love in their own fellowship (1 John 4:7ff). For this reason, the Church receives the governing ethic of the Kingdom of God to "love the Lord your God with all your heart, with all your soul, with all your strength, and with all your mind and love your neighbor as yourself" (Luke 10:27). The Church, as that which participates in the triune life through Jesus Christ, comes to reflect its mutual relations of reciprocal love in its own structures and way of being.

The Ecclesial Communion

The Church is a creature of the Word and Spirit of God. The Church is brought into being by the act and call of God. The structures of the Church, e.g., its orders and its modes of governance, should be determined by its divine provenance. When our first questions run along these lines, matters of Church order will be in their proper place, inseparably connected to who God is and the manner of his action in calling it into being in the first place.

If ecclesial communion does, in some sense, bear a resemblance to the divine communion, then what is the method by which that resemblance can be grounded? What is the mechanism by which to apply belief about the triune God to the Church? Colin Gunton, for example, has argued that deficiencies in many ways of understanding the Church arise from a failure to establish what we think about the Church on the triunity of God.[36] His diagnosis of the problem is that "the conception of God as triune community made no substantive contribution to the doctrine of the Church," which has led to a variety of views of the Church which are either non-communal or exclusively institutional and hierarchical.[37] The cure, Gunton suggests, is to propose that the Church imitates the triune communion. In so doing, Gunton argues that the best way to describe the Church is a communion which reflects the divine communion: "The Church is what it is by virtue of being called to be a temporal echo of the eternal community that God is."[38] A similar view of the Trinity as a model for human community is advanced by Marjorie Hewitt Scuhocki, who says that "the *model* of a trinitarian God, irreducibly diverse yet one, suggests a world community of irreducibly

36. Gunton, "Church on Earth," 48–80.
37. Gunton, "Church on Earth," 52.
38. Gunton, "Church on Earth," 75.

diverse communities, each of which is itself richly created in and through the irreducible diversity of its members."[39]

The problem with a bare notion of imitation is that it has the capacity to establish the human community as a parallel *response* to God's action rather than as something fully integrated with what God has done in our humanity and what he has made us to be in Jesus Christ. For this reason, a more suitable way forward is given in Paul Fiddes's view that imitation is valid but needs to be supplemented by *participation*.[40] For Fiddes, the Church imitates the triune communion because it has been drawn to participate in the relation of Father and Son in the power of the Spirit. Fiddes's development is absolutely crucial because it establishes the life of the Church as an act of God's grace, not a human effort made in response to God's self-revelation. The Church as a creature of the grace of God which is wholly caught up in God the Son whose vicarious humanity has accomplished our entire part in the dialogue between God and creation cannot be a parallel response to God without, that is, betraying the inner essence of what the Church is as the body of Christ. The Church does not only make its response to God the Father through Christ. The Church as the body of Christ shares in the movement of the Son's self-giving love to the Father in the power of the Spirit.

This chapter concludes with an exploration of three ways in which the triune life of God shapes the ecclesial communion: the Church as community, the relationship between the universal and the local Church, and also the character of the Church as an ordered communion. Driving this account is a construction that follows on from Fiddes's prioritizing of participation in the triune relations through incorporation into the incarnate Son. The Church as a communion reflects the relational being of God inasmuch as it indwells the divine communion through the Son in the power of the Spirit.

The Church as Communion by Participation

Just as God has his being in communion, the Church's mode of being is communion. The Church is not an event we attend or an experience to enjoy (or to not enjoy, as the case may be); it is a communion to which we belong. God has his life in communion, and this is reflected by the Church, which also has its life in communion. Crucially, however, this is not a mirroring that takes place by a human appraisal of God's self-revelation as triune and corresponding application of certain principles such as mutuality

---

39. Suchocki, "Introduction," x–xi.
40. Fiddes, *Participating in God*, 29.

or collegiality. Nor is it a doxological act in which our worship of the triune God compels us to more profound fellowship.[41] Instead, it is an organic growing alongside through the indwelling of the Church in the triune relations on account of our corporate inclusion into Jesus and the empowering of our fellowship by the Spirit who eternally unites the Father and Son in love. Just as the Spirit empowered Jesus Christ to live the life of the Son in his human particularity, so also the Spirit is at work in the Church enabling us to live the life of the people of God in communion with God and one another in Jesus Christ. In other words, the Church is a communion that reflects the triune communion by the redemptive acts of God. In calling the Church into being, God does not only establish a reciprocal relationship between himself and us, he also establishes us in communion with one another: "[God] not only creates personal reciprocity between us and himself but creates a community of personal reciprocity in love, which is what we speak of as the Church of the Lord Jesus Christ living in the Communion of the Spirit and incorporated into Christ as his body."[42]

Some caution is needed when talking about participating in the divine communion. The idea of the ascent of humanity to take its place within the life of the eternal and the transcendent is an old idea and if we are not careful some unhelpful and alien forms of thinking can intrude at this point. We are not, for example, thinking in terms of Platonic participation in the realm of the eternal and its Gnostic counterpart of the soul elevating to the heavens after it departs the restrictions of the body. Nor are we talking about the elevation of the human nature by the cultivation of virtues by the infusion of divine grace and the aid of the Holy Spirit. Instead, this is participation in the divine life that is predicated upon God the Son becoming a human and gathering us up in himself through the Holy Spirit and returning us to the Father in love. As Julie Canlis has written, with characteristic insight and clarity, our participation in the divine life is "neither a matter of the soul's latent powers nor of conscientious Christian endeavour but of communion: it is a participation in Christ's own response to the Father."[43]

John Zizioulas has had a profound impact on thought about the Church from the latter half of the twentieth century to the present day. Rowan Williams has written of Zizioulas's seminal *Being as Communion* that it "has a fair claim to be one of the most influential theological books of the later twentieth century; it had a lasting effect on ecumenical discussion and

41. LaCugna, *God for Us*, 366–68.

42. Torrance, *Atonement*, 360.

43. Canlis, *Calvin's Ladder*, loc. 84.

on the vocabulary and assumptions of many Churches."[44] For Zizioulas, that God has his life as Trinity means that the central category in which we understand God and the Church should be communion: "God *is* Trinitarian: He is a relational being by definition ; a non-trinitarian God is not *koinonia* in His very being. Ecclesiology must be based on Trinitarian theology if it is to be an ecclesiology of communion."[45]

The foundation-stone of Zizioulas's complex body of thought is a conviction that a person is not a modification of abstract being, but the person is actually the cause of being.[46] A person, in Zizioulas's estimation, is constituted by a real existence as a particular (*hypostasis*) who transcends one's own boundaries (*ekstasis*) bringing about a differentiated and integrated unity (communion). A person, in other words, is an individual-in-relation. Moreover, for Zizioulas, this individual-in-relation is the ground of being. Consequently, Zizioulas is critical of any theological approach which thinks of God first as one nature and only then considers him as three persons. The reality, he argued, is quite the reverse. For Zizioulas, the cause of the being of God is the person of the Father (this is Zizioulas's *personalism*).[47] The result of this, Zizioulas argues, is the difference between freedom and necessity. If God's personal existence were simply the result of the way he had his being then this compromises his freedom. If, on the other hand, the person of the Father constitutes the divine being by willing the generation of the Son and the procession of the Spirit then the being of God is the product of a personal will to communion. It is worth quoting Zizioulas at length.

> When we say God "is," we do not bind the personal freedom of God—the being of God is not an ontological "necessity" or simple "reality" for God—but we ascribe the being of God to his personal reality. . . . God as a Father, and not as a substance, perpetually confirms through "being" His *free* will to exist. And it is precisely His trinitarian existence that constitutes this confirmation: the Father out of love—that is, freely—begets the Son and brings forth the Spirit. If God exists, He exists because the Father exists, that is, He who out of love freely begets the Son and brings forth the Spirit. Thus God as person—as the

44. Williams, "Foreword," xi–xii.

45. Zizioulas, *One and the Many*, 49.

46. Zizioulas, *Being as Communion*, 39. For a fuller discussion of Zizioulas's ontological revolution and the engagement with the Cappadocian Fathers by which he reached these conclusions, see Grenz, *Rediscovering the Triune God*, 133–42.

47. Zizioulas, *Being as Communion*, 40.

hypostasis of the Father—makes the one divine substance to be that which it is: the one God.[48]

For Zizioulas, then, the life of God as communion exists by the Father's will to communion: "this communion is a product of freedom as a result not of the substance of God but of a person, the Father . . . because the Father as a *person* freely wills this communion."[49] The implication of this, Zizioulas contends, is a richer foundation upon which to understand what it is for God to be love. Love is not a property of God; it is the very mode of God's existence as the Father chooses to extend beyond his own particularity and love the Son and the Spirit. The being of God, therefore, is the orientation of the divine persons toward one another in love. Relationality, therefore, constitutes the very essence of God (this is Zizioulas's relational ontology). Difference and love are inherent to the divine being: love is what "makes God what he is, the one God."[50]

There are grounds for some misgivings with the specific trinitarian mechanics of Zizioulas's account.[51] Not least among these are the concern that understanding the Father as the cause of the divine being may be open to the accusation that this subordinates the Son and the Spirit to the Father as lesser forms of deity. Certainly, Zizioulas's flexibility with the fundamental distinction between being and willing creates the possibility for category confusion along the lines of Arianism. Moreover, one could object that this proposal does not really think of the threeness and the oneness of God simultaneously as personhood has been made the cause of being. Against the specifics of Zizioulas's trinitarian theology, but with his association of being and communion, it may be preferable to think of the begetting of the Son and the procession of the Spirit from the Father, as the way in which the being of God necessarily has life. In this way, the essence of God is understood to be a relational essence: God's being is "inherently altruistic, *Being for others, Being who loves.*"[52] Even if this criticism and counterproposal were to be accepted, then there is still common ground upon which to build, which is conviction that the being of God is a relational reality.

Zizioulas's distinctive trinitarian theology provides the foundation for his ecclesiology. The point of connection is Zizioulas's anthropology and corresponding soteriology. Zizioulas describes salvation as the transfer

---

48. Zizioulas, *Being as Communion*, 41.

49. Zizioulas, *Being as Communion*, 44.

50. Zizioulas, *Being as Communion*, 40-41.

51. For a full discussion, see Torrance, *Persons in Communion*, 293–94.

52. Torrance, *Christian Doctrine of God*, 12.

from "biological to ecclesial existence."[53] All humans are born into what is described as a biological existence. This form of human existence (which is more ordinarily spoken of as humanity in its fallen state) has two fundamental problems, according to Zizioulas. First, it does not possess freedom inasmuch as it did not choose to exist and it is tied to "natural instinct" and "impulse."[54] The biological mode of existence is humanity driven by the law of its being, not the freedom of personal will-to-communion. The second problem is that of separation. This form of existence behaves in a way that prioritizes the individual which is ultimately expressed in death as the final cessation of connection to others, the sealing of this biological mode of existence.[55] Paul McPartlan, a commentator on Zizioulas, helpfully summarizes the thrust of Zizioulas's view of how sin has impacted humanity: "The Fall did not damage the *naturas* of things, but broke their *communion* with God; it made difference into division and persons into individuals."[56]

Ecclesial existence is a corresponding mode of existence in which the biological existence undergoes a new birth into a mode of existence that is free from the necessity that inhibits freedom and forestalls communion: "The first and most important characteristic of the Church is that she brings [humans] into a new kind of relationship with the world which is not determined by laws of biology."[57] The means by which this happens is baptism for it is in the Church where existence "is not determined by the laws of biology."[58] By this Zizioulas means that entrance into a ecclesial mode of existence creates the possibility of a nonexclusive love that is utterly free from impulse and self-interest. The Christian, in other words, is the one who is free from biological necessity and capable of engaging as a person (that is with the freedom to transcend oneself), rather than an individual. It is out from this tension between freedom and biological necessity that the implications for Zizioulas's ecclesiology emerge into plain view: "As an ecclesial hypostasis [existence] man thus proves that what is valid for God can also be valid for man: the nature does not determine the person; the person enables the nature to exist. Freedom is identified with the being of man."[59] The chief expression of this, Zizioulas argues, is in the Eucharist in which "the terms 'father,' 'brother,' etc. lose their biological exclusiveness and reveal, as we have seen, relationships of

53. Zizioulas, *Being as Communion*, 49–65.

54. Zizioulas, *Being as Communion*, 50.

55. Zizioulas, *Being as Communion*, 51.

56. McPartlan, *Eucharist Makes the Church*, 152.

57. Zizioulas, *Being as Communion*, 56.

58. Zizioulas, *Being as Communion*, 56.

59. Zizioulas, *Being as Communion*, 57.

free and universal love."[60] In other words, it is in the Church that the human person is set free from a mode of existence characterized by necessity and individualism and enabled instead to exist in the freedom of persons orientated beyond themselves toward communion.

The heart of what it is to be saved, Zizioulas argues, is the "eternal salvation of the human person . . . as loving and being loved."[61] The mechanism of this salvation is participation in the personal communion of God through Jesus Christ and realizing this personal communion in our human existence. To be saved is to participate in the relationship of the Son and the Father in the power of the Spirit. It is, as Zizioulas put it, to "enter by grace into the sonship which is conveyed to us by the living relationship between the Father, the Son and the Spirit."[62] At the center of this is Jesus Christ who is not savior "because he brings the world a beautiful revelation, a sublime teaching about the person." Instead, Christ is savior "because he realizes in history *the very reality of the person* and makes it the basis . . . of the person for every [human]."[63] To be incorporated into Christ as his body is to share his mode of existence and so participate in the communion of Father and Son in the power of the Spirit.

The implications for Zizioulas's vision of the Church are significant. It is pretty well axiomatic for Zizioulas that "ecclesiology must be situated within the context of trinitarian theology."[64] What it means for God to be communion carries implications for what it means for the Church to have its life as a communion. Within trinitarian theology as it has been parsed by Zizioulas, then, diversity within the Church is not a challenge to the communion but is essential to it: "There is no model for the proper relation between communion and otherness either for the Church or the human being other than the Trinitarian God."[65] The diversity of the Church is not in spite of our communion but is constitutive of communion. There needs to be difference in order for us to move beyond ourselves and stand in positive relation to others. For Zizioulas, then, "otherness is *constitutive* of unity, and not consequent upon it."[66]

The analogy of relation is central to any attempt to establish some correspondence between the divine communion and the ecclesial

60. Zizioulas, *Being as Communion*, 60.

61. Zizioulas, *Being as Communion*, 49.

62. Zizioulas, *Communion and Otherness*, 306.

63. Zizioulas, *Communion and Otherness*, 238.

64. Zizioulas, *One and the Many*, 137.

65. Zizioulas, *Communion and Otherness*, 4.

66. Zizioulas, *Communion and Otherness*, 4.

communion. We cannot decide upon our own direct analogy between the human community and the divine communion. We only walk the path that has been beaten down by Jesus Christ. In God the Son incarnate, the divine communion is lived out in human history. This means that in the power of the Spirit, Jesus Christ lives the life of God the Son among us and before us. God the Son incarnate makes known the Father, and his love for the Father, by obeying the Father's will in unity of the Spirit. The love of God the Father for the Son is made known in the resurrection of the Son incarnate by the power of the Spirit.

However, this is not just a demonstration of divine love that goes on before our eyes but above our heads. Wondrously, mercifully, this is a manifestation of the divine communion that *actually invites us in*. This is demonstrated by the full sweep of the work of Christ from incarnation to ascension. In taking our humanity into personal union with himself by the agency of the Spirit, God the Son identifies himself with us and establishes a fraternal relationship with us. Through the full course of his life, he lived the life of God the Son as a human through which divine faithfulness is met by an answering human faithfulness. In bearing our humanity to death, God the Son incarnate provokes the full depravity of humanity in our contradiction of God in that, when God came among us, we despised him. Drawing this sin into his body on the cross, God the Son incarnate became a curse for us, blotted out the stain of sin and turned away the wrath of God. Going with us into the lowest point of death and estrangement from the Father, God the Son catches us up with him and includes us in his resurrection from the dead. Now a corporate person as we are united to him through his incarnation, death, and resurrection, Jesus ascends to the Father and, in him, we are "partners in a heavenly calling" (Heb 3:1). We, together, are welcomed into the very communion of the divine life because we are in the Son who has returned to the Father: "you have died, and your life is hidden with Christ in God" (Col 3:3).

The ecclesial communion is derived from our participation in the triune communion of God's life through Jesus Christ. As John put it, "We proclaim to you what we have seen and heard, so that you may have fellowship with us. And our fellowship is with the Father and with his Son, Jesus Christ" (1 John 1:3). The communion of the Church is a shared participation in communion with the triune God. The inseparability of the Church as a communion of humans and the Church in communion with God is reflected in a number of scriptural designations for the Church. The Church is the people of God (1 Pet 2:9–10); the temple of the Holy Spirit (1 Cor 3:16–17); the bride of Christ (Rev 21:2); and, of course, the body of Christ (1 Cor 12:27). All of these terms express both a relationship with God on account of which individual human beings share a corporate existence and have communion with one another. It is within our shared participation in Christ by the power of the Spirit that we are also in relationship with one another. As one influential ecumenical document puts it, "this communion is participation in the life of God through Christ in the Holy Spirit, making Christians one with each other."[67]

Fiddes's own discussion of our participation in the triune relations functions through the idea of taking part in the movement of the divine relations by being incorporated into the Son. By being one with the Son, the Church is included in the divine movement of self-giving to the other.[68] The inner-wiring of Fides's position rests on the commitment that the divine persons do not have relations but that they *are* the relations (subsistent relations).[69] There is no Father and Son at either end of their relationship of generation; instead the Father is the relation of unbegotten source and the Son is the relation of the begotten. This means that to be included into the Son does not mean to be included in a person who has a relationship; it means to be included into the filial relationship itself. Importantly, therefore, Fiddes establishes that the axis of the intersection between us and our incorporation into the eternal movement of God's life is the human sonship of Jesus as he lived the life of the Son as a human so that we might share in his Sonship.[70] In other words, it is as the body of Christ that we participate in the divine relations. The development of this idea is the major burden of the next chapter.

At this moment, though, I would like to apply Fiddes's insight in a different way. If the ecclesial communion is what it is through participation in the divine communion through Christ, then this must be expressed in connection with the invisible, vertical, and the visible, horizontal aspects of the Church. The communion of the Church is both (i) invisible and vertical and (ii) visible and horizontal with the former being the ground of the latter and the latter reinforcing the former. The communion of the Church is vertical in that it is communion with God and it is horizontal in that it is communion with one another, and these two aspects belong inseparably together within the Church.

The vertical communion of the Church is the people of God who are grasped by the saving work of God and drawn to have their place in the triune communion. It is our adoption as the children of God by sharing the status of

---

67. "Church as Communion," para 13.
68. Fiddes, *Participating in God*, 37.
69. Fiddes, *Participating in God*, 34.
70. Fiddes, *Participating in God*, 42–43.

sons by our inclusion into the Son in the power of the Holy Spirit. This vertical communion is not a loose coalition or an arbitrary connection. Instead, it is a vibrant participation in the reciprocal love of Father, Son, and Spirit. There are three core elements of this vertical communion: the Son, the Spirit, and the ministry of the Church in proclamation and celebration.

God the Son has assumed humanity into a personal union with himself "in order to redeem those who were under the law, so that we might receive adoption as children" (Gal 4:5). In bearing our humanity to the Father, the Son received the penalty of the law in his body thus "erasing the record that stood against us with its legal demands" (Col 2:14). As one of us and for all of us, he offered to the Father a human life of utter obedience ("yet not what I want, but what you want" [Mark 14:36]) and trust ("Father, into your hands I commend my spirit" [Luke 23:46]) and the resurrected Christ was welcomed into the presence of the Father. In Jesus' love of the Father and the Father's love of the Son, the eternal divine love is lived out within our human history. In other words, in the person, life, death, resurrection, and ascension of Jesus Christ, the debt of sin is erased, and the life of a human covenant partner is made real and God opens his divine being for human participation.

Through Christ and by the Spirit, God has revealed that he eternally has his life as a communion of love and has provided the means of our participation in that love as his children. In doing so, God creates a human community of reciprocal love, which is the Church, which is a sign pointing beyond itself to the eternal love of God (1 John 4:7–21).[71] This is why the body of Christ metaphor is of such importance to our understanding of the Church. At one and the same time, it says that the Church is incorporated into the divine communion by its incorporation into Jesus Christ through baptism, and therefore the Church is a communion of believers who are united together on account of our common participation in Jesus Christ (1 Cor 12:13, 27).

Our communion with God means that we are in communion with one another. The spiritual reality has a necessary visible expression. Paul describes the Church as a community of believers who bear a God-given responsibility and relationship to one another. There is a common concern for one another built upon a solidarity of shared experience: "if one suffers, all suffer together with it; if one member is honoured, all rejoice together with it" (1 Cor 12:26). There is a pneumatologically grounded mutual commitment within the body as each is gifted in a certain way for the good of the community (1 Cor 12:19–21, 28–30). Moreover, the common inclusion

---

71. Torrance, *Trinitarian Faith*, 251.

into the body of Christ disregards division and reconciles, "Jews or Greeks, slaves or free are all alike baptized into the one body" (1 Cor 12:13). In Jesus, all things are being reconciled, that is drawn together, under one head (Eph 1:9) and as such "there is neither Jew nor Greek, there is neither slave nor free, there is neither male nor female; for you are all one in Christ Jesus" (Gal 3:28), because "in his flesh [Christ] has made both groups into one and broken down the dividing wall, that is, the hostility between us" (Eph 2:14). This unity is also sacramental (as will be developed in the next chapter), we are one body because we all share in one bread (1 Cor 10:16–17) and we are baptized into one body (1 Cor 12:13).

It is in the power of the Holy Spirit that believers are united to Christ and are adopted into communion with God by sharing in the relation of the divine Son to the Father. Our invisible communion with God through the Son is established and constantly renewed by the Holy Spirit. In his famous letters to Serapion, Athanasius of Alexandria articulated his belief in the divinity of the Spirit on the grounds that the Spirit communicates to humans the divine life and actually enables believers to participate in it. This is because the Spirit is the Spirit of Jesus Christ who communicates to us is the very presence of Jesus Christ and is the light of God that shines in our hearts by which we can see the light of the glory of the Father in the face of Jesus (2 Cor 4:6). For this reason, another great theologian of the fourth century, Basil of Caesarea, established his thinking about the Holy Spirit on the foundation of Paul's statement "No-one can say Jesus is Lord except by the Spirit" (1 Cor 12:3).

> Just as the Father is made visible *in* the Son, so also the Son is recognized *in* the Spirit. To worship *in* the Spirit implies that our intelligence has been enlightened. . . . The Holy Spirit cannot be divided from the Father and Son in worship. If you remain outside the Spirit, you cannot worship at all, and if you are in him you cannot separate him from God. Light cannot be separate from what it makes visible, and it is impossible for you to recognize Christ the Image of the invisible God, unless the Spirit enlightens you. Once you see the Image, you cannot ignore the light; you see the light and the image simultaneously. It is fitting that when we see Christ, the Brightness of God's glory, it is always through the illumination of the Spirit.[72]

By the Spirit, believers are baptized into the one body of Jesus Christ (1 Cor 10:16-17; 11:23–29). The Son is sent so that we may receive adoption, but it is by the Spirit that we may appropriate the reality of that adoption,

---

72. Basil, "On the Holy Spirit," 26.64.

for it is by the Spirit that we are bound to Christ. This is why it is only by the Spirit that we cry "Abba! Father!" (Gal 4:4–6). It is, then, by the Spirit that believers are referred to by Paul as being "in Christ" (2 Cor 5:17; Col 1:27–28), and as we are in Christ we share his relationship to the Father and so are welcomed into the triune communion.

The word of God proclaimed and received by faith and the sacraments are the concrete and effective means of our incorporation into Christ and so the filial relation with the Father. It is as we hear Scripture proclaimed and explained that we are pointed to the Word of God incarnate and are enabled by the Holy Spirit to respond in faith that the faithfulness of Jesus Christ as the Son of God is counted as ours. It is as we are baptized that we are united to Jesus Christ, a unity we sustain by Eucharist. Very importantly, however, the proclamation of the gospel and the sacraments are not only the means of our participation in the triune communion, *they are also the elements that are the very visibility of the Church.* It is as we share the one bread, that we manifest that we are the one body and it is as we sit under the word that we are manifested as a community in solidarity under the Lordship of Christ. It is in the sacraments and in preaching, therefore, that the vertical and invisible communion with God intersects with the horizontal and visible communion of the Church. Any analogy, therefore, between the divine communion and the human community is inseparable from the sacraments and from the preaching of the word because through these means we participate in the divine communion through Christ and recognize our communion with one another.

Focusing our attention on the person of Christ and the means of our incorporation into him and so into the filial relation of Father and Son in the power of the Spirit establishes our thinking about the connection between the divine communion and the human community of the Church on the priority of grace. The community of the Church is a creation of grace. It is not the best instincts of human beings to a communal existence coalescing into an objective institution. The failure of any such project is writ in large on the walls of each political prison and mass grave of every Marxist state of the twentieth century. The community of the Church is a work of grace. This is very important because, in order to understand this community, we cannot look at it with the eyes of anything other than faith. Because the Church is a community of believers that is established by the work of the triune God and is actually established on account of a shared inclusion into the communion of the triune God through Jesus Christ, the communion of the Church takes its distinctive character and form from the communion of the triune God.

The divine communion is not simply a model for the Church. The divine communion is that in which the Church has its life as a corporate body. This is very important because it is for this reason that the Church is a communion. The Church does not exist aside from this incorporation into the movement of the Son beyond himself, transcending his own boundaries and concerns to be united to the Father in the power of the Spirit. The very context of the Church's existence is self-offering and other-receiving. Moreover, it is in this act of self-offering to the Father in which we are corporately drawn that we are brought into a corporate relationship with others. The Son's self-transcendence accomplishes in us a corresponding self-transcendence as the Greek and the Jew are reconciled to one another through the cross. In other words, as a creature of grace, the basis and character of the Church's existence is as a community of those who are made open to others by the openness of Jesus Christ. In Zizioulas's terminology, Jesus is the personalizing person because he is the one who establishes us as persons by being orientated beyond ourselves and freed from biological necessity to be in positive relations with others.

This brings us fairly close to delineating the communion of the Church in terms of *perichoresis*. There are two senses in which *perichoresis* may be helpful in further parsing the ecclesial communion. First, as was outlined above, it is possible to think of *perichoresis* in terms of the dynamism and movement of the divine persons orientated toward one another in self-giving love. Such an account of the divine communion means that in being included into the Son, which is itself the incorporation into the relation of Sonship itself, the Church is included in the movement of that relationship.[73] As Christ prayed "as you, Father, are in me, and I am in you, may they also be in us" (John 17:21). In this sense, *perichoresis* offers a way in which to describe the Church's participation in the triune communion. The Church as a community should be set on this foundation. Paul could write that those who are reconciled to God form "one body in Christ and are individually members of one another" (Rom 12:5). This means that, in our very personal identity, we now make room for one another as we, in a very real way, belong to one another by our common inclusion into Christ and participation in the Father-Son relation. Just as the term "Father" and "Son" are relational, reciprocal names and so contain the other in the identity of the one, so now we carry in ourselves all our brothers and sisters in Christ.

However, we, living in space, cannot mutually interpenetrate one another as the divine persons do. Perhaps, though, it is possible to distill the principles of *perichoresis* out and consider how the Church through

73. Fiddes, *Participating in God*, 72–81.

indwelling the triune life reflects these in its own life. The divine persons are within one another and their identities are determined by one another. This structural and formal personal reciprocity and mutual belonging encases a dynamic idea of a ceaseless movement of love toward one another. The relations between human persons in the Church can function with the same *movement*, if not with the same structure of mutual interiority. The New Testament presents the Church as a profound and affectionate fellowship bound together in love. The fellowship of the Church is one in which we share one another's joys and sorrows (Heb 10:33), we serve one another in love (Gal 5:13), pray, eat and worship together (Acts 2:42), share material possessions for the good of others (1 Cor 16:1–13), and share our very lives with one another (1 Thess 2:8). This orientation to one another in love includes spiritual gifting, also. God gives a variety of gifts to his Church through the Holy Spirit (1 Cor 12:8–11), and these gifts are given "for the common good" (1 Cor 12:7), for the fullness of the life of the whole Body of Christ (1 Cor 12:14–21). For this reason, the gifts are not to be exercised in self-aggrandizement, but in the aggrandizement of Christ in his Church. They are to be used in love to bind the fellowship of believers ever more securely. Just as the perichoretic relations of the Father, Son, and Holy Spirit rebound into the unity of the one God, so also the reciprocal relations of love and mutual gifting of each believer rebounds into the unity of the one Church.[74]

However, within the similarity of the divine perichoresis and the ecclesial mutual commitment to one another, there are very significant differences. This is very important because the Church is the creation of God and while it resembles the divine communion in its own patterns of communion, it does so in a creaturely way. The divine fellowship is eternal and uncaused by any other, whereas fellowship of the Church does not cause itself but is established by grace. This means that our participation with one another in relations of love is an act of grace. As was explored above, the unity of the Church is established by God, not by the good intentions of humans. This is very important because if we can establish this point very firmly in our minds, it means that we will not get the direction of causation between the structural and the dynamic elements of the Church as community the wrong way around. The fellowship of the Church is not characterized by mutually belonging to one another *because* of our mutual affection for one another or because of our exercise of spiritual gifting for the common good. Instead, we love one another and exercise gifting for the common good because we have been made members of one another by the work of Jesus Christ and the power of the Holy Spirit. Our perichoretic-like unity is established by

74. Volf, *After Our Likeness*, 211.

the reconciling act of God by which we are mutually included into Christ and as such become members of one another. If we get the causation the wrong way around the Church will be no different from any other human community the existence of which is dependent on the commitment of its members. Furthermore, we can only correspond to the perfect communion of the triune life in a broken and limited way. As Miroslav Volf has written, "ecclesial communion on this side of God's new creation can correspond to the perfect mutual love of the trinitarian persons only in a broken fashion."[75] The individuals who are part of the community of the Church get things wrong, we are orientated to ourselves and our own good and we are hurt by others in the fellowship who do wrong to us. However, it is in this that we are reminded that the ultimate ground of our reciprocal relations of love is not dependent on us, but rather on the grace of God in drawing us to participate in the triune relations through our incorporation into Jesus.

The Universal and Local Church

The triunity of God informs the relation of the universal and the local Church. The Church is one and many and, as with God, neither the one nor the many is to exercise dominance over the other. This has both an economic aspect in the way we think of the work of the Son and the Spirit in mutuality in establishing the Church as the body of Christ and also an immanent aspect as we derive principles for the relation of the one and the many from the way in which God has his life. It is imperative that the economic aspect is supplemented by the immanent aspect because, without it, the economic aspect has a center of gravity that leans to the priority of the local Church over the universal.

The aspect of the universality, or catholicity, of the Church with which we are currently interested is *the mystery of the whole Church that is in spiritual union with Jesus Christ*. This is the primary meaning of catholicity from which all other dimensions of its meaning are derived. In this primary sense, catholicity is correlate to the designation the body of Christ, which is developed further in the following chapter. Certainly, this is the sense in which the term was first used by Ignatius of Antioch when he wrote that "wheresoever Jesus Christ is, there is the catholic Church."[76] The one, universal Church is inseparable from Jesus Christ because it is the whole Church that is united to him as the body of Christ. The Church must be considered in its unity because its defining relationship to Jesus both establishes

75. Volf, *After Our Likeness*, 207.
76. Ign. *Smyrn.* 8.2.

and treats it as a totality. This universal incorporation into Christ means that wherever there is a fellowship of believers, no matter how small or uncertain, the whole Church is there by merit of a shared inclusion in Jesus.[77] This is the mystery that is the Church and why the Church can never be analyzed accurately from non-theological (better, non-Christological) grounds. The Church is catholic because she is the body of Christ and our catholicity is not contingent on us behaving as such. The catholicity of the Church, therefore, is not an ethos or a morality of openness to all. The catholicity of the Church is, as Zizioulas rightly says, by the presence of Jesus Christ who unites us together into one reality.[78] The catholic ethos and morality of universal openness is derived from the essence of catholicity which is a shared participation in Jesus.[79]

However, this does not mean that local Churches should be thought of as derivative, concrete expressions of the universal Church. If this were the case, then lying above and before the local Church is a universal Church which has dominance over the local. Scripture does not always speak of the Church with an eye on its totality, but also speaks of it in its locality. Letters are written to believers within a particular city or province. The seven letters at the beginning of the book of Revelation address seven Churches in different localities. Paul writes to the Philippians as "saints in Christ Jesus who are in Philippi" (Phil 1:1). In this he refers both to the invisible fellowship in Christ which is shared by all Christian believers and also to their physical location in that particular city; the former is the Church in its universal, invisible aspect and the latter is the Church in its local and visible aspect. How should we hold the universal Church as the body of Christ in relation to these local Churches, without marginalizing one in the place of another?

John Zizioulas provides a very helpful starting point. For Zizioulas, the local Church is local because the sacraments must be celebrated in a locality.[80] However, unlike other versions of this sacramental ecclesiology, this, Zizioulas suggests, does not lead to the dominance of the local over the universal. Zizioulas's proposal stands against that of Nicholas Afanasiev who thought of the local parish Church as the heart of all ecclesiology: "Where there is the Eucharistic assembly there is Christ, and there is the Church of God in Christ."[81] Zizioulas's reticence to prioritize the local over the universal is established upon a synthesis of the work of the Son and

77. See also Küng, Church, 300.

78. Zizioulas, Being as Communion, 158–60.

79. Torrance, Conflict and Agreement, 198.

80. Zizioulas, Being as Communion, 247.

81. Afanasiev, "Una Sancta," 14.

the Spirit in the work of salvation, whereby the Son is made incarnate and enabled in his mission by the Spirit such that the Spirit is recognized to be constitutive of salvation.[82] In the same way, Zizioulas argues the Spirit is constitutive of the Church: "the Spirit is not something that 'animates' a Church which already somehow exists. The Spirit makes the Church *be*."[83] It is as the Spirit incorporates us into Christ as his body through the sacraments that the Church is actually constituted. Therefore, both the many local Churches or sacramental communities and the one universal Church of our unity in Christ are constitutive of the Church.

There is a lot that is very helpful in Zizioulas's approach. There is a strong affirmation of the mutually constitutive roles of the Son and the Spirit in establishing the Church upon their mutuality in the divine economy. The body of Christ is always formed by the Spirit: it is by the Spirit that the Son is made incarnate and it is by the Spirit that believers are baptized into the body of Christ. The catholicity of the Church as the one body of Christ can't be thought of independently from the Spirit because the body of Christ is always the work of the Spirit. Therefore, the one universal Church cannot be thought of independent from the local congregations within which the Spirit binds us to Christ through the sacraments and, the proclamation of the gospel.

While Zizioulas's willingness to see the catholicity of the Church in its pneumatological and local perspective as well as its Christological perspective is necessary, it is also incomplete. The centre of gravity in Zizioulas's thought falls on the local Church, as if the universal Church were the aggregation of the local eucharistic communities. Perhaps this is to be expected given the character of personalism to Zizioulas's trinitarian ontology. The simultaneity for which Zizioulas reaches ultimately eludes him. Zizioulas's fundamental contribution can be affirmed with respect to the mutuality of the Son and the Spirit in the divine economy of salvation and the constitution of the Church. However, it needs to be supplemented by the recognition of the implications of the way God has his life in his nontransitive relations as three-in-one for the way in which we relate the one and the many in the case of the Church. In this way, the simultaneity of the universal and local Church will be protected from both the front and the back.

It is characteristic, particularly of Paul, to speak of the Church at one and the same time as universal and local. This is why Paul can speak of the Church of God which is in Corinth (1 Cor 1:2; 2 Cor 1:1), for example. As with the visible and the invisible Church considered above, the Church as

82. Zizioulas, *Being as Communion*, 126–32.
83. Zizioulas, *Being as Communion*, 132.

catholic and as regional needs to be thought of as two dimensions, which are not in competition but in mutuality. These two dimensions are both *necessary but insufficient* to the fullness of the Church. The catholic Church is inseparable from the multitude of local Churches, and *vice versa*. The catholic Church depends upon the local Church for concrete, historical existence and constitution, while the local Church depends upon the catholic Church for its basic identity as the body of Christ. For this reason, the universal Church and the local Churches need to be spoken of in simultaneity and reciprocity. So, we need to find a way of speaking of the relationship between the one and the many in which one does not cause or dominate the other. It is precisely here that we turn to the triune relations of God to learn how to hold these aspects of the Church in complementarity. The triunity of God provides us with a way of thinking in which the one does not exert monolithic control over the many and the many do not undermine the one.[84]

The doctrine of the triune God does not start either from the unity of the divine essence or the plurality of the divine persons. Similarly, the doctrine of the Church must not begin with wholeness of the catholic Church or the plurality of local Churches. As the one divine essence has no priority over the three persons, but rather has subsistence as and in the three persons, so also the universal Church does not have priority over the local Churches, but rather is dependent upon them for visible expression in history and actual constitution in the power of the Spirit. However, this does not mean that the local Churches are prioritized over the universal Church any more than the persons are prioritized over the essence. Just as the three divine persons are the personal modes of subsistence of the divine essence, so the local Churches do not have any inner being aside from as the subsistent mode of being of the universal Church. The local Churches, therefore, are the visible manifestation or realization of the invisible reality of the one Church united to God through Jesus Christ. The universal Church cannot be without its historical manifestation and pneumatological constitution and the local Churches cannot be without their essence.

Writing from a Free Church perspective, Miroslav Volf is deeply critical of the Roman Catholic Joseph Ratzinger for what Volf considers to be a "pyramidal dominance of the one" in Ratzinger's trinitarian theology which flows out into Ratzinger's vision of the Church in which the one universal Church is prior to and exerts dominance over the local Churches.[85]

---

84. Gunton, *One, the Three and the Many*.

85. Volf, *After Our Likeness*, 216–17. There might be some veracity to this given that Ratzinger has said that the universal Church "is a reality ontologically and temporally prior to every individual Church." Ratzinger, *Letter to the Bishops of the Catholic Church on Some Aspects of the Church Understood as Communion*, 9. See also, Ratzinger,

This corresponds to Volf's mentor Jürgen Moltmann's explosive claim that monotheism lies at the root of authoritarian power structures.[86] While Volf's criticisms are overstated (Ratzinger's trinitarian theology is significantly more nuanced than Volf's analysis indicates), it does indicate how a lack of balance in trinitarian theology might feed through into how the Church is thought of. Let's say, for the sake of argument, a theologian were to prioritize the one divine essence over and above the threeness of the persons, to the effect that the distinctions between the Father, Son, and Spirit are smudged over. Such a foundation would have a correlate of the universal Church as an idealized communion which has its life aside from and antecedent to the concrete, historical reality of local Churches. In such a scenario the—almost Platonic—catholic Church would dominate local Churches and absorb their differences into a more fundamental oneness.

However, what if, in the quite understandable desire to avoid the "pyramidal dominance of the one," we were to oversteer in the other direction? We might think, along with the social trinitarians, that the oneness of God is nothing other than the community of the three persons united in relations of love. In this way of thinking it is very hard to think of the one God as having anything other than a conceptual existence as the combination of the three. The ecclesial correlate of this would be local Churches that are logically prior to the one Church and that are considered to be sufficient in and of themselves. The catholicity of the Church would become the aggregate of all the local Churches, if indeed we deigned to retain it at all. The one Church may, in other words, cease to be anything at all beside the nominal congregation of all the local fellowships each of whom have their own distinctive theologies and offices.

We are faced, once again, with the problem of thinking two things at once. The challenge is to try to find a middle route which will avoid both the monolithic dominance of the one over the many and the erasing of real unity through the prioritizing of the many. Just as the universal Church does not exist before and independent from the local Churches, the local Churches do not exist before and apart from the universal Church. The metaphor of the body of Christ is crucial to framing this reciprocity in a way that coheres to the fundamental grammar learnt from trinitarian theology. The universal Church can only be understood as a Christological and Pneumatological reality. The universal Church is the one Church that is united to Jesus Christ through baptism in the power of the Spirit and so elevated to participate in the triune communion. For this reason, the catholicity of the Church is a

---

Church, Ecumenism and Politics, 75.

    86. Moltmann, *Trinity and the Kingdom of God*, 129–32.

statement of faith, and not an empirical phenomenon in and of itself. God
has established one Church by the inclusion of believers into Christ in the
power of the Spirit. This one Church exists in relation to God in its totality. Catholicity, in other words, is a divine act of grace not a human act of
combination or by the unifying power of an institution.

However, this common inclusion into Christ as his body must have
empirical and local expression. Just as the one divine essence has its subsistence in the three divine persons, so the universal Church is given concrete
expression in the local. The local Churches are the various manifestations
of the universal Church. The universal Church cannot be without the local
Churches any more than the invisible aspect of the Church can be without
the visible, or the essence of God can be without the persons. The universal
Church exists in space and time with distinct communities of believers in
a variety of locations who, nevertheless, all make present the one universal Church. In this sense, the universal Church is instantiated in the local
Church. This means two things. First, that the universal Church does not
have concrete expression in and of itself but only in and as the local Church.
Second, that the local Church does not have any content aside from its being
a manifestation of the universal Church. However, this does not imply the
dominance of the one over the many, for just as the perichoretic relations
of the three persons of the triune God return us to the unity of the divine
essence, so also the local eucharistic communities are not only the presence
of the one body of Christ but also the localities in which the Spirit actively
includes us in the body of Christ. This is a relationship of reciprocity which
touches on the character of perichoretic relations in that each dimension, the
catholic and the local, carries within itself the fact of the other.

One of the advantages of thinking of the universality of the Church as
a Christological reality is that this acts as a prophylactic against thinking of
catholicity as an institutional abstraction. The one universal Church does
not have any content aside from the whole Church in union with Christ
and it has no historical extension aside from the local Churches. It is for this
reason that the earthly apparatus of catholicity cannot be accepted. Because
if it did, then we could identify the universal Church with whatever institutional framework we desired and exclude others from it. The error here is
that two elements of catholicity get smudged together: the catholic Church
as the worldwide communion and the catholic Church understood as the
communion of believers in spiritual union with Jesus Christ. It is vital that
we keep these elements of catholicity separate because if we do not then we
will transpose the spiritual reality of the whole Church into institutional
form and ignore that the catholicity of the Church is a Christological, transcendent, and invisible reality.

This does not mean, however, that the universal Church does not have historical, institutional expression. As we are real human beings who exist in history with one another, our spiritual union with Jesus Christ can never be without historical expression. This is one aspect of the importance of the apostolicity of the Church. The apostolicity of the Church is not only its being sent out in mission to the world or its conformity to the apostolic gospel (although these are of course crucial aspects of apostolicity of the Church). Apostolicity is also about the apostolic office which is a focus of unity, drawing the variety of local Churches into the oneness of the catholic Church. This apostolic function was not an addition to the community Christ established, but, as Michael Ramsey has shown, emerges out from the very essence of the gospel which has united humanity in the fellowship of the one Church by our common inclusion into Christ.[87] The central function of the episcopacy is to be the instrument and expression of the unity of the Church. It is only possible because of our common and spiritual union we share by our common inclusion in Jesus Christ. The diocesan bishops embody the reciprocity of the universal and the local Church. At one and the same time, the bishop reminds the Church of the mystery of its catholicity and also the fact of its localized existence. It is with this that we turn to think about the order of the Church.

The Church as Ordered Community

The third way of thinking of the Church in correlation to the triune being of God concerns the question of Church order. How do we relate the organic life of the community and the more formal structures of the institution in our understanding of the Church? Throughout the majority of its history the Church has been organized into clear orders of episcopacy, presbytery, deacons, and laity. There are three general reasons for this. First, Christ established his Church with apostles as its head and this fundamental ordering continues today. Second, the Church is given its own reality as a visible, human entity and must embrace and live out this humanity, part of which is human organizational structures. The first and second reasons are expanded upon in chapter 5. The third reason, which is more pertinent to the subject-area of this chapter, is that God has his life in an ordered communion and the Church reflects that in its own ordered communion.

Miroslav Volf has constructed a sophisticated case which argues that an understanding of the character of the Church as a community which is shaped by the triunity of God must be egalitarian because this is the

---

87. Ramsey, *Gospel and the Catholic Church*, 68–77.

character of divine communion. Volf argues that any idea of hierarchy in the Church is improper because it does not correspond to the triune communion. Volf is critical of his Orthodox and Roman Catholic colleagues Zizioulas and Joseph Ratzinger for their hierarchical understandings of the divine life which flow out into their hierarchical understandings of Church order. For Ratzinger, Volf suggests, this hierarchical character is rooted in the supposed predominance of the one divine nature over the persons expressing itself in the universal institutional jurisdiction of the Pope. For Zizioulas, this hierarchical character is rooted in the view of the Father as the source of the triune life which is expressed in the episcopacy and the marginalizing of the laity to an undifferentiated unity having "the same liturgical function."[88] For his part, Volf advocates a trinitarian theology which is, supposedly, free of hierarchy which unfolds into a non-hierarchical Churchmanship. In other words, Volf argues for egalitarian relationships within the Trinity which corresponds to an egalitarian understanding of the relationships within the Church.[89]

However, Volf's proposal has a significant problem in that the trinitarian relations do suggest some degree of personal priority in the relations of Father, Son, and Spirit. The Son and the Spirit come out from the Father and the Father does not come out from any other. Fundamental, therefore, to Volf's egalitarian account of the triune life is a rather strange distinction between the "constitution of the persons and their relations."[90] For example, he suggests that the Son may well be begotten from the Father, but this is about how the Son is constituted as a distinct person, an individual standing aside from the Father and the Spirit. However, he suggests that this does not tell us anything about the actual character of the relationship between the Son and the Father: it "says nothing as yet about *how* the relations between them are structured."[91] The effect of making this distinction is to provide a justification of removing linear and hierarchical relations from the triune life. The actual relations between the persons, Volf insists, are characterized by egalitarian, or perichoretic, love. In other words, the Father may well be the source of the Son in their constitution as distinct persons, but this does not bleed into the character of their relationship to one another. Therefore, while the Son may well come out from the Father, this does not mean that the *relationship* between them is characterized by

88. Zizioulas, *Being as Communion*, 89.
89. Volf, *After Our Likeness*, 217.
90. Volf, *After Our Likeness*, 216.
91. Volf, *After Our Likeness*, 217.

an order.[92] The relationships the persons have, Volf argues, is free to be nonordered and characterized by equality and mutuality thus removing the need for a hierarchical order in the triune life. The corresponding understanding of the Church is one without hierarchy, but a thoroughgoing equal priesthood of all believers.[93]

The distinction drawn by Volf makes the significant assumption that the modes of origin of the divine persons have no bearing on the relations of God's triune life. However, the suggestion that the constitutive element of the divine persons has no connection to the relationship between the persons is hardly compelling. Even if the association between personhood and relation was understood to be that the relation distinguishes the persons (rather than actually being the persons), then to differentiate between mode of origins and relational identity is impossible. The Father is the Father *because* of his relation to the Son. The attempt to differentiate between modes of origin and constitutive relations does not make sense, precisely because they are the same thing. For this reason, Volf's proposal risks resulting in two Trinities: the hierarchical relations of origin which constitute the persons and the egalitarian relations those persons have with one another. Undesirable enough in itself, this has the added problem of raising the following question: To which aspect of this artificial division between God's substantive and egalitarian relations do we establish an understanding of the Church in correlation?

Undergirding Volf's trinitarian mechanics is a particular understanding of personhood that is, at the very least, suboptimal. At the heart of Volf's distinction between the modes of origin which constitute the persons and the relationships that the persons are in to one another is a view that *a person is an individual which has a relationship*. In other words, Volf is antagonistic to the idea of subsistent relations, being the view that the divine persons *are* the relations. For Volf, the person comes before the relationship as the individual which is capable of being in relationship. Therefore, the eternal begetting of the Son from the Father is the mode by which the divine person has subsistence, and this person subsequently has a relationship with the Father and the Spirit. Of course, that the person is the basis of relationship is a justifiable position to hold.[94] The problem with this view, is that it is heavily reliant on

92. A very similar approach is taken by Gary Badcock who argues that the relations of the divine persons "are not immediately derivative of the processions." Badcock, *Light of Truth and Love*, 245.

93. In this, Volf's approach to ecclesiology is very similar to that of Colin Gunton, *Promise of Trinitarian Theology*, 71–77.

94. See, for example, McFarland, "Personhood and the Problem of the Other," 204–20.

seeing the person as a subject who possesses relationship as a property, as if divine personhood envisages some basis of subsistence aside from relationship. Volf's solution to this problem is to advance modes of origin as a basis of subsistence which can possess mutual and nonhierarchical relations. Once again, we arrive at the problem of the questionable validity of a distinction between the modes of origination and relational identity.

If, on the other hand, modes of origin and personal identity are treated as synonymous, then the communion of Father, Son, and Spirit is an ordered communion. The Father is alone the source of the Son and the Spirit. The economy of salvation is God's outward relation to creation which is governed by the inner order of the triune relations. The Son is sent out by the Father into time in correlation to the Son eternally coming out from the Father in the Godhead. The Spirit is poured out on believers by the Father through the Son as the Spirit eternally proceeds from the Father through the Son. The Father is not superior to the Son and the Spirit. However, the Father is the source of the Spirit and the Son. This is not a hierarchical relation, but it is an ordered relation. The ordering is not about power or authority but about precision and specificity in personhood. It is axiomatic of Zizioulas's ecclesiology that the Church is "a reflection of the very love of God" on account of which "hierarchy and authority are thus born out of relationship and not of power."[95] This has bearing directly on Church order and authority. As Catherine Mowry LaCugna has put it, "the trinitarian doctrine of God, as the basis for trinitarian ecclesiology, might not specify the exact forms of structure and community appropriate to the Church, but it does provide the critical principle against which we can measure institutional arrangements."[96] The principle LaCugna advances is the principle of communion. The Church should be characterized by "inclusiveness, interdependence and cooperation, structured according to the model of *perichoresis* among persons."[97] LaCugna's appeal to perichoresis as a model of mutuality and collegiality is instructive because it establishes authority in a relational perspective. The Church leader "should be *part* of the community and not stand above it as an authority in itself. All pyramidal notions of Church structure vanish in the ecclesiology of communion."[98] This does not mean an absence of difference or hierarchy so long as it is acknowledged

---

95. Zizioulas, *Being as Communion*, 223–24.

96. LaCugna, *God for Us*, 402.

97. LaCugna, *God for Us*, 402.

98. Zizioulas, *One and the Many*, 54.

that the Church is "hierarchical in the sense in which the Holy Trinity itself is hierarchical: by reason of specificity in relationship."[99]

The ecclesial correlate is an ordered communion predicated upon relational specificity, not power. The ordered relations of bishop, priest, deacon, and laity are not artificial additions to the simple pure community of believers but are necessary expressions of the Church as a community that is shaped in accordance with the triune life of God. The ordering of the Church is derived from the very life of God by the power and gifting of the Holy Spirit. By the will of the Father, humans are incorporated into Jesus by the power of the Spirit and in Jesus we are lifted into the very life of the Godhead. By this participation, the Church begins to resemble the triune character in its own being and structures as the Spirit gifts parts of the body of Christ to the end of the enrichment of our common life. In other words, the charismatic organization of the Church into diverse orders is the mode of being of the Church as a communion. The priest is a mode of being within the body of Christ that has a specific relational orientation to the rest of the body, which is expressed in certain functions, being the preaching of the gospel, pastoral care, and the celebration of the Eucharist. Likewise, the layperson is a mode of being within the body of Christ that holds a specific relational orientation to the rest of the body and so also the bishop and the deacon. These ecclesial modes of being interrelate and complement one another such that one carries within itself the fact of the others. Church order is a diversification within the unity of Christ's people for the purpose of sustaining and giving visible expression to that communion. The ordered relation of the Church has its source in God's triune being and act and its purpose is to maintain and strengthen our common unity in Christ, as is developed in some length in chapter 5.

Church order, then, does not emerge from the Church itself. The formalizing of relations is not the result of a self-referential human institution attempting to perpetuate itself through the maintenance of a rigid hierarchy. Instead, Church order is dependent on the action of God in calling and gifting. In other words, the charismatic and the institutional are not at loggerheads, but rather are interconnected. This is what is represented by the ancient act of the laying on of hands. At one and the same time, this act is the election of the Church to the particular ministry in recognition of God's calling and it is the prayer that God would enable them for it. This inseparable relationship between the charismata of God's calling and gifting and the institutional act of choosing leaders has been put with great clarity by Joseph Ratzinger.

99. Zizioulas. *Being as Communion*, 223.

> That this structure element of the Church [orders of ministry],
> which is the only permanent one, is a sacrament, means that it
> must be perpetually recreated by God. It is not at the Church's
> disposal, it is not simply there and the Church cannot set it up
> at its own initiative. It comes into being secondarily through a
> call on the part of the Church. It is created primarily by God's
> call to this man, which is to say, only charismatically-pneumato-
> logically. By the same token, the only attitude in which it can be
> accepted and lived is one unceasingly shaped by the newness of
> the vocation, by the unmanipulable freedom of the *pneuma*.[100]

There is a complementarity of gift and order. The ordering of the Church is a necessary response to the gift of God. As the Church of England Book of Common Prayer Ordinal has it, the God who "didst give to thy holy Apostles many excellent gifts" continues now in the same way in that he "hast appointed divers orders of ministers in thy Church." This unity of charism, calling, and Church order gives a very particular orientation to how we might understand ordination.

A similar view is articulated by Zizioulas, who stresses the *relational* character of ministry within the Church.[101] Zizioulas holds an understanding of ordained ministry in which the different orders of the Church are constitutive of the community of the Church. Zizioulas rejects the two traditional alternatives of ordination which emphasize either clericalism or the priesthood of all believers because both of them see the Church as somehow before or causing ordination. The community of the Church, Zizioulas argues, does not exist prior to the diverse ministries that make up its life. Instead, the Church in its unity as a community and its diversity need to be thought of at the same time. At the center of this view is baptism and Eucharist. For Zizioulas, the baptized person is baptized into a body with many different parts, into a eucharistic assembly with different orders of ministry within it. The Spirit unites us into Christ at the same moment as diversifying believers through the giving of different gifts.[102] Baptism, in other words, is an ordination into the person and ministry of Jesus (on which more will be said in the next chapter) in which diversity of orders is a function of the Eucharist (on which more will be said in chapter 5).

Zizioulas's understanding of ordination stresses that it is a direct act of God in which the Spirit unites us to Christ and gives us diverse gifts within the body of Christ. By making the connection between baptism and ordination,

---

100. Ratzinger, "Theological Locus of Ecclesial Movements," 480–504.

101. Zizioulas, *Being as Communion*, 214.

102. Zizioulas, *Being as Communion*, 216–17.

Zizioulas is able to argue that "ordination is understood as constitutive of the community," and so the ministry of the Church "can be described as a complexity of relationships within the Church."[103] The community, in other words, is united in its diversity by the orientation of its gifts to one another in the fellowship of the Spirit. It is this, Zizioulas argues, that renders the Church a "relational reality, i.e. a mystery of love reflecting here and now the very life of the trinitarian God."[104] Ordained ministry, therefore, cannot be viewed as an individual office with its own character aside from the wider community. Its purpose is to serve the body of Christ by being the means through which Christ tends to his body by the Spirit in gifting some for this specific mode of relation to the body of Christ.

The ordering of the Church is both a charismatic reality and an institutional reality. The Spirit incorporates us into Christ and the gifts of the Spirit are poured out on every member of the body of Christ. Some of these charismatic gifts pertain to Church leadership. This connection between charism and order means that the communion of the Church should not be like that of a hierarchical institution in which one advances beyond the other by merit of their greater capacity or achievements. Such a conception would lead inevitably to competition, jealousy, and cronyism. The act of ordaining some into the ministry of pastoral care, sacrament, and preaching is at one and the same time a divine and a human act. The act of ordaining is a recognition of the Church of the gifting and calling that have come from God. In this sense, it is a witness to God endowing his Church with gifts. However, in the ordination as an act of the Church, God is at work to equip those being ordained with that which is required. In this sense, therefore, ordination may be described as sacramental. It is a human act that embodies the fact that God has acted to choose and gift his Church, and through this act God actually does do something to choose and gift.[105]

Fundamentally, the ordination of some into the mode of being of deacons, priests, and the further consecration of others into the mode of being of bishops, is in service of a setting aside for participation in the ministry of Christ that is more fundamental. Peter says of the Church: "you are a chosen race, a royal priesthood, a holy nation, God's own people, in order that you may proclaim the mighty acts of him who called you out of darkness and into his marvellous light" (1 Pet 2:9). The whole Church is set aside as God's own people, a universal priesthood, for the purpose of being a witness to the world

---

103. Zizioulas, *Being as Communion*, 220.

104. Zizioulas, *Being as Communion*, 220.

105. For more on this, see Avis, "Revision of the Ordinal in the Church of England 1550–2005," 101–6.

of God's redemptive works, ministering Christ's reconciling love in the power of the Holy Spirit, and participating in Christ's sacrifice of praise to the Father. All other subsequent ordering of the Church is a corollary of this one.

> Q. Who are the ministers of the Church?

> A. The ministers of the Church are lay persons, bishops, priests and deacons

> Q. What is the ministry of the laity?

> A. The ministry of the lay person is to represent Christ and his Church; to bear witness to him wherever they may be; and, according to the gifts given to them, to carry on Christ's work of reconciliation in the world; and to take their place in the life, worship, and governance of the Church.[106]

In this sense, there is a universal ministry which is shared by the whole Church. As participation in Christ's mission is a calling shared by all believers, so the gifting of the Holy Spirit is shared by all believers.

From within this shared calling as the people of God, there are some who are set aside specifically to serve the Church and equip it to undertake the charge God has given it. This specific calling is a gift to God's people to sustain and lead through the ministries of pastoral care, preaching, and sacrament. As is written in the Berkely Statement, which is signed by thirty of the thirty-seven Anglican Provinces, affirms that all believers are baptized into the person and mission of Jesus Christ to be active participants in God's mission of reconciling humanity to God. Baptism is therefore the fount of a universal priesthood of all believers as through baptism we are incorporated into the body of Christ and so to the ministry of the body of Christ. However, completely continuous with this is its affirmation that "in order that the whole people of God may fulfill their calling to be a holy priesthood, serving the world by ministering Christ's reconciling love in the power of the Spirit, some are called to specific ministries of leadership by ordination."[107] These convictions are reflected in the 2005 Common Worship Ordinal which states that "to serve this royal priesthood, God has given particular ministries,"[108] deacon, priest, and bishop. These are modes of being, which each have their own specificity but yet are all orientated to one another in mutual service. There will be a great deal more to say about

106. *Book of Common Prayer*, 855.

107. Gibson, *Berkeley Statement*, 2.

108. *Common Worship: Ordination Services*. For a more detailed discussion on this, see Irving, "Baptismal Ecclesiology," 203–24.

these different orders, particularly the character of priesthood such as it is derived from Christ who is the true priest as the reality of God's redemptive action toward us and the human response of faith and obedience, in chapter 5. Discussion of the distinct character of ordered ministry within the Church will wait until setting properly the foundation from which it derives its actual essence, which is Jesus Christ.

4

The Body of Christ

THE THEMES THAT HAVE been considered separately throughout the previous chapters converge in the designation of the Church as the body of Christ. In the first chapter, the idea of Christ as the perfect covenant partner of God was introduced with the associated notion that to be saved is to be included in him and share in his relation to the Father in the power of the Spirit. In the second chapter, the continuities between the Church and creation were highlighted. Like creation, the Church is brought into being from nothing by the act of God and, in that absolute dependence, it has its own distinct existence as the Church. In the third chapter, the ecclesial communion was set in relation to the triunity of God through its participation in the triune communion through incorporation into the Son. Both of these aspects of the Church (its being a creature of the word of God and its indwelling in the triune relations) are derived from the central reality of the Church that constitutes its very existence: the Church is the body of Christ.

God has done something in his creation to bring the Church into being. This new thing that God has done has its life wholly by its inclusion into the person of Jesus Christ by the Spirit. Just as the human nature of Jesus Christ is dependent upon being assumed into union with God the Son for its existence (*anhypostasia*) but once it has been assumed has a real, full existence as humanity within the person of God the Son (*enhypostasia*), so also the Church is dependent upon being assumed into union with God the Son for its existence (the *anhypostatic* aspect of the Church) but once it has been assumed into personal union with Jesus, it has a full human existence in its incorporation into Jesus Christ (the *enhypostatic* aspect of the Church). Once again, this is not to undermine the unique reality of the incarnation. Instead, it is to say that the inner logic of the union of the divine and the human in Jesus Christ gives us the fundamental principles by which we can understand the relation of God and creation more generally, including in our consideration of the Church.

The next two chapters examine the *anhypostatic* and *enhypostatic* aspects of the Church. This current chapter will consider the Church in its dependence on being assumed into personal union with God the Son by the Holy Spirit (i.e., its *anhypostatic* aspect). This is the Church as a miracle of the grace of God. The next chapter will consider the Church in its full humanity as it emerges out from being included in God the Son as the human gathering and institution of the Church (i.e., the *enhypostatic* aspect). The Church is *anhypostatic* in that the Church has no existence aside from being called into existence by the act of God. However, the Church is *enhypostatic* in that it is given its own real human existence, with real historical particularity, within the person of the Son. In other words, the person of Jesus Christ gives us the grammar by which we are to understand his Church.

One of the major benefits in following this line of approach is that it will keep us out of a costly tug-of-war between a theological perspective that insists that the Church is an event of God's grace and another that insists the Church is a divinely established institution that continues through time. When we take Jesus Christ as providing us with our laws for understanding then we will see that the dependence of the Church on God as being brought into existence by the act of God is not in competition with its institutional and historical particularity. Put in Christological terms, the *anhypostatic* aspect of the Church (the Church as the event of God's grace) is compatible with its *enhypostatic* aspect (the Church in its historical, institutional continuity). Indeed, the Church in its historical continuity as a human community and institution is not possible aside from the Church as event, called into being by the grace of God and the Church as called into being by the act of God has a necessary expression as an earthly-historical entity. The earthly-historical reality of the Church persists within the person of Jesus Christ, as his body. The calling of the Church into being does not exist in some non-physical ideality. The Church as the event of God's grace exists as historical continuity in the collection of Christian believers who all share a common inclusion in Christ and for that reason are bound one to the other, which is expressed in a range of organizational and liturgical frameworks.

In establishing our thinking of the Church as the body of Christ on these Christological foundations, a way of conceptualizing the Church as an institution with particular historical, human existence and as a creature of the word of God is possible. The dominant accent of some Protestant ecclesiology can relativize historical continuity through bishops in favor of conformity to the apostolic gospel (an implication of understanding the Church to be brought into being by the word of God heard by faith), but it also includes a marked concern for Church order as a gift of God to accommodate our frailty.[1] Likewise Roman Catholic ecclesiology may well lay particular stress on historical continuity through the episcopate, but it also affirms very clearly that the visible structures of the Church and its orders are of a divine origin in terms of call and gift.[2] In order for the Church to be true to its foundations in Jesus Christ, both sides must be stressed. The Church is both brought into existence from nonexistence by the act of our being united in the person of Jesus Christ (the Church is the event of being included into Christ) *and because of that* it has a true human existence within the person of the Son. There is priority to the act of God in bringing the Church into being, on account of which the Church cannot exist as a human institution aside from the divine act.

In this connection, a thoroughly Christocentric ecclesiology provides a perspective from which to think of the marks of the Church not as aspirations but as divinely established properties of the Church. The Church is one, holy, catholic, and apostolic because it is made as such by the act of God through Christ by the Spirit. Within some Protestant approaches to the Church, there is a reluctance to treat the marks of the Church as established reality.[3] On one level, this reticence is deeply understandable because it is conscious that our tendency to idolatry can lead us to view the Church as an infallible institution that is unable to depart from that which Christ established it to be. Certainly, the Church, as made up by fallible believers, is very capable of living in a way that is not one, holy, catholic, and apostolic. Moreover, it is an unavoidable fact of historical demonstration that the Church in its visible aspect does not necessarily manifest these attributes.

All of these historical failures, however, must not shroud the fact that the Church really is one, holy, catholic, and apostolic. This is what the Church is made to be as it is united to Christ as his body in the power of the Spirit. In its *enhypostatic* aspect, the Church often fails to uphold and demonstrate its essential attributes in its historical existence. This is the reason why, in the *enhypostatic* aspect of the Church, we must shape our order and polity on the practices of the Church that bind us to Christ, which are preaching and the sacraments. As will be developed in the next chapter, the Church as a divine institution must be shaped in its structures by the pulpit, font, and communion table, for it is in these ways it continues its participation in Christ and in these ways that it truly is one, holy, catholic, and apostolic. In all our thinking about the Church we must not

---

1. Calvin, *Inst.* 4.1.1–4.
2. Paul VI, "Dogmatic Constitution on the Church (*Lumen Gentium*)," 2.
3. For example, Berkouwer, *Church*, 11–17.

allow ourselves to get dragged into the old tug of war between Church as continuity and Church as an event of God's activity. The Church was, is, and will be *both*. The Church is an event of being called into existence by God's grace, which incorporates us into, and continues our participation in, the person of Jesus Christ. At the same time, this creature of the word of God has its existence as a creature.

This chapter thinks about the Church as that which is brought into being by the act of God through incorporation into Christ by the Spirit. The Church exists on account of its participation in Jesus Christ. This gives priority to the body of Christ as the primary designation with which to describe the Church. Just as the human nature of Jesus Christ had no personal existence aside from being incorporated into union with God the Son, so also in assuming us into union with himself, Jesus brings the Church into existence, which it could have in no other way. From the perspective of this *anhypostatic* aspect, the Church has no existence other than its relation of dependence to Jesus. The Church exists as an event of divine action. The primacy of divine act in the Church is explored through the notion of salvation as participation in Jesus which has its correlate in the designation of the Church as the body of Christ. Placing front and center the designation of the body of Christ acts as something of a handbrake against any separation of the sacramental activity of the Church and the complete work of Jesus Christ. The very essence of salvation is that Jesus unites us to his own person by the Holy Spirit, whereby we share all he is before the Father. By establishing our thinking on this foundation, any subsequent analysis of the Church as a human institution will not fall into seeing the human actions of the Church as a response to God which is parallel to but not fully joined to Christ.

Incorporation into Christ

Throughout Paul's letters, the use of the phrase "in Christ" is utterly pervasive. There are several ways in which Paul uses this phrase. He uses it to refer to what God has done "in Christ." For example, Paul writes of the "grace of God that has been given you in Christ Jesus" (1 Cor 1:4) and that "God was in Christ reconciling the world to himself" (2 Cor 5:19). He uses it as part of an encouragement of his readers to a particular course of action: "we command and exhort in the Lord Jesus Christ to do their work quietly" (2 Thess 3:12). However, the use of the phrase with which we are most interested is the *position of the believer as being in Christ*. For example, Paul writes that Christian believers "must reckon yourselves dead to sin and alive to God in

Jesus Christ" (Rom 6:11). Closely correlated to this use are the occasions in which Paul writes of the deep confluence of the life of Christ with the life of the believer: "it is no longer I who live but Christ who lives in me" (Gal 2:19–20). Clearly Paul understood himself to be caught up in the person of Jesus such that his own life was inseparable from Jesus to such an extent that Jesus could be described as the believer's life itself (Col 3:4).

Salvation as Participation in Christ

For Paul, to be brought into Christ is synonymous with salvation. Jesus' incarnation, death, resurrection, and ascension together constitute a new beginning, a new human existence free from the power of sin and death and in fellowship with the Father through the Son in the power of the Spirit. To be saved is to "be set free from the present evil age" (Gal 1:4), "rescued from the power of darkness and transferred into the Kingdom of his beloved Son" (Col 1:13), through the transfer from Adamic humanity to the new humanity under the headship of the risen Jesus Christ. This transfer is brought about, so Paul writes, by the mystery of inclusion into Jesus Christ's risen humanity by being made one with him in his death (Rom 6:1–11), through the sacrament of baptism effective in the power of the Spirit (1 Cor 12:13). For Paul, salvation is not some commodity that is received aside from Jesus. Paul will not allow us to think of grace as something that we receive that is separate from or external to Christ. The opening doxology of his Letter to the Ephesians celebrates the blessings of God which are received by our inclusion into Christ. This gives a profoundly trinitarian character to the Christian idea of salvation: to be saved is to be included in the risen Lord in the power of the Spirit on account of which we share in Christ's relation to the Father. To be united with Jesus is not just one aspect of the gospel. It is not one of the benefits we receive by the grace of God. Instead, participation in Christ *is* the gospel. It is by taking our place and our share in all that Jesus is and has done that we are adopted as the children of God. To be a Christian is to be united to Jesus and share in all he is and all he has done as one of us and for all of us. By our inclusion into Jesus, the perfect righteousness of Jesus Christ before the Father is given to us and we are given a share in his sanctified, risen humanity which has been received to the right hand of the Father.

Prioritizing the theme of participation in Christian thought about salvation means that the person and the work of Jesus Christ are not artificially separated. To be saved is not simply receiving the *benefits* that Jesus has won for us. Instead, it is to participate in *Jesus himself* and receive the blessings of his life and his relation to the Father. This is the inner essence of the doctrine of adoption. Justification, for example, is not only a forensic legal status that is pronounced over us which we appropriate by faith in Jesus' sacrificial death (although it certainly is that), it is also our right standing with the Father on the grounds that we are counted as one with Jesus, the one who is truly faithful to the Father. Could it be that the long-running exegetical dispute over Romans 3:23 is the product of the inherent double emphasis in Paul's grammar and theology? If so, it would require that *pistis Christou* operates as both a subjective genitive and an objective genitive. It is both that we are justified by faith in Jesus and by the faithfulness of Jesus. Likewise, the renewal of our humanity must not be alienated from its primary reality, which is the Spirit-empowered incarnate life, obedience, and resurrection of Jesus Christ. The risen Jesus is the human who is righteous in the eyes of the Father and who stands at the head of a new sanctified humanity. In union with Christ, we share the renewal already achieved and in the same Spirit who actualizes that renewal within our lives.

A corollary of the separation of Jesus from the benefits he bestows on us is that it causes us to think in a way that detracts in very different ways from the centrality of Jesus as the mediator between God and humanity. It is in Jesus Christ that God has moved toward humanity in reconciling love and in whom humanity moves toward God in sanctifying obedience and faith. The purity of the priestly work of Christ is diluted by alien mediators, being either our personal faith by which we appropriate the benefits Christ offers us or the Church through which we receive the grace by which our own humanity is restored. Salvation is not something external to Jesus. Salvation is to be united to Christ who is the one mediator between God and humanity, to share in his righteousness before the Father and to share in his sanctified, risen humanity.

We can view the problem from another angle. Take the popular distinction in soteriology between the Son changing our objective status before God in justification and the Spirit changing our inner state through sanctification. This account of salvation sees the work of the Son and the work of the Spirit going on to quite different ends and in quite distinct spheres of influence. Not only is this problematic from the perspective of the grammar of trinitarian theology, it is out of step with the character of salvation. The Son and Spirit are each involved in the one work of God which is to restore humanity to God. Justification and sanctification are each the work of the Son and the Spirit together. By the Spirit, God the Son became one with us and lived a life of perfect obedience in the power of the Spirit. In so doing he lived the life of the second Adam in the flesh of the old. In the power of the Spirit, he offered our humanity up to the Father in his own obedient and faith-filled life. In obedience he was put to death, exhausting the penalty and stain of our sin in his

body on the cross. By the Spirit he was raised from the dead as new humanity
and that new humanity was lifted to the Father in the ascension. The Spirit
unites us to Jesus through baptism, incorporating us into the body of Christ.
The righteous status of humanity and the sanctification of humanity are both
realities in Jesus Christ through the power of the Spirit.

We would do altogether better, then, if we thought of salvation in
more rigorously *trinitarian* terms. Salvation as participation in God the
Son incarnate, Jesus Christ in the power of the Holy Spirit by whom we are
adopted as the children of the Father. What, however, is meant by participation? Most plainly, this is not imitation. This is not participation as we might
participate in the example of another. The sort of participation described in
the New Testament is the participation of indwelling, of engrafting, of, in a
very real sense, being in Christ. This sort of participation is incorporation
into Jesus such that all he is, his very life, becomes ours also. John Calvin
had this theme at the center of his theology.[4]

Union with Christ in the Soteriology of John Calvin

Calvin articulated a robust and sophisticated account of the gospel as incorporation into Christ, through whom God has moved toward humanity in
reconciling love, bearing the penalty and guilt of sin in his body on the cross
and in whom humanity has moved toward God in sanctifying obedience and
faith through which our broken humanity is resurrected and returned to the
Father in love. As such, it is axiomatic to Calvin's understanding of salvation
that the "whole of salvation is not to be sought anywhere else than in Christ."[5]
Likewise, the introduction to Calvin's commentary on Ephesians makes clear
that all parts of our salvation are placed in Christ alone, such that we may not
seek anything elsewhere.[6] Calvin's focus falls on the belief that the gifts which
God gives are indivisible from the person of Jesus. Therefore, it is only by
being united with Jesus that we receive forgiveness of sins, resurrection from
the dead, and any other benefit of the gospel. Christ alone is our redemption
and Christ alone is our righteousness.

This Christological focusing of salvation does not betray an unsatisfactory trinitarian theology. For Calvin, the saving act of God is the work of
Father, Son, and Spirit. God the Son, in obedience to the will of the Father,

---

4. For a more detailed analysis, see Billings, *Calvin, Participation, and the Gift*,
25–67. See also Hart, "Humankind in Christ and Christ in Humankind," 67–84; and
Slater, "Salvation as Participation," 39–58.

5. Calvin, *Calvin's Commentaries*, 17:123.

6. Calvin, *Calvin's Commentaries*, 21:191–93.

lives the life of the Son as a human by the power of the Spirit. However, this does not mean that salvation is something that goes on above our heads from which the benefits eventually trickle down to us. Instead, this reconciliation is lived out within the heart of our human existence by the incarnation of God the Son to whom we are joined by the work of the Holy Spirit. The reconciling activity of God is not a divine drama played out beyond us. It is the act of God by which we are laid hold of and adopted as the children of God by our inclusion into the Son. It is because God the Son descends to be one of us so that he can lay hold of us and lift us up to share in his relationship with God the Father.

> As long as Christ remains outside of us, and we are separated from him, all that he has suffered and done for the salvation of the human race remains useless and of no value for us. Therefore, to share with us what he has received from the Father, he had to become ours and to dwell within us. For this reason he is called "our head [Eph 4:14] and "the first-born among many brethren" [Rom 8:29]. We also, in turn, are said to be "engrafted into him [Rom 11:17] and to "put on Christ" [Gal 3:27]; for, as I have said, all that he possesses is nothing to us until we grow into one body with him.[7]

What saves, so far as Calvin is concerned, is not the legal status Christ earns for us or the righteous life Christ lives on our behalf. These are of no consequence to us so long as we are not grafted into him. The lynchpin of salvation is to be incorporated into Jesus Christ, and through participating in Jesus we receive the blessings he has won for us: "as soon as you become engrafted into Christ through faith, you are made a son of God, an heir of heaven, a partaker in righteousness, a possessor of life."[8] It is by being one with Jesus Christ that we share in his relation to the Father and in the blessings of that relationship.

> We await salvation from him not because he appears to us afar off, but because he makes us, ingrafted into his body, participants not only in all his benefits but also in himself. . . . But since Christ has been so imparted to you with all his benefits that all his things are made yours, that you are made a member of him, indeed one with him, his righteousness overwhelms your sins; his salvation wipes out your condemnation. . . . We ought not to separate Christ from ourselves or ourselves from him. Rather we ought to hold fast bravely with both hands to that fellowship

7. Calvin, *Inst.* 3.1.1.
8. Calvin, *Inst.* 3.15.6.

by which he has bound himself to us. . . . Not only does he cleave
to us by an invisible bond of fellowship but with a wonderful
communion day by day he grows more and more into one body
with us, until he becomes completely one with us.[9]

Christ, therefore, is a "fountain open to us, from which we may draw
what otherwise would lie unprofitably hidden in that deep and secret spring,
which comes forth to us in the person of [Jesus]."[10] It is by our inclusion
into Jesus that we share in the blessings of being the children of God.

I confess that we are deprived of this utterly incomparable good
until Christ is made ours. Therefore, that joining of Head and
members, that dwelling of Christ in our hearts—in short, that
mystical union—are so accorded by us the highest degree of importance, so that Christ, having been made ours, makes us sharers with him in the gifts with which he has been endowed. We
do not, therefore, contemplate Christ outside of ourselves from
afar in order that his righteousness may be imputed to us, but
because we put on Christ and are engrafted into his body—in
short, because he deigns to make us one with him. For this reason we glory that we have fellowship of righteousness in him.[11]

For Calvin, the center point of salvation is the inclusion of the believer
in the person of Jesus Christ on account of which we share in all that Jesus
is and all that he has done for us.

The foundation stone of our incorporation into Christ is the incarnation of God the Son. It is because God the Son became a human and shared
fully in all we are that we are able to share fully in all he is. For Calvin, the
incarnation is not just a means to an end so that the Son could suffer the
judgement of the Father. Instead, in Calvin's estimation, Christ shares all
that we are so that he might meet us in our fragility, follow that path right
down to death from where he lifts his brother Adam from death up with
him to the right hand of the Father.

becoming Son of Man with us, he has made us sons of God
with him . . . by his descent to earth, he has prepared an ascent to heaven for us . . . by taking our mortality, he has con-
ferred his immortality on us; . . . accepting our weakness, he
has strengthened us by his power; . . . receiving our poverty
unto himself, he has transferred his wealth to us; . . . taking the

9. Calvin, *Inst.* 3.2.24.
10. Calvin, *Inst.* 3.11.9.
11. Calvin, *Inst.* 3.11.10.

weight of our iniquity upon himself . . . he has clothed us with his righteousness.[12]

Similarly, Irenaeus of Lyons thought of the incarnation as God the Son assuming our humanity so to include us in his own relation with the Father: "For this is why the Word became a man, and the Son of God became the Son of man: so that man, by entering into communion with the Word and thus receiving divine sonship might become a son of God."[13] So also Calvin writes that "certainly for this reason Christ descended to us, to bear us up to the Father, and at the same time to bear us up in himself, inasmuch as he is one with the Father."[14]

What is remarkable about the incarnation as Calvin presents it is the fullness of God the Son's humanity. This was not dipping his toe into our human existence, but a whole sharing in everything it is to be a human, right down to our relationship with God. God the Son stands before the Father as a creature intended for covenant fellowship. However, where Adam lived this existence in disobedience, Christ lived it in obedience and love. Moreover, Jesus does this vicariously; that is, he does it on our behalf and as our substitute. God the Son shared in our humanity, so that we might share in his. God the Son grasped hold of us by becoming one with us so that we might be adopted as the children of God by being drawn in to participate in all he has done as one of us and for all of us. We share in Christ's relation to the Father as his brothers and sisters because Christ has become our brother at the incarnation.

> Who could do this unless the Son of God should become the Son of man and so receive what is ours as to transfer to us what is his, making that which is his by nature to become ours by grace. Relying on this in earnest, we trust that we are sons of God, because the natural Son of God assumed to himself a body of our body, flesh of our flesh, bone of our bones, that he might be one with us; he declined not to take what was peculiarly his own, and thus might be in common with us both Son of God and Son of man. Hence that holy brotherhood which he commends with his own lips, when he says, "I ascend to my Father and your Father, to my God and your God." In this way, we have a sure inheritance in the heavenly kingdom, because the only Son of God, to whom it entirely belonged, has adopted

---

12. Calvin, *Inst.* 4.17.2.

13. Irenaeus, *Haer.* 3.19.

14. Calvin, *Inst.* 1.13.26.

us as his brethren; and if brethren, then partners with him in the inheritance.[15]

By taking our human body as his own, the incarnation of God the Son is the possibility of our incorporation into his body. God the Son grasps hold of the whole of humanity by his incarnation, providing the basis upon which we may be united with him. We can be the children of God because the eternal Son has become one of us and has lived the life of the eternal Son, the life of perfect love of the Father in the power of the Spirit, within our humanity. We can be joined to this perfect covenant partner of God and share in his relationship to the Father: "he is by nature the only Son of God; and he communicates this honour to us by adoption, when we are engrafted into his body."[16]

To be united with Jesus brings about, what Calvin calls, the double grace of justification and sanctification. The declaration of innocence and the healing and restoration of our humanity are Christological realities first, and they become ours through our participation in him. It is precisely this emphasis which enables us to steer in between the two sets of rocks in which the blessings of the gospel are something external to Jesus Christ. Moreover, if we follow Calvin in thinking this way, we do not insert an unnecessary division between the work of the Son in justification and the work of the Spirit in sanctification. Instead, our humanity is seen to be justified and sanctified in the incarnate work of the Son which is lived by the power of the Spirit by whom we also are grafted in to the resurrected, sanctified humanity of Jesus Christ.

> Christ was given to us by God's generosity, to be grasped and possessed by us in faith. By partaking of him, we principally receive a double grace: namely, that being reconciled to God through Christ's blamelessness, we may have in heaven instead of a Judge a gracious Father; and secondly, that sanctified by Christ's spirit we may cultivate blamelessness and purity of life.[17]

So, while Calvin keeps a clear distinction between our legal status as justified before the Father and our moral state as those who are in the process of being sanctified (this distinction is essential to not mistake salvation for a process which is contributed to by our moral attainment), they have a common source in the believer's incorporation into Jesus. To be justified is to share in the righteousness of the obedient, resurrected, and ascended

15. Calvin, *Inst.* 1.13.26.

16. Calvin, *Calvin's Commentaries*, 17:124.

17. Calvin, *Inst.* 3.11.1.

Son. To be sanctified is to share in Jesus' humanity which has died to sin and risen a new sanctified humanity. So, while justification and sanctification are distinct from one another they are utterly inseparable because they are both derived from being included into Jesus.

> As Christ cannot be torn into parts, so these two which we perceive in him together and conjointly are inseparable—namely, righteousness and sanctification. Whomever, therefore, God receives into grace, on them he at the same time bestows the spirit of adoption [Rom 8:15], by whose power he remakes them to his own image. But if the brightness of the sun cannot be separated from its heat, shall we therefore say that the earth is warmed by its light, or lighted by its heat? . . . The sun, by its heat, quickens and fructifies the earth, by its beams brightens and illumines it. Here is a mutual and indivisible connection. Yet reason itself forbids us to transfer the peculiar qualities of one to the other.[18]

The analogy drawn is that as heat is to light with respect to the sun, so justification and sanctification are with respect to Jesus. Like heat and light, justification and sanctification are in a differentiated unity that derive from a more fundamental reality. Heat and light are different aspects of the brightness of the sun; justification and sanctification are different aspects of incorporation into Jesus Christ. While it is essential that we do not confuse them (because our acceptance by the Father is not contingent on our moral improvement but on the righteousness imputed to us by Christ) it is equally important that we do not separate them because both are necessarily related to incorporation into Christ. We are engrafted into Christ and share his righteousness before the Father and we participate in his risen and sanctified humanity, whereupon we are progressively transformed into his likeness.

To be justified, then, is a real sharing in the righteousness of Jesus Christ. Its foundation lies in Jesus' incarnate life including his death, resurrection, and ascension. Jesus stands as the fully righteous human before the Father and as we are engrafted into him we share the benefits of all he has accomplished. It is in Jesus' vicarious humanity lived on our behalf that we are justified. This is the lynchpin of Calvin's dispute with the Lutheran Anders Osiander. Osiander argued that Jesus is able to make us righteous by the operation of his divine nature within our humanity. The reality, Calvin argued, is quite the reverse. It is precisely in his humanity that Jesus lives the life of the perfect covenant partner of God. In so doing, Jesus is not simply

18. Calvin, *Inst.* 3.11.6.

the agent who has won justification for us, he is the one in whom we are justified before the Father: "we do not, therefore, contemplate him outside ourselves from afar in order that his righteousness may be imputed to us, but because we put on Christ and engrafted into his body. . . . For this reason, we glory that we have a fellowship of righteousness with him."[19] In other words, as those who have become sharers in Jesus Christ, we share in his human righteousness before the Father. He does not come as a mere example to help us reach righteousness. *Jesus is our righteousness.*[20]

Likewise, Calvin considers sanctification as something that has been accomplished in our humanity by the vicarious life of Jesus. In a discussion on repentance, Calvin says that repentance and conversion mean the same thing as the "true turning of our life to God" and that this is made up of the putting to death of our old way of life and the new life of the Holy Spirit,[21] the "transformation, not only in outward works, but in the soul itself."[22] This true turning of our life to God "happen[s] to us by participation in Christ."[23] We take our place in Jesus' death so to die to the rule of sin and we share in Jesus' resurrection whereby we are raised up to newness of life in the power of the Holy Spirit. The inner heart of sanctification, therefore, as our progressive transformation into the likeness of Jesus Christ and the turning of our selves to God in obedience and love is both our participation in the death and resurrection of Jesus Christ and our subsequent sharing in the same Spirit who enabled him to offer his life as a sacrifice of praise to the Father. Our incorporation into Jesus is an incorporation into his death to Adamic humanity and into the resurrected humanity of Jesus. We are incorporated into the one in whom our humanity has already been sanctified by his life of obedience on our behalf. A particularly pronounced version of this has been put forward by T. F. Torrance:

> What Jesus did was to make himself one with us in our estranged humanity when it was running away into the far country, farther and farther and farther away from the Father, but through his union with it, he changed it in himself, reversed its direction and converted it back in obedience and faith and love to God the Father.[24]

---

19. Calvin, *Inst.* 3.11.10.
20. Calvin, *Inst.* 3.15.5.
21. Calvin, *Inst.* 3.3.5.
22. Calvin, *Inst.* 3.3.6.
23. Calvin, *Inst.* 3.3.9.
24. Torrance, *Mediation of Christ*, 84.

This is not to say that there is need for our own personal decision and faith. However, it does mean that our faith and conversion is grounded in the act of God the Son as one of us and for all of us. In this sense, the regeneration of the individual believer is the actualization in the human person of what has already been accomplished for them by Jesus.

It is with Calvin's comments on the work of the Spirit in our salvation that we see the fully trinitarian character of Calvin's doctrine of salvation: "the Holy Spirit is the bond by which Christ effectually unites us to himself."[25] Again, "the Spirit alone causes us to possess Christ and have him dwelling in us."[26] It is through the Spirit that we are united to Christ and thus come to share in all he is before the Father. Clearly Calvin has in his mind here the principle that the acts of God are indivisible. By the will of the Father, humanity is gathered as the people of God through our incorporation into Jesus by the Holy Spirit.

A satisfactory understanding of the Church must take very seriously the centrality of union with Christ such as Calvin envisaged it. What it is to be the body of Christ is inseparable from salvation as that work of God to gather us up in the Son through the Spirit. In other words, this discussion has really been quite a lengthy preamble by which to say that when Paul says the Church is the body of Christ, he really means it.

The Body of Christ

What it means for the Church to be the body of Christ is shaped by the sheer centrality of the believer's incorporation into Jesus by the Spirit. As the body of Christ, the Church is not an institution alongside other human creations. The Church does not have some independent existence with its own reason for being and rationale for being the way it is aside from Jesus. The Church does not have its identity or its meaning in its own structures such as its liturgy, its canon law, or any other internal factor. As the body of Christ, the Church cannot look to itself to know what it is. If the Church is to understand what it is, it needs to look to Christ who has assumed it into oneness with himself and, in so doing, brought it into existence in the first place. If we try to think about the Church from any other angle, then we will get quite a skewed view of it. Very much like the limited vision of the logical positivists, we will know the Church only in the shallows of how we experience it in history. When, though, we think of the Church primarily in terms of its union with Christ (and so, therefore, in the power of the Spirit and

25. Calvin, *Inst.* 3.1.1.
26. Calvin, *Inst.* 4.17.12.

in relation to the Father) then we will know it in depths of its inner nature, which is Jesus Christ himself.

The Oneness of Christ and His Church

As the body of Christ, the Church has no existence and no essential content other than that which it receives from Jesus. It does not exist by itself or for itself. This is demonstrated by the very founding of the Church as the gathering of the messianic community around Jesus. Jesus proclaimed that the kingdom of heaven was active and operative in his person. In so doing, he gathered a small community around himself who became his true family (Matt 12:49). This new community was congregated around Jesus Christ and was taught by him and inducted into a life as his followers such that the teaching, prayer, and mission of Jesus would give form and structure to the community that had gathered around him. Jesus went further and incorporated his followers into his own messianic mission as he sent them out to preach the presence of the kingdom of God, to perform miracles and to baptize.[27] The existence of this new messianic community was formalized at the Last Supper, which, as Rowan Williams has pointed out, constituted a transition into the new solidarity of those united to God and one another by a shared participation in Jesus Christ.[28] This new community is formed, in other words, by the act of becoming united with Christ in his death and resurrection such that the life of Christ becomes inseparable (although distinguishable) from the life of the society he establishes: "he who eats my flesh and drinks my blood abides in me, and I in him" (John 6:56). By this common abiding of one in the other, by this intertwining of the life of Jesus and of the society formed by being united to him, the life of Christ and his Church becomes as indivisible as the life of the vine and its branches.

It is this deep union between Jesus and his Church that makes the designation of the body of Christ so profoundly powerful, even when considered alongside the other ways Scripture speaks of the Church. Within the dense thicket of terms of symbols layered one upon the other, the body of Christ affirms in a unique way the mystery of the union of Jesus and his Church: Jesus is the head of which the Church is his body. This is the natural way in which to speak of the Church once the centrality of participation in Jesus is identified as the dominant key of New Testament soteriology. Lying underneath this designation is the twofold reality of the life of Christ and of our inclusion into him. In the incarnation, death, resurrection, and ascension,

27. *Catechism of the Catholic Church*, 176.
28. Williams, "Sacraments of the New Society," 209–21.

Jesus Christ grasped hold of us, lived our human life down to its depths, and gathered us up in his new life and his return to the presence of the Father. The Spirit causes us to hear the gospel and respond in faith, in baptism we are transferred into Jesus Christ, and we renew that incorporation through the Eucharist. The body of Christ, in other words, refers to the new existence of believers as inseparably united to Jesus Christ.

If the Church is the body of Christ, then Jesus makes room in his identity for his Church. The whole Christ (*totus Christus*) now includes Jesus and his Church in one differentiated unity. The real oneness and communion between Christ and his Church is such that Jesus and the Church together make up the whole Christ. The Church is one with Christ and his full identity now includes within it his Church. This is what Thomas Aquinas meant when he wrote "head and members form as it were one and the same mystical person."[29] Just as the head has no existence aside from the body and the body no existence aside from the head, Christ no longer has his existence aside from the Church, and the Church never had existence aside from Christ.

We may correlate this to the doctrine of *perichoresis*. Just as the Father, Son, and Spirit make room in their own personal identities for the other two, Christ has made room in his own identity for us. For this reason, Zizioulas argues that Christ has become a corporate person, a relational reality in whom we are included.[30] To describe the Church as the body of Christ is not like the metaphor of the body politic to speak about the state. The body of Christ is not some sort of supra-personal existence like a society or an institution which has many individual members occupying a role or place within it. Instead, the body of Christ is inseparable from the very person of Christ. To say that the Church is the body of Christ is the same as to say that the Church and Jesus Christ have become one variegated reality, he is the head of which we are the body. As Lionel Thornton put it, "we are members of that body which was nailed to the cross, laid in a tomb and raised to life on the third day. There is only one organism of the new creation; and we are members of that one organism which is Christ."[31]

The logic of the hypostatic union provides us with the grammar by which to understand the identity of the Church as the body of Christ. The incarnation is the event in which God the Son united his divine nature to our human nature in his person. Without having been assumed in this personal

29. Aquinas, *Summa Theologica*, III.48.2, cited from *Catechism of the Catholic Church*, 184.

30. Zizioulas, *Being as Communion*, 110.

31. Thornton, *Common Life in the Body of Christ*, 298.

unity, the human nature of Jesus would have no personal existence. In Jesus Christ, this unity of divine nature and human nature is irreversible. Also, this personal unity does not change either the divine nature or the human nature. This structure of personal unity alongside the retention of differentiation is at work in the designation of the body of Christ. There is the same distinction within personal unity. Christ has incorporated his Church into an unbreakable unity with himself. This personal unity, however, has not turned the Church into Christ any more than it has turned Christ into his Church. This is very important because without this clarification we could arrive at a conclusion that the Church is in some way an extension of the incarnation. This Christological logic of the doctrine of *totus Christus* brings us back around to the fundamental theme of this chapter: the *anhypostatic* aspect of the Church. Just as the human nature of Jesus had no personal existence aside from being assumed into union with God the Father, so the Church has no true existence aside from Jesus incorporating it into himself.

This union means that Jesus has shared in all that we are such that we might have a share in all he is. The Church participates in Christ and draws its life and nature from him, sharing in his life as the incarnate Son of the Father. It is a realistic designation which identifies something at the very heart of what the Church is as that which Jesus draws to himself by the Spirit to share in all he is and has in relation to the Father. It articulates the reality of the union of Christ and his Church. It speaks about the Church most directly as that which has been united to Christ such that it has become one with him. Dialogically speaking, the Church has been incorporated into the perfect relation of divine love and human faith. As the body of Christ, the Church shares in the Son's relation to the Father. This is the ultimate root of the doctrine of adoption, for we are adopted as those who have been assumed into union with the rightful Son and we stand before the Father in him alone. For this reason, everything that was said in the third chapter is a corollary of our incorporation into Jesus Christ. To think of the Church as that which has been included into the triune communion is comprehensible only in terms of our participation in the life of the incarnate Son who has returned to the Father in the power of the Spirit.

One way the logic of the hypostatic union can act as the governing structure of ecclesiology is with respect to Paul's elaboration of the designation in which Christ is the head of which the Church is the body. While Jesus and the Church have become one personal reality without division and without separation, they remain distinct from one another without confusion or change. Jesus Christ is the head of which the Church is the body. Jesus Christ is not the Church for he is the Lord of his Church. However, he is the Lord of the Church who exists in such intimate union with his people that the Church and Christ need to be spoken of as one entity although distinct as that one entity. Christ may well have his existence now only in unity with the Church, Christ may give himself to dwell in the Church by his Spirit, but he is never contained by the Church such that he becomes indistinguishable from it. This means we should be very suspicious of the claim that the Church and its sacraments are the *continuation* of the incarnation. To say this is to nullify the distinction between Jesus and his Church, to discount the difference of the body and the head. God the Son assumed a unique and unrepeatable incarnate presence in Jesus Christ, not the Church. The Church may well share in all Jesus is, including in his mission but it does so as his servant, not his continuation. Just as the divine unity incorporates the personal specificity of the Father's will and the Son's obedience, whereby Christ is the sent of the Father, the unity of the body of Christ incorporates difference as the Church is the servant which is sent out by its Lord.

This affects the form of our discussion of the Church. Ecclesiology is not an independent division of theology. Ecclesiology can only ever be a derivative locus that is inseparable from Christology. Materially, when we describe the Church as the body of Christ, we are saying that the Church must be understood primarily in terms of what we can say about Christ. This is important because it means that we should not take any historical manifestation as normative of what the Church actually is. The Church is what it is by union with Jesus Christ and thus takes its essence, life, and mission from the essence, life, and mission of Jesus Christ. The Church has no meaningful existence apart from Christ. This means that we must learn to think of the Church in such a way that is determined from the very outset by Jesus Christ.

This being said, the designation of the body of Christ is not uniquely a Christological reference; it is also a pneumatological one.[32] The Spirit does not become the focus of our encounter with God. Instead, it is through him that we recognize and respond to Christ.[33] However, the Spirit does not only work after the fact of Jesus. The Spirit is active in the saving work of Jesus and in the establishment of the Church. It is by the Spirit that the person of Jesus is actualized in our history and it is in the power of the Spirit that Jesus was anointed and empowered for his saving work and then resurrected from the dead. Just as God the Son was made incarnate by the Spirit, so also the body of Christ, the Church, is brought into being by the Spirit as he unites us to Jesus in baptism. The Spirit is the one through whom God

---

32. For a helpful discussion of the pneumatological character of the designation the body of Christ, see Zizioulas, *Being as Communion*, 110–14.

33. See Smail, *Giving Gift*, 30–55.

the Son becomes embodied and the Spirit is the one through whom we are incorporated into the body of Christ. It is with this in view that we move to consider the sweep of Pauline soteriology as the liberation from the body of sin by being incorporated into the body of the incarnate savior.

Human Embodiedness and the Body of Christ

It is not a surprise that it was Paul who called the Church the body of Christ. It is a designation of the Church that is fitting both for his experience and for his understanding of salvation. As a persecutor of Christians, Saul, as he then was, encountered Christ who said to him, "Saul, Saul, why are you persecuting me? . . . I am Jesus whom you are persecuting" (Acts 26:14; 9:4-5; 22:7). At the heart of this experience was Jesus' self-identification with his Church. It is easy for us to lose the importance of this in the narrative of the conversion of Saul, but the impact on Paul of this personal identity between Jesus and his Church appears to have been of central importance to his thought from that point on.

The construction "in Christ" pervades Paul's thought like oxygen in the air. The great event of the transition from the "present evil age" (Gal 1:4), from the epoch dominated by sin and death to the new humanity free from death and living by the Spirit is through inclusion into Jesus Christ in his death and resurrection. On account of this inclusion, we are no longer one with Adam, but we are one with Christ (Rom 5:11-19). The old divisions that separated people groups have been overcome by merit of a common incorporation into Jesus Christ (Gal 3:28; Eph 2:14-15). The focus of the sacraments for Paul is orientated to our incorporation into Jesus. It is in the Spirit and by baptism that we enter the body of Christ (1 Cor 12:13) and it is in Eucharist that we who are many become one body as we renew our incorporation into Jesus by eating his flesh and drinking his blood (1 Cor 10:17). In other words, the designation the body of Christ carries organic connections to the central motif of Paul's view of salvation.

John Robinson's little book *The Body* is a helpful study arguing that the theme of the body forms an arc that continues all the way through Paul's soteriology.[34] At one level, this is clear from the difference between apostolic Christianity and its gnostic perversion: salvation is not being saved from bodily existence but being transferred into a different type of bodily existence (from being human in Adam to being human in Christ). Perhaps unsurprisingly, the starting point of Paul's body theology comes in his anthropology. Paul has two words for the embodied nature of

---

34. Robinson, *Body: A Study in Pauline Theology.*

human existence, *sarx* (often translated "flesh") and *sōma* (often translated "body"). Robinson's insightful analysis demonstrates that the interplay between these two terms introduces a dynamic into Paul's anthropology which is addressed in his notion of salvation as death to the flesh (*sarx*) and incorporation into Christ as his body (*sōma*).

Of the two, *sarx* communicates a sharper analysis of the human condition. The range of ways Paul uses *sarx* is quite baffling. He can use it to refer simply to the physical stuff that makes up the human body. He can also use it to describe the seat of the malevolent force of sin within our humanity.[35] Are we to think of this term referring simply to the substance of human physical existence or as the beachhead of a force that leaves us in a state of existence that is antithetical to our being made as the covenant partners of God? The answer appears to be that we should think of it as both and everything in between. Underlying the array of ways Paul uses *sarx* in his letters is a common theme of mortality and the associated weakness or frailty. At the physical level, *sarx* is perishable (1 Cor 15:50) and experiences illness (2 Cor 7:5). At the moral level, it is on account of our flesh that no person may justify themselves before God (Rom 3:20). The reason for this is that *sarx* is the seat of sin's power within the human person (Rom 7:5, 18). Therefore, it is in *sarx* that Christ had to defeat the power of sin (Rom 8:3). The use of flesh in Paul's thought then refers to the weakness of human existence and its vulnerability to sickness and corruption. It is precisely this weakness of *sarx* that makes it vulnerable to coming under the force of the power of sin such that the human person becomes overthrown. In this sense, the human bodily existence is not in itself wrong, but it is *frail*.

The vulnerability of the flesh is exploited by the power of sin (Rom 7:17, 20). The way in which *sarx* is influenced by this power is of determinative importance for understanding Paul's account of salvation which provides the framework of meaning within which to appreciate what is going on in designating the Church as the body of Christ. As a power, sin is that which prevents humanity from living in accordance with their creatureliness and so in dependence upon its Creator and turning us inward upon ourselves and the things of creation. It is precisely this power of sin that causes human beings to be those who belong to and are orientated only to the world. To live according to the vulnerable flesh that has been overcome by the power of sin, therefore, constitutes a distortion of the relationship of the creature to God in which the human person who was made to live in the world as the covenant

---

35. For a fuller analysis of the spectrum of ways Paul uses *sarx* see Dunn, *Theology of Paul the Apostle*, 64–66.

partner of God now lives in the world and for the world.[36] It is by sin that the human flesh is utterly consumed by worldly affairs such that the creature is turned in on itself, turned away from loving dependence and faith toward the Creator and towards a self-serving self-sufficiency. This is, of course, the essence of idolatry. By the power of sin, living according to the flesh has become a denial of humanity's dependence on its Creator, which is replaced by a self-reliance in our own moral attainment (Gal 3:3) and knowledge (2 Cor 1:12; Col 2:18). This leads inevitably to "living according to the flesh," the self-glorification of the human creature in setting itself up on the strength of its own creatureliness.[37] Connected with this is the self-destructive spiral into death for it is in its denial of the true reality of the human situation as a creature the human turns away from the source of its life, and, if you turn from life, there is nowhere to go but death. In assuming our flesh (*sarx*), Jesus did not assume our sinful state but he did assume our vulnerability and from within the flesh lived a life of obedience to the Father in the power of the Spirit, carrying us with him from death to life.

Like *sarx*, *sōma* has a broad spectrum of meaning. Certainly, it refers to the physicality of human existence (2 Cor 10:10; 1 Cor 5:3). However, we should not take from this that what Paul meant is exactly what we mean when we say the word "body." We tend to think exclusively of the physical presence, whereas Paul's intellectual heritage contained a more nuanced idea. More importantly, we should not think that Paul meant what the Greek-thinking culture around him meant by body, which is something not essential to the person, but like clothes which the person has around them and will one day put off. Paul uses *sōma* with an eye on the human being as an embodied reality which is in a reciprocal relationship to other entities around it in space.[38] In this sense, *sōma* means a great deal more than simply physical existence; it is the physical existence which enables human beings to be in relationship with the world and with one another.[39] This relationality inherent in the conceptual content of *sōma* undergirds its covenantal undertones in Paul's usage. While *sarx* has come to mean humanity-in-distance from God, *sōma* is used in a sense consistent with the dialogical framing of God and creation. Paul uses *sōma* in such a way that expresses the reality that humanity is made as the covenant partner of God: "the body [*sōma*] is made for the Lord, and the Lord for the body [*sōma*]" (1 Cor 6:13). For Paul, *sōma* contains within its conceptual range that fundamental reality of

36. Robinson, *Body*, 25.
37. Robinson, *Body*, 31.
38. Dunn, *Theology of Paul the Apostle*, 56–57.
39. Dunn, *Theology of Paul the Apostle*, 55–61.

human existence which is that it is made to be the covenant partner of God. Humanity has its life as a being-in-response to God. It is for this reason that our bodily existence is central to our obedience as we "present your bodies as a living sacrifice" (Rom 12:1).

There is quite a lot of overlap between *sōma* and *sarx*. There is a degree to which the human *sōma* is implicated in the same vulnerability of *sarx* to the power of sin and death. *Sōma*, like *sarx*, is weak before the powers that would corrupt it. It is the "body [*sōma*] of sin" that is destroyed as we are included in Jesus' death (Rom 6:6). Driven to desperation by the power of the law of sin that wages war against the law of God, Paul asks "who will rescue me from this body of death?" (Rom 7:24). Even in the new situation of inclusion into Christ the believer is to "put to death the deeds of the body" (Rom 8:13). The overlap between *sōma* and *sarx* is so powerful that their identification is confirmed by the phrase "the body [*sōma*] of flesh [*sarx*]" (Col 2:12). *Sōma* penetrates the same deep and looming blackness as does sarx. However, unlike *sarx*, the conceptual content of *sōma* is not exhausted by the turn from Creator to death. The body is not identical to the flesh. While *sōma* carries the same idea of human frailty, it also diverges from this desperate condition through the redemptive significance of the body (*sōma*) of Christ.

So, while *sarx* has come to mean humanity in our distance from God which implicates *sōma*, *sōma* continues to carry a covenantal undertone that recognizes that humanity is made for God. Even though, in our frailty, our vision has become earthbound, the reality of who we are is those who have been made for God. In this context, *sarx* is the subversion of human existence for God. Seen in this light, the frailty of *sarx* has led to the terrible contradiction of *sōma*. In this, the full awful reality of *sarx* is made clear: it is our *dehumanization*. Humans are not living as we were made to be but have turned away from our identity as the focal point of the covenantal relation between God and creation and becoming bent downwards to creation itself and inwards to our own desires and fears (Rom 1:19–25).

The question with which Paul's anthropology leaves us is how can the embodied human being leave behind the compromised aspect of its embodied existence and experience a new form of bodily existence that is free from the power of sin and death? Paul's answer is that *God the Son assumes our embodied existence so to incorporate us into his embodied existence.* He assumes our flesh to make us his body. God the Son became what we are at the incarnation, and he identified with our body of flesh at his baptism and he carried it to its inevitable conclusion at the cross. However, Jesus Christ lived the life of the body of flesh as an act of unbroken obedience and worship to the Father. In this way, Jesus accomplished in our frail humanity what no one else could: a life of covenantal faithfulness to God. In the case of Jesus Christ, the *sōma* is not compromised by the dehumanizing impact of the vulnerability of *sarx* to the power of sin. This is the redemptive significance of the incarnation: God the Son becomes just as we are and by his obedience breaks the dominance of sin, bears our frail humanity to death, and, in his resurrected and ascended body, opens up for us a new and living way to God.

In other words, the designation of the body of Christ is inseparable from the movement of the gospel as God the Son descends to be one of us so to incorporate us into himself and so include us in his ascent to the right hand of the Father. Jesus penetrates into the very depths of our human existence. He took the form of a slave (Phil 2:7) just as we are enslaved under the power of death (Gal 4:3). He shared our flesh in its frailty to sin (*sarx*), though he did so without sinning (Rom 8:3). Though Jesus himself never strayed from the will of the Father, he was made to be sin for us (2 Cor 5:21). He was born under the law so to redeem us who had fallen under the curse of the law by becoming a curse for us (Gal 3:13). He meets us in the far country of our separation from God and alliance with death and, grasping hold of us, drags us up with him in his new humanity.

The link between the incarnation and crucifixion is important here. God the Son took on our human existence in full at the incarnation. He took on our flesh with its weakness and its fragility to sin. However, he lived in our human flesh a new life of perfect obedience. The full course of his life was a continual resistance of the weakness of the flesh. A continual fight against the impulse to turn away from God and toward self-preservation and the glory of created things (surely this is the nub of the devil's temptation of Christ in the wilderness) and to live instead as the perfect covenant partner of God. In his death, Jesus achieved the perfect "anti-*sarx*" act as he surrendered his life as an act of worship and obedience to the Father. It is this that becomes the basis of the possibility that the Christian believer may "put off the body of flesh" because we share in this great act of Christ in which he lived a full human life to the glory of its Creator and not to ourselves.

Jesus taught that, on the cross, he would draw all people to himself (John 12:32). In his death, he made room for us in himself and drew us to himself. As the spear pierced the side of Christ, a figurative space was made in his body for our participation. For Paul, this gathering into Jesus at the cross is intensified to mean a participation in the death of Jesus. The incarnation and the crucifixion, therefore, act as parallels to one another, or as two parts of the one act of unification. At the incarnation, God the Son united himself to us such that his life was now inseparable from the human experience. At the crucifixion, God the Son united us to himself such that our life is now lived only as his body. In some way, the Christian has really and truly died in and with the crucified body of Jesus (Rom 6:6; 7:4; Gal 2:19) and this participation in the death of Jesus is the means of participating in his resurrected life: "I have been crucified with Christ; and it is no longer I who live, but it is Christ who lives in me" (Gal 3:19–20). The incarnation is not a temporary thing from which God the Son emerges again into a spiritual existence. Instead, at the incarnation, God the Son binds himself to our embodied existence once and for all, so to unite us to his embodied existence once and for all.

T. F. Torrance has argued that when we think of the Church as the body of Christ, we set ourselves up to think of the Church in terms of the incarnation and atonement.[40] At the heart of Torrance's association of atonement and the designation of the body of Christ is the gathering up of humanity into the person of God the Son incarnate who lived a life of human obedience to the Father's will and suffered the death of our unfaithfulness on our behalf and in our place. If the body of Christ designation means that the whole Jesus now includes Christ and his Church, then this can only be grounded on the prior movement in which God established reciprocity between himself and humanity at the incarnation. God the Son assumed humanity and, in so doing, took hold of everything we are and bound it to himself. By the incarnation, then, God the Son establishes a bond, a brotherhood, with us. In his identification with us, he stepped into our unfaithfulness to God and took the end of that into his own body on the cross. This is the act of God as a human, standing in our place offering a filial obedience where we had offered only unfaithfulness. The fraternal connection Jesus established with us at the incarnation and crucifixion is why the Church can be the body of Christ.

> In the human nature which He united to himself, the Son of God redeemed [humans] and transformed [us] into a new creation by overcoming death through his own death and resurrection. By communicating His Spirit to His brothers, called together from all peoples, Christ made them mystically into his own body.[41]

Jesus shared our embodied existence as the true and faithful covenant partner of God and he incorporates us into his person so that we may share in all he is: "he the sinless One incorporated Himself into our flesh if sin that

---

40. For a full analysis of this theme, see Torrance, *Conflict and Agreement*, 238–62.
41. Paul VI, "Dogmatic Constitution on the Church (*Lumen Gentium*)," 20, para. 7.

through substitutionary atonement we who are sinners might be incorporated into Him as His body."[42] For Torrance, Christ's substitution in our place is the foundation of our incorporation into him as we are included in his death and resurrection (Rom 6:4–5). This participation in the risen Christ extends to the ascension as the Church is that whose life is hid with Christ in God (Col 3:3). As Calvin writes, "The Lord, by his ascension to heaven, has opened up the access to the heavenly kingdom, which Adam had shut. For having entered it in our flesh, as it were in our name, if follows, as the apostles say, that we are in a manner now seated in the heavenly places."[43]

All of this, the sweep of Paul's soteriology, is lurking within the subject of Paul's designation of the Church as the body of Christ. Certainly, for Paul, the Church and Jesus Christ cannot be separated because they have been united as one reality in the incarnation, crucifixion, and resurrection. As Michael Ramsey has said to call the Church the body of Christ is "to draw attention to it not primarily as a collection of [people], but primarily as Christ himself in his own being and life."[44] The Church is not merely a society with a common life and set of beliefs. The Church is that which has been incorporated into the person of Jesus Christ, such that its very essence is Jesus Christ. Jesus will not be without his Church for he has united it to himself in his incarnation and death. For Jesus, to be without the Church would be to be without an aspect of himself. The Church, meanwhile, will not be without Jesus for in dying to the flesh, it has no life other than his resurrected life. As the body of Christ, the Church has no essence and no existence apart from its participation in the person of Jesus, died and resurrected. This is the proper context within which to understand the nature and purpose of sacraments.

Sacraments and the Body of Christ

So far, the designation of the Church as the body of Christ has been aligned to the conviction that the center of salvation is inclusion into Jesus Christ in his death and resurrection. The theme of participation in Jesus Christ in the theology of John Calvin was outlined as a helpful presentation of this salvific reality. It is this sense of salvation as co-extensive with incorporation into Jesus Christ that provides the fundamental nexus of meaning for Paul's description of the Church as the body of Christ. This connection between incorporation into Christ and the Church has been explored through Paul's anthropology,

42. Torrance, *Conflict and Agreement*, 1.245.

43. Calvin, *Inst.* 2.16.16.

44. Ramsey, *Gospel and the Catholic Church*, 35.

specifically as it pertains to human embodied existence. It has been suggested that there is a continuity in Paul's thought between the fragility of human embodied existence (*sarx*) and the incarnation. God the Son became flesh (*sarx*) and shared our vulnerability to sin, though he did so without sinning. In so doing, he lived the vicarious life of the perfect covenant partner (*sōma*) as one of us and for all of us. By joining our embodied existence at the incarnation, Jesus Christ drew us to share in his embodied existence on the cross and in his risen life at the resurrection. The Church shares in all that Jesus is in his relation to the Father, and so have a part in Jesus' calling to return to the Father's right hand. The body of Christ is a central designation for the Church because it carries within it the essence of the gospel, which is to be gifted our position as the faithful covenant partner of God via inclusion into the person of Jesus Christ. In other words, salvation is a complete event which becomes a reality into which we enter as we are incorporated as the body of Christ. The sacraments of the Church need to be understood in connection to this participatory account of salvation.

The Church as the people of God has no existence or essence other than its union with Jesus. The means by which believers are joined to Jesus is, therefore, integral to the reality of the Church as the Church. In the preaching of the word of God and its reception by faith, in baptism, and in Eucharist the Church has its life as the body of Christ. Sacraments and the ministry of the word of God are the means by which the word of God comes to us, establishing and strengthening our union with him. The centrality of the sacraments to the Church are a product of the fact that the Church does not have its life within itself, but instead derives it from beyond itself. It is only by continual return to that source beyond ourselves that the Church continues to exist. In other words, preaching and the sacraments are not only the means through which we look back and remember. These are not merely grateful human responses to commemorate and keep in our minds what God has done for us. However, to say that sacraments are more than commemoration to stimulate saving faith is not the same as saying that sacraments are a constitutive part of salvation in and of themselves. Just as there are places in between London and Newcastle, there are places in between a merely ethical and a constitutive understanding of sacraments.

> It would, I think, be an exaggerated objectivity that would lead one to hold that the sacrament achieves its effect without regard to the disposition of the one who receives. On the other hand, it would be seem to be a denial of God's action in the sacrament if we made its efficacy depend on the faith of the subject to whom it is ministered. If Catholics have erred in the direction of an

exaggerated objectivity, Protestants have sometimes been guilty of making our human faith the foundation of the sacrament.[45]

If, though, Christ is at the center of our sacramentality, then the objectivity of divine action and the subjectivity of human faith may coexist. The sacraments are the ways in which Christ is at work in the Church today, reaching out to us and binding us to himself, making effective in the Church the complete work of salvation that he has won for us.[46] This means that the sacraments cannot be thought of in the flats of either an aid to the individual faith of the believer or as containing their efficacy within themselves. Instead, they need to be thought of in relation to the act of God in Jesus Christ.

Jesus: The Primary Sacrament of God

This strong association between sacrament and the act of God means that whatever a sacrament is it cannot be thought of in the abstract. Certainly, at the heart of the problem of understanding sacraments is the relationship between an earthly reality functioning as a sign (*signum*) and a supernatural or heavenly reality that is signified (*res*). The proliferation of religious practices, beliefs, and objects around the world and throughout human history gives a sense of the deep religious urge that humans have. Humans have always used the things in the world around us to, in some way, point toward the reality of the divine and to, in some way, effect its agency in relation to creation.[47] Within Christianity, while we may inherit some derivative formula from our tradition such as *effective sign* or *visible sign of an inward and invisible grace*, all such phrases run the risk of receiving their meaning from the theological system we happen to inhabit. These headlines do nothing to help us think about the relationship between the sign and the thing signified. Those raised within a Protestant hermeneutic will tend to understand them in one way and those within a Roman Catholic hermeneutic will tend to understand them in another way. However, if we try to do the hard thing of stepping outside the internal coherence of our respective theological systems and allow Jesus Christ to determine what we think we mean by sacrament, we may find we stand a better chance of understanding what it means. Jesus Christ is the primary and the ultimate Sacrament of God. The sacraments of the Church and anything else which can be described by the designation "sacramental" are so by merit of participation in Jesus.

45. Macquarrie, *Guide to the Sacraments*, 53.
46. Davison, *Why Sacraments?*, 1.
47. Macquarrie, *Guide to the Sacraments*, 1–11.

This is an understanding of the sacraments that has been clearly articulated by Torrance.

> [Sacraments] are traced back to their ultimate ground in the incarnation and in the vicarious obedience of Jesus Christ in the human nature which he took from us and sanctified in and through his self-offering to the Father. This means that they have to be understood as having to do with the whole historical Jesus Christ from his birth to his resurrection and ascension, for their content, reality and power are constituted not simply by the saving act of God upon us in Christ but by the act of God fulfilled in the humanity of Christ. . . . That is to say, the primary *mysterium* or *sacramentum* is Jesus Christ himself, the incarnate reality of the Son of God who has incorporated himself into our humanity and assimilated the people of God into himself as his own body, so that the sacraments have to be understood as concerned with our *koinonia* or participation in the mystery of Christ and his Church through the *koinonia* or communion of the Holy Spirit.[48]

For Jesus to be the primary sacrament means that the sacraments of the Church derive their essence from him. The reality into which the Church is incorporated by its derivative sacraments is the primary sacrament, Jesus Christ who is the *actualization of communion between God and creation*. He is God the Son with us, acting as one of us and for all of us; acting on our behalf within the worldly realities in which we have our life establishing positive union with God the Father in the power of God the Spirit.

In Paul's thought, this finds expression in the notion of the mystery (*mysterion*) of the will of God which is set forward in Jesus Christ, which is to gather up all things as one in Jesus (Eph 1:9). Something very similar is said in Colossians in which the mystery of God's will is that Christ should be within his people and this union is the hope of glory (Col 1:27). This means that the mystery of God's saving intent is revealed in Jesus. In his very person, Jesus is a sign of reconciliation: the personal unity of God and humanity.[49] However, Jesus is not only a sign of the will of God. In Jesus Christ, revelation and reconciliation come as a piece. Jesus Christ effects the saving will which he signifies, accomplishing the union of God and humanity in his very person. In a very real way, then, Jesus Christ can be thought of as the mystery (*mysterion*) of God (Eph 3:1). He reveals the love of the Father towards his creation and

---

48. Torrance, *Theology in Reconciliation*, 82.
49. See Torrance, *Incarnation*, 161–80.

the will of the Father that it should be restored to him in covenantal fellowship *and* he accomplishes that which he reveals.

Thomas Aquinas articulates something fairly similar when he describes Jesus as "the fundamental sacrament, insofar as his human nature, as the instrument of divinity effects salvation."[50] However, Aquinas's formulation does not give account to the reciprocal response of humanity. A fuller account of Jesus as the primary Sacrament comes from Edward Schillebeeckx's notion of Jesus as the Sacrament of encounter with God. Schillebeeckx develops Aquinas's idea by his recognition of God's act of salvation incorporating our human response. For Schillebeeckx, Jesus Christ is God at work on creation as a human. With Aquinas, Jesus is the sign and the effective cause of God's saving power toward us. Jesus is the revelation of God's love for the world by actually being the bestowal of it.[51] Beyond this, though, "Jesus is not only the offer of divine love to [humanity] made visible, but at the same time, as prototype (or primordial model) he is the supreme realization of the response of human love to this divine offer."[52] Not only does Jesus unveil and accomplish God's saving will, he also represents us in his response of faith and love. Jesus both uncovers God's will toward us and he uncovers our eyes and ears to the will of God.[53] Through the full course of his life he accomplishes an agreement between the Word of God's love to humanity and the word of human obedience, faith, and love to God. Jesus, in Schillebeeckx's own terminology, in his very person is the Sacrament of *encounter*. We might put this in terms we have already used and talk of Jesus as the covenant partner who perfectly fulfills the dialogue between God and creation by himself being the event of that dialogue (e.g., both the Apostle and High Priest). God has both acted within his creation from the side of God and God has acted from the side of humanity to respond to divine grace with obedience and faith.

Whatever else sacraments might be, our understanding of them must be established on the primacy of Jesus as the Sacrament of encounter between God and humanity. The sacraments of the Church do not have any power or purpose isolated from Jesus. As such, the power of the sacraments is that by them we are drawn to participate in the one true Sacrament, which is Jesus Christ in whom God and humanity are drawn into the union of positive encounter.[54] How exactly sacraments effect this

---

50. Aquinas, *Summa Contra Gentiles*, IV a.41.

51. Schillebeeckx, *Christ the Sacrament*, 13–17.

52. Schillebeeckx, *Christ the Sacrament*, 19.

53. Torrance, *Incarnation*, 167.

54. See Davison's lively discussion of sacraments as used by Christ to bind us to

participation is far less important than *what* is taking place. Alongside his own incarnation, crucifixion, and resurrection and the sending of the Spirit, the sacraments of the Church are the means by which Jesus draws us to participate in his reality as the primary and ultimate Sacrament: the one in whom God's will to communion with humanity is both revealed and achieved. This does not mean to downplay the centrality of preaching, the significance of which in relation to our incorporation into Christ is explored in more detail in the next chapter.

The Church as a Sacrament of Jesus Christ

As the body of Christ, the Church has a share in everything that Jesus is. Jesus is the revelation and the accomplishment of God's covenantal love for his creation and creation's response of love and praise to its Creator. The Church has been drawn to participate in Jesus' reality. This participation in Christ is the Church's sacramental character. To describe the Church as a sacrament of Christ is to say that it participates in Jesus as the covenant partner of God.

It may be objected that, in light of what has just been said about Jesus as the ultimate Sacrament, to describe the Church itself as a sacrament is unhelpful or contradictory. Certainly, it would be if what was meant by calling the Church a sacrament were that the Church replaces or adds to the complete encounter of God and humanity in Jesus Christ. This is a concern that stands for all the right reasons. However, what is necessary is not an addition to what Christ has done, but a means of access, a means of encounter with the sacrament of encounter. We don't require an elongation of the incarnation, but a way of being joined to the incarnate Christ. This is precisely what is intended by the idea of the Church as a sacrament of Jesus Christ: the Church is a sign and instrument of God's act.[55] The Church is both the *sign* of having been united to Jesus as the body of Christ, and it is the *effective means* through which Christ draws us in to share in himself as the one ultimate Sacrament of God. As the World Council of Churches' statement *The Nature and Mission of the Church* has it, "those Churches who use the expression 'Church as Sacrament' do so because they understand the Church as an effective sign of what God wishes for the world: namely, the communion of all together and with the Triune God,"[56] a communion which has its reality only in the person of Jesus Christ.

---

him. Davison, *Why Sacraments?*, 4.

55. *Nature and Mission of the Church*, 11, para. 43.

56. *Nature and Mission of the Church*, 12, para. 48.

The former Bishop of Norwich Graham James held a particular distaste for the idea that one of his priests might speak of "my ministry." "It's not your ministry," he would say, "it's the ministry of Jesus Christ into which you are included." Of course, he was quite right. The ministry of the Church is nothing other than the ministry of Jesus Christ, as the activity of the body of which Jesus is the head. This means that when we are talking about the sacramental character of the Church, any hackles raised by a suspicion of an arid institutionalism or of ecclesial replacement of Jesus should come down. To discuss the Church in terms of sacramentality, as Rowan Williams has said, must have Christology at its heart.[57] Such Christocentrism is the only basis upon which it is possible to integrate sacramentality into a doctrine of the Church. The Church is an event of being encountered by Christ in word and sacrament through which it is joined to the true Sacrament, which is the encounter of God and humanity in Jesus Christ. The mystery of God's will set forward and accomplished in Jesus Christ is not continued in or replaced by the Church. The Church is sacramental inasmuch as it is a sign which testifies to union with Christ and accomplishes the union of which it is a sign. Jesus Christ is the true essence of the union of God and humanity and the Church is the worldly reality which gives witness to that great act of salvation and facilitates our participation in it.

So, if we can think about the Church as a sacrament which derives its sacramental character by its connection to Jesus Christ, then we can begin to see that the Church is a sacrament inasmuch as it is a sign of unity with Jesus who draws us into union with the Father in the power of the Holy Spirit *and* it is an effective means through which Jesus unites humanity to himself. Jesus makes the Church "His sign and instrument which he uses to carry out his work of renewing and reshaping humanity, to the glory of His Father."[58] As such, the Church is "a kind of sacrament or sign of intimate union with God" and an "instrument for the achievement of such union."[59] At one and the same time, the Church is the visible sign of unity with Jesus and it is also the effective means through which Jesus causes that unity to be established and strengthened. We find ourselves here circling back around to where we were before in thinking about the Church as a creature of the word of God. The same basic logic is at work when we think about the Church as a sacrament.[60] These two designations are two sides of the same

57. Williams, "Church as Sacrament," 117.

58. Vorgrimler, *Sacramental Theology*, 34.

59. Paul VI, "Dogmatic Constitution on the Church (*Lumen Gentium*)," 15.

60. The correlation between the Reformed notion of the Church as creation of the word of God and the Catholic notion of the Church as a sacrament of God has been highlighted in the World Council of Church's 1990 report, *Towards a Common*

coin, one expressed in the Protestant dialect and the other in the Catholic dialect: the Church is brought into being by the direct act of God to have its own discrete identity and existence which remains wholly dependent on God's action in bringing it to being. Certainly, the Church is brought into being upon hearing the word of God read and proclaimed. However, the sacraments of the Church are also a form of God's word establishing and renewing the Church in union with Christ.

The sacramentality of the Church is derived from the reality of Jesus' life as the saving power of God at work on creation and the corresponding human obedience and faith. The Church is an effective sign of the union of God and humanity in Jesus Christ inasmuch as it does itself participate in that union through unity with Jesus. The sacraments of the Church, therefore, have no other foundation or content aside from the incarnate life, death, resurrection, and ascension of Jesus Christ. In such a context, we need to think about the sacraments of baptism and Eucharist in what T. F. Torrance described as their "dimension of depth."[61] By this phrase he meant that the phenomena of the Church's sacraments should not be isolated from their underlying structures of meaning (he used the same phrase against the philosophical modality of logical positivism which separated phenomena as it disturbed sensibility from its underlying ontic structures). This means that we don't think of sacraments in the flat as ritual events which objectively contains its meaning and potency in the Church's performance of it. Nor do we think of the sacraments in the reverse subjective flats where it has meaning and efficacy only in the personal holiness of the cleric officiating or the faith of the recipient. Instead, the content and power of the sacraments is sourced within the actual person of Jesus Christ who is God among us in our reality in power to save and also a human being who responds to the work of God with obedience and faith. In such a perspective, we will not think of the Church being the mediator of salvation. Nor will we think of our faith as a work we must hold in addition to the work of Christ and that being the thing that saves us. Instead, we will think of the sacraments as the means through which Jesus Christ acts upon his people to draw them into an ever-maturing participation in his body.

As Schillebeeckx rightly observes, "through the sacraments we are placed in living contact with the mystery of Christ the high priest's saving worship."[62] Sacraments are the means through which we enter into the dialogue of God and humanity in Jesus Christ. The purpose and goal of the sacrament is to

---

Understanding of the Church.

61. Torrance, *Theology in Reconciliation*, 83.

62. Schillebeeckx, *Christ the Sacrament*, 54.

bring about unity with Jesus Christ, and in that unity, a union with God. In this way a sacrament may be seen as a "reaching out in faith and love to take hold of Christ's redemption."[63] All importantly, though, the Church is not the primary agent in bringing that union about. The Church and its sacraments are the effective sign that Jesus uses in order to unite his people to himself such that they may share his relation to the Father in the power of the Spirit. The human agency of the Church is subsumed within the person and work of Jesus Christ. In baptism, therefore, Jesus is actively including the believer into his own life of death to the self and life to the Father through the obedience of the Church in baptizing believers. In the Eucharist, Jesus himself includes us into the act of the self-giving of God to humanity and the self-giving of humanity to God which is the substance of the crucifixion through the Church's act of celebrating the Eucharist.

The sacraments of the Church, in other words, are not merely witnesses to the act of God, they are the means through which Jesus draws us to share in his embodied existence and so his vicarious obedience lived on our behalf whereby the primary sacrament of his encounter with God is the joyful reconciliation of God and his human covenant partner. To bring us round full circle to where we began, this is the basic thrust of John Calvin's teaching on sacraments and preaching. These are the means of grace by which the Holy Spirit unites us to Jesus through the "communication of Christ."[64] The sacraments have no power aside from Jesus for only he is the "substance of all the sacraments; for in him they have all their firmness and they do not promise anything apart from him."[65]

Baptism and the Eucharist in their Dimension of Depth: Thomas Torrance

These fairly lengthy comments about what sacraments are, how they relate to Jesus and whether the Church can truly be described as *sacramental* provide us with a platform upon which to consider baptism and the Eucharist. There is a closely packed set of relationships at work here, which needs further clarification. On the horizontal dimension, the sacraments of baptism and the Eucharist refer to one another. They are two aspects of the one reality of reconciliation through unity with Jesus. By baptism we are incorporated into Christ, and this incorporation is renewed and maintained through the Eucharist. Adopting again the language of the body,

63. Schillebeeckx, *Christ the Sacrament*, 165.

64. Calvin, *Inst.* 4.4.17. See also Billings, *Calvin, Participation and the Gift*, ch. 4.

65. Calvin, *Inst.* 4.14.16.

we are incorporated into the body of Christ at baptism, in which we are sustained at the Eucharist. However, we are not solely concerned with the internal logic of sacraments any more than we are concerned uniquely with the syntactic relationship between statements. We must not think of sacraments as formal logicians think of symbolic notation. This means that we must establish what we think is going on at the horizontal dimension with a different vector. On the vertical dimension, the Eucharist and baptism share a common reference beyond themselves to the foundation and essence of what they are effective signs of, which is the incarnate life, death, and resurrection of Jesus. As such, baptism and the Eucharist are both instruments through which Jesus is at work to bind people to himself through which we participate in him.[66] Such an understanding of the sacraments can be expanded upon in conversation with both a Reformed and a Roman Catholic perspective. Thomas Torrance held that baptism and the Eucharist were the means through which Jesus included us in his own vicarious life of self-offering to the Father. Upon this view, the sacraments are shared between Christ and his Church, with Christ being the primary agent and the Church being drawn in to share in Christ through them. In the perspective of Henri de Lubac, sacraments (specifically the Eucharist, although we can broaden this to include baptism) are the means through which the Church is constituted as the body of Christ. These perspectives are complementary, orientated in the direction of the Church as participating in Christ.

If baptism and the Eucharist are understood in their relation beyond the ritual act or the faith of the individual, then they will be more properly established in relation to the act of God in Jesus Christ. They are not human ethical responses to the love of God separate from the act of God itself and nor are they supplementary to the work of Christ. Salvation is in Christ alone, but Christ works through the Church and its sacraments such that baptism and the Eucharist become modes of our participation.[67] Specifically, sacraments are the forms of the one saving act of God which unites us to what he has already done as a human on our behalf. The sacraments of the Church are derivative from the primary Sacrament, which is Jesus Christ. They unite us to the positive encounter between God and humanity in the person of Jesus Christ in whom the faithfulness and love of God is met by the faithfulness and love of humanity.

66. Calvin, *Inst.* 4.15.6.

67. George Hunsinger has demonstrated that this is the contribution of T. F. Torrance's sacramentology which charts a middle course between the ambiguity of Calvin's participatory sacramentology and Karl Barth for whom the sacraments are as human ethical responses to what God has done. Hunsinger, "Dimension of Depth," 155–76.

Once again, we find the designation of the body of the Church to be in the foreground here: in baptism, we are baptized into the body of Christ and at the Eucharist we take his body into ourselves and (in a wonderful reversal of normal digestion) instead of incorporating what we eat into ourselves, we become incorporated into what we eat. This brings us back around to where we came in at the third chapter: the Church must be thought of in the dimension of its inclusion into the very life and love of God. In the Son, God has established a binding relationship with us. Through the Spirit, we are enabled to respond and receive what has been done through the Son in the sacraments of the Church. By this participation in the Son by the power of the Spirit, the Church participates as body of Christ in the relation of the incarnate Son with God the Father and so we are adopted as the children of God.[68]

Baptism is the effective sign through which Jesus causes us to participate once and for all in him and so in the community of those who are the body of Christ. For Torrance, this constitutes a real participation in the life and work of Jesus Christ.[69] Torrance argues that there is one baptism that is held in common between Christ and his Church and through the sacrament of baptism, the believer is united with Jesus' own baptism. This is what Torrance calls thinking of baptism in its dimension of depth. The "content, reality and power" of the sacraments is the "act of God fulfilled in the humanity of Christ."[70] The point of intersection is the humanity of Christ, because underlying our union with Jesus in his baptism, is his vicarious sharing our human existence (we share in his body because he has shared our embodied existence). Jesus lived in our place and on our behalf. In him our human nature has already been cleansed from sin and offered to the Father in a sacrifice of praise. Through sharing in him through baptism, our salvation is "more by way of realization or actualization in us of what has already happened to us in him than as a new effect" resulting from what he has already done.[71] Baptism needs to be thought of in its dimension of depth because it is joining us to a reality that is complete quite aside from it making us "partake of a redemption that has already been accomplished for us in Christ."[72] For Torrance, then, baptism points beyond itself and is the means used by Christ to effectively join believers to the reality to which it points: "the one saving act of God in Jesus Christ. . . . When the Church baptizes in his name, it is actually Christ himself who is savingly at work,

---

68. Calvin, *Inst.* 4.15.1.

69. Torrance, *Theology in Reconciliation*, 82–105.

70. Torrance, *Theology in Reconciliation*, 82.

71. Torrance, *Theology in Reconciliation*, 89.

72. Torrance, *Theology in Reconciliation*, 89.

pouring out his Spirit upon us and drawing us into the power of his vicarious life, death and resurrection."[73]

Clearly, Torrance's account of baptism places heavy emphasis on the doctrine of Christ's vicarious humanity (that Christ was a human as one of us and for all of us and that we share in the benefits of that via our participation in him). For example, arguing that the full course of his saving life, death, resurrection, and ascension is present in Jesus' baptism, Torrance holds that this participation in Christ's baptism constitutes participation in the entire vicarious life of Jesus Christ.[74] The great strength of this is that it is impossible to separate baptism from the gospel itself. In obedience to the will of the Father, God the Son numbered himself among the sinners as he had already done at the incarnation and would do again on the cross. Jesus was announced by the Father in terms that equated him to the suffering servant of Isaiah and he was anointed by the Spirit to be the one who would undertake this role and open up the way to the Father's presence. Jesus is affirmed as the Son of the Father as he would be again at the resurrection and the ascension. It would appear that the baptism of Jesus is a moment in time which contains in embryonic form the entire event of salvation. When we share in Jesus' baptism, we are being joined to the full course of Jesus' obedient self-offering to the Father and also to his acceptance by and ascension to the Father: "hence the reality of our baptism is to be found in the objective reality of what has already been accomplished for us in Jesus Christ and is savingly operative in us through union and communion with Christ effected by the Spirit."[75] If we restore the terminology used in the first chapter, Jesus Christ is the true and perfect covenant partner of God, accomplishing in our humanity our response to the Father. He shared our embodied existence so that we might share in his as the perfect covenant partner of God. At his baptism, God the Son associated with us in our lostness from the Father so to include us in his own faithfulness. When we are baptized, we become the body of Christ and share in this act of human faithfulness and obedience to the Father.

This means that ecclesial baptism "is not a separate or a new baptism but a participation in the one all-inclusive baptism common to Christ and his Church."[76] For Torrance, there is just one baptism and it is held in common between Jesus and his Church. However, the Church and Jesus engage in this baptism in different ways. For Jesus, baptism was being identified with

---

73. Torrance, *Theology in Reconciliation*, 83.

74. Torrance, *Theology in Reconciliation*, 83–85.

75. Torrance, *Theology in Reconciliation*, 94.

76. Torrance, *Theology in Reconciliation*, 88.

the sinners and set apart by the Father as the one who would bear our un-righteousness in obedience to the will of the Father. However, all the time believing that this would include the Father's affirmation and vindication. For us, baptism is becoming one with Jesus and sharing in all he has done on our behalf.[77] The salvation of humanity has already taken place. In baptism, we are united with Jesus as his body; we share in the salvation that has been worked out in his human life: "this is why baptism is understood properly only in that dimension of depth reaching back into Jesus Christ himself, for it belongs to the peculiar nature of baptism that in it we partake of a redemption that has already been accomplished for us in Christ."[78] Baptism, therefore, is the effective sign of our inclusion into Christ in his death and resurrection such that we may participate in him as his body and share his status as the perfect covenant partner of the Father. In this sense, baptism should not be thought of in terms of something the Church does, but rather as something that Christ has done for us and continues to unite us to through his Spirit, who incorporates us into Christ's body through baptism.

Torrance's doctrine of baptism has a trinitarian structure.[79] The char-acter of the saving acts of God is from the Father through the Son and in the power of the Spirit. The Church's action in baptizing someone is not an act of obedience that is separate from God's act; it is included in the work of the triune God acting to save. The human life of the Son is the essence of baptism and this is shared in by the Church. By the Spirit we are enabled to participate in Christ *through* baptism. Moreover, as was discussed in the third chapter, it is by our participation in Christ that the Church participates in the com-munion of the Father and the Son in the power of the Spirit. God, Torrance writes, has "opened his divine being for human participation."[80]

The sacrament of Eucharist shares a very similar logic to that of bap-tism. Once again, Torrance insists that it be understood in its dimension of depth. Just as the sacrament of baptism is grounded in the vicarious baptism of Jesus Christ (which carries with it the entire course of his incarnate life, death, and resurrection), so also the sacrament of the Eucharist is grounded in Jesus' own obedient self-giving to the Father. As such, the Eucharist has its own dimension of depth in that it is established upon the Last Supper and through it to the full course of Jesus' life, lived to the glory of the Father which culminates in the great act of self-giving obedience on the cross: "The

77. Torrance, *Theology in Reconciliation*, 87.

78. Torrance, *Theology in Reconciliation*, 89.

79. Torrance, *Theology in Reconciliation*, 99–105. See also the excellent discussion in Hunsinger, "Dimension of Depth," 165.

80. Torrance, *Theology in Reconciliation*, 101.

key to the understanding of the Eucharist is to be sought in the vicarious humanity of Jesus."[81] Just as with baptism, there is one Eucharist (one thanks offering to the Father) which is the self-giving of Jesus in obedience to the Father's will on the cross. The sacrament of the Eucharist has been given to us through which we may participate in that thanks offering. Therefore, as with baptism, there is one Eucharist that is held in common between Jesus and his followers, albeit shared in different ways. Jesus is the one who is active, offering his life in obedience, thanksgiving, and praise to the Father. This is the essence of the Eucharist. The Church shares in this self-offering passively as we call to mind his self-offering in the eucharistic prayer and unite ourselves to him through bread and wine. The Eucharist is what Jesus has done in the full course of his life in his vicarious life of prayer, obedience, thanksgiving, and self-giving to the Father. The sacrament of the Eucharist is the means by which Jesus has given us to be included in what he has done vicariously for us in pouring out his life in obedience to the Father. Jesus Christ is the content of eucharistic worship.

This, of course, raises the question of the eucharistic sacrifice. The whole idea of the Eucharist involving some form of sacrifice has received serious objections.[82] There is the concern that this notion undermines the complete sufficiency of Jesus' sacrifice of himself by implying that we need to in some way repeat that sacrifice to ensure our forgiveness. There is another concern which is that if the purpose of the eucharistic sacrifice is to enable believers to existentially appropriate that sacrifice for ourselves by mirroring it in our liturgy, then does that say that the agent of the sacrament of the Eucharist is really the Church, not Jesus Christ actively uniting us to his own self-giving at Calvary? If so, does this not make the Church and its priests some stratum of mediation aside from Jesus, which is quite irreconcilable with the essence of the gospel? There is a lot in the complaints made against the idea of the eucharistic sacrifice that constitutes a useful caution in our use of the term. If what is meant by the phrase is that the saving work of Jesus needs to be repeated or completed, or that the Church serves as a mediator of the benefits of that work, then it should be resisted. However, following the footsteps of Rowan Williams in his excellent booklet *Eucharistic Sacrifice*, it is my view that an account of the Eucharist which takes seriously the imperative to ground the sacrament of the Eucharist on the vicarious life and obedience of Jesus Christ allows us to use this term as an important aspect of our sharing in the self-offering of Jesus.

81. Torrance, *Theology in Reconciliation*, 110.
82. For a survey of these, see Williams, *Eucharistic Sacrifice*, 9.

Once again, the sacramentology of Thomas Torrance is a useful guide. Torrance insists that the ritual of the Eucharist must not be detached from the actual self-offering in thanksgiving to the Father, which is the life of the incarnate Christ.

> The mystery of the Eucharist is not to be understood in terms of external causal relations between Christ and the Eucharist or between the Eucharist and ourselves, but in terms of our participation through the Spirit in what the whole Christ, the incarnate, crucified, risen and ascended Son is, in himself in respect both of his activity from the Father towards [humankind] and of his activity from [humankind] towards the Father. . . . In so far as the Eucharist is the act of the Church in his name and is also a human rite, it must be understood as an act of prayer, thanksgiving and worship, i.e. as essentially *eucharistic* in nature, but as act in which through the Spirit, we are given to share in the vicarious life, prayer, worship, thanksgiving and self-offering of Jesus Christ to the Father, for in the final resort it is Jesus Christ himself who is our true worship.[83]

Jesus has already given himself as a perfect self-offering to the Father. This is an established event which does not need to be repeated. As a human, God the Son incarnate has already offered to the Father a human life of faithfulness and love to answer his own faithfulness and love of creation. At the sacrament of the Eucharist, we do not repeat or add to what has already taken place. Instead, at the Eucharist, Jesus unites us to his own vicarious self-offering to the Father: "Thus the eucharistic sacrifice means that we *through the Spirit* are so intimately united with Christ, by communion with his body and blood, that we participate in his self-consecration and self-offering to the Father."[84] There is no content to the eucharistic sacrifice aside from the self-offering of Jesus Christ. What has changed, is that we have been included in Jesus' sacrifice of praise.

I once heard a tutor of a theological college say that the direction of travel at the Eucharist is all from God to us. Certainly, this is correct inasmuch as the Eucharist is not an independent act done by us in response to what Christ has already done. Even so, this is hard to accept, especially as eucharistic liturgy of the Church has always included the lifting up of our hearts to the Lord! Moreover, in the Eucharist we are bringing our sacrifice of praise, our self-offering to the Father (Rom 12:1). What my tutor's perspective totally misses is that the sacrament of the Eucharist is the means

---

83. Torrance, *Theology in Reconciliation*, 109.
84. Torrance, *Theology in Reconciliation*, 134.

through which we take part in the life of human obedience and thanksgiving that Jesus lifts up the Father in his sacrifice of himself. A lot depends on the strength of the connection we keep between the ritual act of the sacrament of Eucharist and its objective reality in Jesus' eucharistic self-offering as the mediator between God and humanity. We offer our sacrifice of praise to the Father by being joined to Jesus' sacrifice of praise to the Father. So, while we do lift up our hearts and our very selves in worship of the Father, we only do so by being joined to Jesus' self-offering.

Eucharistic Ecclesiology: Henri de Lubac

If by the sacraments of baptism and Eucharist, we are united to Jesus and participate in all he is and has done before the Father, then the Church itself is brought into being by the sacraments it celebrates. Such an understanding of the sacraments is positively related to a participatory view of salvation in which God the Son takes our body so that he might vicariously live the life of the perfect covenant partner to the Father and assume us into incorporation with his body through baptism and renewing that unity at the Eucharist. Baptismal ecclesiology and eucharistic ecclesiology express the idea that the Church is brought into being as the body of Christ through the sacraments by which it is united to Jesus. The heart of this approach to ecclesiology is an inversion of the chain of causation between Church and sacrament. Instead of thinking that the Church is the institution which causes the sacraments to be celebrated, the Church is brought into being by the sacraments which are effective signs of its unity with Jesus Christ. Henri de Lubac is more properly associated with eucharistic ecclesiology, but for the purposes of completion, this discussion will include a few comments on baptismal ecclesiology, also.

Baptismal ecclesiology has been received with particular enthusiasm in certain parts of the Anglican Communion. The Episcopal Church of the United States of America (USA), for example, has reenvisioned its own ordination rites from the perspective of a view of the Church as a "community formed by baptism and empowered by baptism."[85] Subsequently, both the Sixth International Anglican Liturgical Consultation on Ordination[86] and the 2005 *Common Worship* Ordinal service reflect the prominence of the notion that baptism into the body of Christ is the source of the Church. However, as Paul Avis has helpfully demonstrated, Anglican formularies will not allow the absolutizing of baptism, viewing incorporation into

85. Meyers, *Continuing the Reformation*, xvi.
86. Gibson, *Anglican Ordination Rites*.

Christ as a process that includes baptism, confirmation, and participation in the Eucharist.[87] In this sense, Ruth Meyers has described baptism as the foundation of the Church in relation to the Eucharist.

> A baptismal ecclesiology understands the Church to be rooted in baptism and nourished by the Eucharist. Baptism forms the body of Christ, a community which is distinct from the surrounding culture and yet is called to participate in Christ's reconciling ministry to the world.[88]

Baptismal ecclesiology has the person of Jesus Christ as its objective center as inclusion into the death and resurrection of Christ through the sacrament of baptism is understood to be that which constitutes the Church. Baptismal ecclesiology thus provides a perspective on the relationship between the sacraments and the Church which undergirds the centrality of the connection between participation and the designation of the body of Christ.

While baptismal ecclesiology has earned the attention of liturgists, it is arguably eucharistic ecclesiology that has more captured the attention of constructive theology. The very point at which the unity of the head and the body is proclaimed and strengthened has proved to be a fertile starting point for thought about the Church. Even so, it should be noted that any attention given to a view that through sharing in the Eucharist, we renew our incorporation into his body, is established upon the prior event of our inclusion into Jesus at baptism. The strong connection between the Eucharist and the Church has been a very popular theme in modern thought on the Church, particularly among Orthodox and Roman Catholic theologians.[89]

Of particular importance in this connection is the Roman Catholic Henri de Lubac. Through the course of his reaction to some of the static categories of a scholastic theological method, de Lubac stressed the dynamic continuity between the Church as the ecclesial body of Christ and the sacramental body of Christ in the Eucharist. The Church, he says, takes the sacramental body of Christ into itself and, in so doing, actually becomes the ecclesial body of Christ. This involves us thinking of digestion in an inverse fashion. When we receive the Eucharist, we are taking Christ into ourselves through the effective signs of the bread and the wine.

---

87. Avis, "Baptism and the Journey of Christian Initiation," 50–63; Avis, "Is Baptism 'Complete Sacramental Initiation'?," 163–69.

88. Meyers, *Continuing the Reformation*, 226.

89. For example, from the Orthodox, Afanasiev, "Una Sancta," 3–30; Zizioulas, *Being as Communion*, 27–65; and from the Roman Catholic Lubac, *Corpus Mysticum*; Ratzinger, *God Is Near Us*. A variant of this view has also been expressed from an Anglican perspective: Williams, "Sacraments of the New Society."

However, instead of the believer incorporating the bread and the wine into their own body, the effective signs of the body of Christ *incorporate us into the body of Christ*. In this connection, de Lubac was influenced by a particular interpretation of Augustine.

> When with St Augustine, [previous Christians] heard Christ say to them: 'I am your food, but instead of my being changed into you, it is you who shall be transformed into me', they unhesitatingly understood that by their reception of the Eucharist they would be incorporated the more in the Church.[90]

De Lubac understood Augustine to have meant that in incorporating Christ into himself or herself at the Eucharist, the believer would not transform the sacramental body of Jesus into their own body, but would rather be incorporated into the body of Christ, that is the Church.[91] The sacraments are the means of grace through which believers are united in Christ as the ecclesial body of Christ. De Lubac's proposal functions through a layering of overlapping motifs upon one another, operative through the body of Christ in three forms. The sign (the bread) of the Eucharist participates in the reality of the thing signified (the incarnate body of Christ) and becomes the body of Christ in sacramental form.[92] In receiving the sacramental body of Christ, the followers are incorporated into the ecclesial body of Christ (the Church), corresponding to the Augustinian notion that the receiver is incorporated into that which has been received. In other words, it is in the celebration of the Eucharist that the community of the ecclesial body of Christ is formed, and the presence of Christ is "real" in the Eucharist in that in participating in the mystical body, the ecclesial body is formed.[93] The Eucharist, in other words, has a pronounced ecclesial significance in being the means of our incorporation into the body of Jesus Christ.

The great benefit of de Lubac's eucharistic ecclesiology is that it acts as a prophylactic against seeing the Church as a divinely established institution which distributes the sacramental grace it has received alongside maintaining the importance of the sacraments as the means through which Jesus unites us to his completed work. In this, Torrance and de Lubac offer compatible accounts of how the sacraments may be understood within a participatory ecclesiology, with the former laying emphasis on the vicarious humanity of Christ as the ground and essence of the sacraments and the latter laying

90. Lubac, *Catholicism*, 99–100. De Lubac cites Augustine, *Conf.* 7, 10, 16.
91. Maloney, "Henri de Lubac on the Church and Eucharist," 333.
92. Lubac, *Corpus Mysticum*, 249–50. See also, McPartlan, "Body of Christ," 159.
93. Maloney, "Henri de Lubac on the Church and Eucharist," 339.

emphasis on the sacraments as effective means of grace through which we become the body of Christ by sharing in the body of Christ.

For both, then, the Church is a community of believers established through our common participation in Jesus Christ. The sacraments, in other words, are situated primarily in the anhypostatic aspect of the Church in its dependence on the act of God in Christ by the Spirit. In other words, the sacraments are parsed within a broader grammatical structure shaped by a realist understanding of the Church as the body of Christ. The invisible Church is the font of the visible Church, being thus united with Christ we are all united with one another in the earthly and historical institution of the Church. It is to that which we turn in the final chapter.

5

The Body of Christ in Historical Extension

IN THE LAST CHAPTER, the Church was examined in the aspect of its being brought into existence by the act of God (i.e., in its *anhypostatic* aspect). The Church is an event of God's act breaking into history and calling into being that which could exist in no other way. The designation of the body of Christ is of foundational importance to such an understanding of the Church, because of the stress it lays upon a participatory soteriology, the variegated unity of Christ and his Church and the dependence on the sacraments as the means of our incorporation and renewal in Jesus Christ. In this chapter, the discussion turns to consider the Church in its discrete earthly-historical existence within its dependence on incorporation into Jesus (i.e., in its *enhypostatic* aspect). This is the visibility of the Church with its ministerial orders, structures of governance, its liturgical framework, etc.

However, even in a discussion determined by these parameters, attention will not fall on the internal patterns of logical connection between the various traditions of the Church considered in and of themselves. These traditions and ways of organizing a common life together only have their distinct earthly-historical existence within that dependence on being assumed into union with Jesus as his body and need to be thought in constant correspondence to that reality. The Church as creature is the creature of the word of God. Therefore, we are focused on the various traditions of the Church inasmuch as they arise out from the gospel of Jesus Christ.

The dynamic at work has been well expressed by Karl Barth. Barth locates one of his earliest discussions of the Church within a broader discussion concerning the outpouring of the Spirit and the subjective reality of revelation. Corresponding to the objective reality of revelation constituted by the particularity of the incarnate Son, the act of the Spirit gives to the human person the freedom to receive God's self-revelation and to be the children of God. Axiomatic to Barth's trinitarian conception of revelation is the rejection of any idea that the Church forms itself.

> [the Church] is not created, formed and introduced by individual [humans] on their own initiative, authority and insight. It is not the outcome of a free undertaking to analyse and come to terms with the self-revealing God by gathering together a community which confesses Him, by setting up a doctrine which expounds and proclaims His truth in the way that seems most appropriate. . . . A Church of that kind has nothing to do with the subjective reality of revelation.[1]

For Barth, the Church has no other origin than the Word of God incarnate and the enlightening of humans to receive it. This means that the existence of the Church cannot be thought of on any other basis than in "strict relation to the revelation of God to us . . . in complete subordination to it."[2] The Church is the community that is drawn by the Spirit in correspondence to the objective revelation of God. The life of the Church, therefore, is both dependent on the incarnate Word of God (in that it is called into being by the act of God) and it is a common life, a visible community.[3]

> The Church, even though it is a human gathering and institution, cannot therefore be regarded as a human production. Although it is in the world, it cannot be thought of as owing its existence to the world. Although we are in the Church, are indeed ourselves the Church, the Church cannot be thought of otherwise as the reality of God's revelation for us, i.e., it is in strict relation to the revelation of God to us, it is in complete subordination to it, yet in that relation and subordination it is equally revelation, it is equally God's own act. If we tried to say anything else, we should have grievously misunderstood the biblical image which so far has served as our main statements, that the Church is the body of Christ.[4]

As will be developed below, there is reason to depart from Barth on the way he parses the dependence of the human community of the Church in terms of obedience to revelation, rather than in terms of participation in Christ. However, in terms of setting the general argument, Barth's approach is instructive. Even though the Church needs to be thought of as a human

---

1. Barth, *Church Dogmatics*, 1.2, 213.
2. Barth, *Church Dogmatics*, 1.2, 221.
3. Barth, *Church Dogmatics*, 1.2, 217.
4. Barth, *Church Dogmatics*, 1.2, 221.

institution with its own historical particularity, if we are to have a rounded view of it, it cannot be thought of in exclusively these terms. It is a creature of the word of God, the body of Christ. For this reason, the humanity of the Church needs to be thought about in necessary relation to the act of God. In other words, if the Church has a distinct human and institutional mode of existence, it does so directly from the gospel itself.

Considered in its *anhypostatic* aspect, every aspect of the life and tradition and thought of the Church is subjected to Christ and is shaped according to who he is, because the Church has no life aside from him. If we accept this point, then the locus of ecclesiology can never stand as an independent field of study any more than soteriology can. Just as soteriology is without content aside from Jesus and the Spirit, so ecclesiology is barren aside from Jesus and the Spirit. Materially, any discussion regarding the practices, the traditions, and the rituals of the Church which is not firmly established on the gospel is speaking empty words into the air. Worse than that, it is to establish the practices of the Church as an independent human response, quite isolated from the vicarious humanity of Jesus.

However, this does not mean that the practices, traditions, and rituals of the Church are meaningless. Instead, we ought to think of these things like language. Language can operate very happily by horizontal reference. Our terms syntactically relate to one another and we can develop sophisticated webs of reference and inference. We could spend our lives studying the logical relations between statements (and some people do). We could even abstract all external meaning derived from the real world by creating a symbolic notation which does not import any content from reality and spend our lives distilling ever more exactly the precise logical relationship between modules of speech (and some people do). So also, in the Church, we could spend our lives studying the internal and horizontal relationships between stuff that the Church does. We could also fall into the trap of abstracting all meaning derived from outside this cultic activity in the gospel of Jesus Christ and distilling ever more precisely the logic of the ecclesial act. We could achieve great conceptual cathedrals of self-reference, towers established on foundations internal only to the human mind.

Just as all syntactical possibilities must be surrendered to being shaped by the state of affairs in reality itself,[5] so also the Church in all its ritual possibilities must be entirely shaped by the gospel. This prioritization of the vertical, semantic reference to reality itself does not mean we abandon the horizontal and the syntactic. The latter remains essential. Just as in the development of knowledge, we experience the world and we are capable of

5. For more on this, see Torrance, *Theological Science*, 203–80.

making iterative statements about it. These statements will be composed of a fundamental pattern arising from the coherence in the world around us. The purpose of the horizontal and the syntactic is to establish and make explicit the implicit relations in what we can say by experience. As we do so, the inner logic of the thing in itself begins to be discernible to us. So also, the ritual acts of the Church. Everything we do in Church arises from the gospel itself. The task of studying the Church is to establish the relationship between these different ritual modes and, in so doing, expose and bring to expression the deep internal coherence of the gospel itself.

Once again, the approach taken here is to treat the relation between God and creation demonstrated in Jesus Christ as the normative account of how God and creation are in relationship, distilling out principles that can be applied in other theological loci, in this instance, the Church. This is not to say that the Church is an extension of the incarnation or in any way impinges on the historical particularity of Jesus. Instead, it is to establish Christ as the normative standard of all theology. So, just as the human nature of Jesus Christ was given existence through its being assumed into union with God the Son and has an uncompromised earthly-historical existence within the person of the Son, so also the Church exists by union with Jesus Christ and has an uncompromised earthly-historical existence within the person of the Son. Both the human nature of Jesus and the humanity of the Church are dependent upon the divine act of grace which gives them existence in the first place. The act of God has brought the Church into existence as a distinct human reality among other human realities by its incorporation into Jesus Christ. To put this another way, the body of Christ as a miracle of the grace of God has a proper and an earthly-historical extension and institutional expression *precisely because of that miracle.*[6]

To focus attention on the embodied, concrete, and historical human existence of the Church, does not mean to turn away from the theological setting of the Church. This is important because even though we are looking at the way the Church appears in the contingencies of history, we are not doing so with the eyes of a sociologist or anthropologist. We are still looking with the eyes of those who know God through Jesus Christ in the power of the Spirit. We are just looking at the visible extension of the Church in such a way that recognizes that the Church is always more than it appears to be. We don't see the Church in the shallows of appearance but in the depth of its

---

6. In other words, this chapter looks to build on the question raised by the World Council of Churches Faith and Order Paper 19, *The Nature and Mission of the Church*, 5, regarding the institutional implications for the Church being the creature of the word of God. The solution offered here is to delineate our thinking about the Church along the logic of the union of the divine and human natures of Jesus Christ.

Christological and pneumatological identity. The visible Church with its traditions, procedures, and rituals is the necessary manifestation of the invisible union with Christ by the Spirit that persists across time and space.

The Church has a human extension in an earthly-historical form which is worthy of study. We study this knowing that, in some ways, it is artificial to separate the *anhypostatic* and *enhypostatic* aspects of the Church. It is a bit like turning off the computer so we can open it up and see how all the wires are connected. We can, temporarily, isolate the Church in its *enhypostatic* aspect for the sake of considering it in its humanity. The purpose of so doing is to reunite the Church in all its human practices, traditions, and rituals ever more securely within its *anhypostatic* aspect in the gospel of Jesus Christ. That is to say, to return all our activity as the Church as the mode of expression of our joining in with the life and work of Jesus.

By correlating the doctrine of the Church in relation to the doctrine of Christ, it is apparent that any error in Christology will bleed into an error in ecclesiology without too much encouragement. It is, for example, possible to have a docetic form of thinking about the Church. Just as the docetic Christ merely appeared to be human but was actually transcendentally beyond the vagaries, sufferings, and changes of human life, so also the Church can be thought of in a way that belies its humanity. A docetic ecclesiology is one in which the Church does not really participate in our human existence but remains a transcendent structure which mediates revelation and the sacraments in a way that is high above the complexities and limitations of humans. A docetic ecclesiology, therefore, could be a view of the Church as pure and unchanging in its dogmas, set forward in a continuous line of divine truth running through human history. Or, it may be a way of thinking about the Church as a spiritual community which should not have any institutional organization, as if the invisible union in Christ had no implications for the present time. On the other hand, we might think of the Church in a way more like the Ebionite Christology in which Christ is seen as a human who is adopted into close fellowship with God owing to his excellence. In this sense, the Church is an empirical institution which emerges out of religious or sociological impulses in humanity, perhaps even as a human response to God's revelatory work. Any view of the Church which takes its own ethical response of obedience to divine revelation as something parallel to but ultimately separated from the response already made in Christ is bound to see the Church only as a human entity of some kind, be it an institution or a community.

A view of the Church that is thoroughly established on Jesus will not embrace either of these extremes. The Church is called into being by the act of God through being included into Christ by the Spirit, but its existence

continues with the rhythms, legislation, and limitations of a human institution. The human institution is dependent on the act and call of God, and it
has a distinct existence as a human entity. What exactly is the relationship
here between the divine act of creation and the human extension that it gives
rise to? Any answer we can give to this question, just as with the doctrine of
creation, needs to be grounded uncompromisingly on Jesus, specifically as
belief about Jesus is set forward in the Chalcedonian Settlement.

Clearly, we must steer away from the rocks of ignoring the humanity
of the Church in its fragility and fallibility. However, we must not do so
in such a way that cynically views everything about the Church and its
proclamation of the gospel as filled with error. It is important, also, to not
follow the route of a less cynical anthropocentrism regarding the Church.
We should hold back from thinking of the Church in its earthly-historical extension as the human response of faith, prayer, and worship to the
creative word of God. Separating out the act of God in establishing the
Church and the human act of obedience by which it is perpetuated would
be to neglect that the human response to the divine act has come in Jesus
Christ. This would insert a damaging dualism into the heart of what we
think about the Church. The worship of the Church is not the action of the
Church in response to the grace of God, which goes on parallel to God's act
but never interlocking. The action of the Church cannot be an ethical response made in parallel response to God's action because *God's action to us
already includes the fullness of the human response to him*. The worship and
ministry of the Church is in the form of our participation in the worship of
God and reconciliation of achieved in our humanity through Jesus Christ.
The wholly human response to the gracious self-revelation has already been
achieved and the Church cannot be conceived of irrespective of that. This
is the same structure as was described in relation to the sacraments: there is
one human response to the grace of God common between Christ and his
Church. However, the agency of Christ and his Church in relation to this
response is different. God the Son incarnate completes this perfect human
obedience and worship of the Father as the active agent. The Church participates in this perfect human obedience and worship as the passive agent.
The institution of the Church in its earthly-historical visibility is the action
of those who are united to Jesus, and we are included as passive participants
in what Jesus has done on our behalf.

Conceived of in this way, the Church in all its rituals and visibility will not get in the way of Jesus. Quite rightly, there is an allure and
a beauty to the rituals and ceremonies of the Church that should be attractive. Moreover, there is an appeal to the institutional certainty of the
Church with the clarity its orders of ministry provide for the pattern of life

and worship which provides the cocooned sense of security and stability. There is a draw to the historical continuity of the Church as it appears to convey the permanence and a certainty so powerful in a world of flux and questions. It is not a problem that the Church is attractive so long as we remember that the gospel of participation in Jesus is the inner essence, basis of existence and the reality that the Church points towards. The actions that the Church undertakes are actions of passivity. The human response to the gracious self-revelation of God has already been made by Jesus Christ. The activity of the Church is that by which the Spirit binds us to Christ as the ones who have been included into the covenant partner of God. The activity of the Church is precisely its mode of passivity as incorporated into Christ who is the true covenant partner. The Church is not the earthly-historical form of the existence of Jesus. Instead, it is the earthly-historical form of our participation in Jesus.

However, the passivity of the Church's role in the one human worship of God does not compromise its integrity. To establish parameters around what the Church is by claiming it to be passive in worship does not mean to bind the worship of the Church to the floor. Instead, it is to operate rather more like the walls of a furnace. It is to establish boundaries around what the worship of the Church actually is so to intensify its blaze. Just as the human nature of Jesus was dependent on the divine but yet was the most human person to have ever lived, so also the Church has the freedom to be a human construction, indeed the most human of constructions. Importantly, the structure of this construction is not arbitrary or dreamt up from the minds of humans looking to give some order to this entity. Instead, the structure of the human institution of the Church is earthed deep in the gospel itself. As such, the Church in its visibility is ordered and determined by the logic of the gospel itself, whereby by its existence it proclaims the glory of God in the face of Jesus Christ.

The earthly-historical extension of the Church absorbs and expresses a pattern nascent in the gospel. This means that the institutional structure of the Church is part of our proclamation of the gospel. This is because in every part of its life, all the Church is doing nothing else than engaging as the partner in the obedience, worship, and ministry of Jesus Christ. In its liturgy, it sets forward the self-offering of Jesus through his life and in his death, resurrection, and ascension in such a way that we are joining ourselves to him and welcomes others to do the same. In its earthly-historical structures and patterns it is shaped by the reality of the saving activity of God in Jesus Christ: its ordained ministers are gifted by the Spirit to continue the ministry of Jesus Christ to his body. It is because Christ is the one true priest that the whole Church exercises priestly ministry in derivative form of inclusion. It is within Christ, the true worshiper of the Father, that the Church may worship. It is because Christ cares for his people that the Church may be mother of believers as the means through which Jesus continues to minister to his people. It is because Jesus Christ has reconciled the world to himself that the Church may be the witness and effective sign of reconciliation in its relation to the world which is the context for its life.

Church Order

One of the most clearly visible aspects of the Church's earthly-historical existence as a human institution has been the fact that, for the most part, it has been organized in orders. The Church has for almost all of its existence been characterized by the succession of bishops and the ministry of priests who are, as one well-known ecumenical document has it, "continually responsible for pointing to its fundamental dependence on Jesus Christ."[7] What is the relationship between this institutional framework and the gospel? For some, the very existence of an ordered society with its signs of difference in robes and distinct clerical responsibilities clashes with and obscures the purity of the message of Jesus and the simplicity of the community he established. For others, the ordering of the community may well be a practical necessity to organize the life of the Church, but it does not have an organic connection to the gospel. Michael Ramsey, on the other hand, argued that the order of the Church is "a development which grew in the gospel and through the gospel, and which expresses the gospel and can be belittled only at the expense of the gospel."[8] For Ramsey, the structure of the Church is the visible means by which believers are united to Christ. Church order, in other words, is the structure of the "organism which grew inevitably through Christ's death and resurrection."[9] The visible order of the Church as a human institution is a product of its being utterly dependent on Jesus for existence but yet having its own discrete identity within that dependence.

The organic relation between Church order and the gospel makes the structure of the life of the Church as an institution very different from the sort of structure that goes on in other human institutions. The Church, which has its existence as a human community, is the body of Christ. It is established in being a human community by the act of God through Christ by the Spirit. The laws and norms by which the Church has its common life are determined by that necessary relation to Jesus. Just as the Church has no

---

7. World Council of Churches, *Baptism, Eucharist and Ministry*, 17.

8. Ramsey, *Gospel and the Catholic Church*, 57.

9. Ramsey, *Gospel and the Catholic Church*, 66.

existence aside from Jesus, its way of organizing itself as a human society is also not independent but is derived from Jesus who is the Lord of the Church and orders his community. The ordering of the common life of the Church is a function of the Lordship of Christ over his Church, as the head of which the Church is the body. Concern with Church order is not, then, a corrupting love of bureaucracy imposing itself on the community Jesus established only around himself. The problem with Church order comes when it is abstracted from its actual source in the way Jesus organizes his people for the purpose of the unity between himself and his Church. In other words, the institutional character of the Church is problematic only if it is separated from its organic root.

As Church order is rooted ultimately in Jesus, it is not ultimately defined by the practical requirements of the worship of the Church. The worship of the Church is not our free response to the act of God, regulated only by the practical necessities for making that response. Instead, in our worship, Jesus is present amongst us, organizing our corporate life as the Church in accordance with his own Lordship. It is in the worship of the Church that the invisible community of those united in Jesus becomes visible as Jesus becomes present within the Christian community through the reading of Scripture and the celebration of Eucharist. The ordering of the Church is established through the means of Jesus' presence to us confirming and strengthening our unity with him. This means that Church order comes from the relationship between Jesus as Lord and the Church as his community. This relationship is the one irreducible criterion for understanding and assessing all aspects of ecclesiastical law. We are not obedient to Church law because we are subservient to some human institution which is valid in and of itself. Instead, we are obedient to Church law inasmuch as it is grounded beyond itself in the person of Jesus Christ. Inasmuch as it is true Church law, it demands our utter loyalty and obedience, as obedience to Jesus himself.

That the law by which the Church is governed is given to it by Christ means that the law of the Church is not from some correspondence to secular authorities. It has its own unique form in that it is shaped by Jesus Christ and is the servant of our unity with him and his Lordship of us. This is to be expected because the Church has no life other than the one that is given to it by the grace of God in Jesus Christ by the Spirit. The regulations by which it has that life are to be established by the means of its life (that is, Christologically and pneumatologically). However, just because the Church's earthly-historical extension as a regulated community does not exist aside from the grace of God (the *anhypostatic* aspect) the Church still has a distinct human life as a regulated community within Jesus Christ (the *enhypostatic*

aspect). Once again there is a need to find a middle route between two extremes: a careless dismissal of order in the Church and a flat legalism which
sees ecclesiastical governance as an end in itself. The former is, of course, a
docetic form of thinking about the Church in which it does not have any
earthly-historical extension that needs to be organized by clear legislation.
The latter is more like an Ebionite form of thinking about the Church in
which the earthly-historical extension is all that there is and the law of the
Church becomes an earthly proxy for the law of Christ.

The approach taken to this problem by Barth is instructive, albeit not
conclusive. For Barth, Church law must take concrete and specific form
but yet it was never to be thought of as absolute. The Church is a human
institution and must bear the regulation required by all human communities. However, it only exists as called into being by the Word and Spirit of
God and its life is lived as a divine act.[10] For Barth, this gives to the Church
a profoundly eschatological character as it moves towards the return of
Christ and the ultimate sanctification of all creation.[11] Considered in this
perspective, the law of the Church is derived from beyond itself and is always able to be more closely brought into correspondence with the word of
God. In the sphere of human history, the Church is the community brought
into being by God's act to bring order into the confusion of the world.[12]
Church order, for Barth, is an expression of the redemptive movement of
God, overcoming the disorder of fallen creation. As such, Church order
cannot be thought of aside from the Lordship of Christ over his Church
and, proleptically, over the whole of creation.

> Jesus Christ is here the Lord and Head, the primary acting Sub-
> ject. It is He who gives them, not only their faith and confession
> and prayer and proclamation, but also the form of their life, the
> law and order of all that they do. The community is not a law to
> itself, least of all in its relationship to Him. In its relationship to
> Him He is its living law. . . . A true inquiry concerning what is
> right in the Church will always be an inquiry concerning His
> ordering and commanding and controlling, and corresponding
> obedience. . . . As such, all valid and projected Church law, if it is
> true Church law, will be clearly and sharply differentiated from
> every other kind of "law." In great things and small, in all things,
> true Church law arises from a hearing of the voice of Jesus
> Christ. Neither formally nor materially does it arise elsewhere.[13]

10. Barth, *Church Dogmatics*, 4.2, 616–18.

11. Barth, *Church Dogmatics*, 4.2, 620.

12. Barth, *Church Dogmatics*, 4.2, 676.

13. Barth, *Church Dogmatics*, 4.2, 682.

The great strength of this is that it respects the law of the Church but recognizes its contingency in relation to Jesus and it is always open to reformulation in the event that we understand better tomorrow than we did yesterday.

However, the danger here is that the organization of the life of the Church comes as a *response* to the grace of God rather than our real and present participation in Jesus. Here the sense that something was not quite right in Barth's correlation between the Church and obedience to revelation comes into sharper focus. For Barth, the Church is formed by its Spirit-enabled correspondence to the objective self-revelation of God: "it is concretely to Scripture that the community has to listen in the question of law and order."[14] Of course this is the case given it is the self-attestation of Christ through the apostles. However, it cannot be all that is said. Given freedom by the Spirit or not, casting Church law as obedience to Scripture treats the Church as response to the word of God. Within Barth's view, there is a danger that the Church as a human institution could be seen as a divinely enabled response to God, which is not fully integrated with the response to God made on our behalf in and through Jesus Christ. Certainly, this is ameliorated somewhat by Barth's Christological grounding of the relation of the Church and the world (see below). However, some, for example, have seen something like a separation of the act of God in Christ and the act of the Church in Barth's view of sacraments as actions of the Church that run in parallel to the act of God.[15] Instead, we would do better to think of the order of the Church as established by Jesus *to facilitate the means of unity between the head and the body*. The law of the Church remains relative to the truth of revelation, but it is not a human response separate and parallel to Jesus'. Instead, it is a human response that consciously participates in Jesus' vicarious human life and takes its shape from this participation. For this reason, Church order is established exclusively by the criterion of the means of Jesus' presence to and formation of his community. Specifically, preaching and the sacraments are the sources of ecclesial order because these are the means of grace by which we are united to Christ in the fellowship of the Holy Spirit.

In chapter 3, discussion concerning Church order was with respect to the triunity of God, specifically focusing on the question of the monarchy of the Father and the corresponding ecclesial order of the episcopacy. In this chapter, we are more concerned with the relationship between the order of the Church and the gospel of Jesus Christ. Specifically, we are interested with the question of how the order of the ecclesial priesthood is related to

14. Barth, *Church Dogmatics*, 4.2, 683.
15. See, for example, Yocum, *Ecclesial Mediation in Karl Barth*, 174–75.

the primary and ultimate priesthood of Jesus Christ. The suggestion that the order of the Church is positively related to the gospel should not be a surprise given what has already been said. The Church is the body of Christ: its entire essence is constituted by the love of the Father and the Son in the power of the Spirit which is manifested in the Son's self-denial and self-offering to the Father on the cross in which we are enabled to share. The existence of the Church is not a response to the event of Jesus' death and resurrection; it is a real and present sharing in it.

The unity of believers in the visibility of the Church is the outward expression of the invisible unity with Jesus by which we are one as the body of which he is the head. This unity in Christ is the inner basis of the Church as the assembly of those who have been called out (*ekklēsia*) by God. The inner basis of unity in Christ is the gospel itself as God the Son shares our embodied existence so that we may share in his through inclusion into his death and resurrection. In other words, there is an organic and essential relation between the earthly-historical Church and Jesus Christ in his self-giving to the Father. The ecclesial institution is not simply an ethical response to the gospel but is actually constituted by the gospel events. The organization of the life of the Church is not the creation of the Church and cannot be understood on the horizontal dimension of institutional justification alone. Instead, it is primarily rooted in the very structure of the gospel itself, whereby the ecclesial structures are derived from and patterned in accordance to the historical events of the life of Jesus.

The order of the Church is neither a matter of no-consequence or of supreme consequence. Church order is positively related to the inner essence of the Church in its union with Jesus through inclusion into his death and resurrection making it both a window into the gospel and contingent upon the gospel. This follows on from what has already been said about the Church as sacramental. The Church in its visible unity manifested in its agreed structures of governance, liturgy, and so on is an effective sign of our spiritual and invisible union with Jesus Christ, through which Jesus continues to establish humanity in unity with himself. The organization of the life of the Church into institutional structure is not a distortion of the pure gospel into a hierarchical entity existing to perpetuate its own power. It is not even a pragmatic way of organizing our response to the saving events of the gospel. Instead, the institutional character of the Church takes its structure directly from the gospel. This underscores the claim that the Church cannot be understood only in reference to itself but only in reference to Jesus Christ.[16] This is why there must be an inseparable relation between faith and order. We should

16. Ramsey, *Gospel and the Catholic Church*, 19–56.

not just think of the tradition of the Church as having value simply for the fact of its antiquity. The antiquity of the traditions of the Church don't have authority by merit of their age but by merit of their primal foundation in the person and work of Jesus Christ. In order to elucidate this, we need to think about the relationship between Jesus as the one true priest of God and the derivative priesthood of the people of God.

The Primary Priesthood of Jesus and Derivative Priesthood of the People of God

The one priest of God is Jesus Christ. Jesus is at one and the same time the Word of God to humanity and the word of humanity to God. As the Word of God to humanity, Jesus is the expression of loving-kindness and, as the word of humanity to God, he is the response of obedience, faith, and praise.[17] He is the redemptive Word of God to humanity and the complete response and witness of humanity to that redemptive word. As Apostle, Jesus is sent and acts from the side of God toward humanity in steadfast love. As priest, he acts from the side of humanity in obedience to the Father. The center of this is the cross of Christ where the truth of God's judgement on sin and mercy upon sinful humanity is revealed and where the human response of obedience and faith is made as Jesus speaks out, "Father, into your hands, I commit my spirit." In so doing, Jesus actualizes in our disobedient humanity a new obedience to the Father and offers himself as a full and sufficient sacrifice to blot out the sins of humanity. Jesus does not bear witness to something else. He is not a cultic response to an act of God. Jesus is priest in the full and final reality of priesthood. There is no other mediator aside from Jesus Christ. The human response to God's saving self-revelation has already been made. This is the irreducible foundation upon which we may talk about the priesthood of the people of God.

T. F. Torrance has sketched out how the actual priesthood of Jesus Christ is related to the priesthood of the people of God as the source is related to its derivatives.[18] It is not that the priesthood of the Mosaic Covenant and the priesthood of the New Covenant are just cultic responses to the actual priesthood of Jesus. It is that these derivative forms of priesthood have as their substance the act of God and humanity in Jesus Christ. This can be put around the other way: the true priest, Jesus Christ, continues his priestly work through the derivative priesthood of the people of God. This means that the priesthood of the people of God can never

17. Küng, *Church*, 363–370.
18. Torrance, *Royal Priesthood*, 1–22.

be separated from the act of God, which includes in it the true human response of praise, sacrifice, and obedience.

The great tragedy of Israel's priesthood and Israel's existence as a kingdom of priests established by the redemptive action of God, Torrance argues, is that *its priestly response became separated from God's act.*[19] In grace, God chose Israel to be his people and saved them from Egypt to be his nation of priests (Exod 19:6). From within that common election of the whole of Israel, the tribe of Levi was appointed to serve in the temple, with fewer appointed as priests and, finally, the high priesthood. The temple priesthood acted as mediators, bearing the word of God to Israel in their teaching and bearing the response of Israel to God in the performance of cultic witness to the mercy of God through the temple sacrifices. Israel as a nation of priests existed as an ordered society. The purpose of this cultic priesthood was to facilitate the entire life of the nation as the nation of priests.

Despite their centrality to Israel's national life, the cultic priesthood did not accomplish anything in and of itself. Even the mystery of the high priest entering the Holy of Holies on the Day of Atonement was a liturgical act which derived its essence and efficacy from elsewhere. The sacrificial system was not a mechanism to provoke forgiveness; it was a sacrament that enabled the people of Israel to appropriate and accept the forgiveness made possible by another act.[20] In this, the sacrifices of Israel looked both backwards and forwards. Certainly, they looked backward to the election of Israel and their redemption from Egypt, including the subsequent mediation of Moses on Sinai in receiving the word of God on tablets of stone, and his appeal to God for mercy on Israel for making the Golden Calf. More importantly, they looked forwards for this Mosaic mediation itself was superseded by Christ. For this reason, the temple worship also looked forward to Jesus Christ, the true High Priest and ultimate sacrifice made in the presence of God, rather than in earthly copies. These events bookend the temple sacrifices and are the acts of God to which the cultic activity of the temple joined the people of Israel. In this way, the priestly work is subordinate to and derivative from God's act.

One of the major narrative tropes of the Old Testament is the clash between the prophets and the institutions of Israel, including its priesthood. The prophets repeatedly exposed and attacked the religiosity of Israel in which they separated the sacrifices of the temple from the direct act of God. It would appear that, as the history of Israel developed, the liturgical witness of Israel's temple cult began to calcify and separate itself from its

---

19. Torrance, *Royal Priesthood*, 5–7.
20. Torrance, *Royal Priesthood*, 4.

substance, which is the act of God. These cultic activities became viewed as self-sufficient in and of themselves, leading to Israel's ill-founded confidence in the performance of the sacrificial rituals (e.g., Mic 3:11). The power of the sacrifices did not reside in themselves, but in the steadfast love of God who had appointed them as the means of liturgically connecting Israel to its foundations in the electing mercy of God maintained through the mediation of Moses and forwards to its ultimate establishment as the people of God through Jesus Christ. As the prophetic critique of the temple cultus made plain, the sacrificial system itself was not the source of forgiveness for Israel, as if it were self-sufficient. The liturgical and cultic worship could not be separated from the act of God to establish Israel as his covenant people and rendered a mechanism for maintaining privilege aside from full life as the people of God. The heart of the prophetic critique is that the cultic activity is to facilitate Israel's national life as a nation of priests, and is, therefore, inseparable from God's act of faithfulness in electing and redeeming them from Israel and establishing them in the land and Israel's answering faithfulness of obedience to his word. In other words, sacrifices had no meaning outside the covenant and if Israel would not live as God's covenant people, then they could hardly appeal to the sacrifices.

For Torrance, the unity of the prophetic and the priestly in Jesus Christ who is both Apostle and High Priest needs to be understood in the context of the clash of these orders of ministry in the nation of Israel.[21] Jesus is both the unadulterated Word of God to humanity coming in action to save, and he is the perfect response of obedience and love. Jesus is the prophet in whom God's word and God's self are one and the same thing, and he is the priest in whom the divine act of salvation is direct within our humanity as he offers himself to the Father as a sacrifice to remove the sins of the people. This submission of Christ to the will of the Father to the point of death and the Father's answering faithfulness in the resurrection constitutes the actual saving events in relation to which any subsequent discussion of the priesthood of the people of God needs to be understood.

The warning of Israel's priesthood concerning the separation of the liturgical act as a parallel response to God's act provides us with the basic orientation we need to understand priesthood within the community established around Jesus. After having healed someone, Jesus would on occasion send the healed person to the priests so that the priests may be witness to the truth of God's saving action in its liturgical worship (e.g., Matt 8:4). Jesus forgave sins aside from the mediation of the temple priests, because this was God himself at work to forgive and reconcile (Mark 2:1–11). You don't

---

21. Torrance, *Royal Priesthood*, 14–21.

need the liturgical connection when you have the real thing in front of you. In doing so, Jesus put the temple priests in their place. He demonstrated to the priestly class of Israel that it was not independent from the act of God but instead existed as a witness to the act of God. The priest has no power or authority aside from this.

In the same way, Jesus established his followers as witnesses to him. He gathered a community around himself and gave them a share in his work. First, the inner circle of the twelve (Luke 9:1–6) and then the wider gathering of the seventy (Luke 10:1–12). At his ascension, Christ commissioned his apostles and poured the Spirit out upon them such that they may be "witnesses in Jerusalem, in all Judea and Samaria and to the ends of the earth" (Acts 1:8). This gives a fundamental orientation to how we understand the Church. If the fellowship Christ established tries to separate their witness from the act of God and appeal instead to the power of the Church as a human institution, then the work of Christ is not being done. The priesthood of the Church is nothing other than in its sharing in Jesus as the true priest and pointing beyond itself to the true priesthood of Jesus Christ. This is the principal foundation on which to think about the priesthood of the Church and how this is related to the ordering of the Church as a visible and hierarchical institution.

Priesthood and the Church

The New Testament letters regularly use priestly and cultic language to describe the Church. The Church is to offer spiritual sacrifices without differentiation between its members (for example, Rom 12:1; Phil 2:17; 4:18; Heb 13:15–16; and 1 Pet 2:5). Importantly, these sacrifices are not in parallel to the sacrifice of Christ and they do not repeat the sacrifice of Christ. Instead, they are sacrifices of thanksgiving, they are eucharistic, rising to the Father through the Son's own self-offering. This was impressed upon me as I worshiped in Merton College Chapel in Oxford (a tradition which was at the time very unfamiliar to me). I remember watching the smoke from the incense rise and, in its path upwards, it ran behind a cross. As I watched, I began to think that my sacrifice of praise ascends to the Father through the Son's true sacrificial self-offering. It is not separate from it, it is not in parallel to it, it does not repeat it; it ascends through it.

In being described in priestly terms, the community of Jesus Christ cannot possibly be thought of in terms separated from Jesus as the true priest. As Hans Küng notes, "all human priesthood has been fulfilled and finished by the unique, final, unrepeatable and hence unlimited sacrifice of the one continuing and eternal high priest."[22] Therefore, the priesthood of the Church is constituted by our participation in Jesus' self-offering and reconciling ministry. Later in this chapter we will consider the meaning of participation in Christ's priesthood in more detail. For now, we are focused on the relationship between Jesus and the visible order of the Church inasmuch as the priesthood of the Church is a sharing in Jesus' priesthood. This is what is in view when Peter describes the followers of Jesus Christ using priestly language by saying "you also, like living stones, are being built into a spiritual house, a holy priesthood, offering spiritual sacrifices acceptable to God through Jesus Christ" (1 Pet 2:5). The distinction between the people of God (the stones) and Jesus Christ (the cornerstone) organizes the wider context of this verse. Jesus is the central reality around which the Church is built, but he does not become subsumed into the Church, remaining distinct from it as the head is distinct from the body. The Church as the stones that are being built together around Christ take a share in all he is and in all he has done. The Church is a priesthood whose sacrifices of thanksgiving to God come to him through the one supreme self-offering of Jesus Christ. The worship of the Church, in other words, is contingent on our incorporation into Jesus Christ and sharing in his life of obedience and worship. The priesthood of the Church is in our witness to the life, death, and resurrection of Jesus.

The worst thing that can happen to the Church, as the history of Israel suggests, is for its priestly work to be separated from the act of God in Jesus Christ. The priestly work of Christ is definitive and substantive. The priestly work of the Church is derivative and ambassadorial. There are a number of ways that a dualism of the priesthood of Christ and the Church can come about. Perhaps most obviously to those with Protestant sensibilities, this can happen when there is an exclusive focus on ritualism and clericalism. The Church can get in the way of Jesus Christ by being seen to offer a ritual service that is efficacious in and of itself. However, the antidote to this is not to oversteer to the point of an exclusive focus on our personal faith. If we take that route then, even though the Church is not put in the way of Christ, the individual response of the believer is, as if it were our faith that saves us and not the faithfulness of Jesus. Certainly, both the sacramental activity of the Church and the faith of the believer are necessary but neither are sufficient in and of themselves. We get into real problems when we fall into thinking of our activity as an active response to the act of God in Jesus Christ as opposed to a passive act of joining ourselves to what God has done on our behalf.

22. Küng, *Church*, 366.

The corollary of this is that the whole Church participates in Christ as one as a holy priesthood.[23] There is not some stratum within the Church that does not share the common reality of being joined to Jesus and given a share in his relation to the Father and his mission to the world. As Zizioulas put it, "there is no such thing as 'non-ordained' persons in the Church."[24] Through the Spirit, God "baptizes us into the life and ministry of Christ and forms us into the *laos*, the people of God, who as signs and agents of God's reign participate in God's mission of reconciling humanity and all creation to God."[25] Baptism is the means through which we are incorporated into the body of Christ and so into the ministry of the body of Christ. Jesus is the one true priest who mediates the things of God to humans and responds to God with obedient self-giving. This one priest opens his life for our inclusion in the power of the Spirit. Therefore, as his body, we are included into the ministry of his ultimate priesthood as a derivative priesthood. So, then, Christ is the source of ministry in the Church, and the Church is commissioned by Christ to be his witnesses. In this sense, as Schilebeeckx puts it, the Church is, at one and the same time, "both community of the redeemed and a redeeming institution."[26] As each a member within the body of Christ, every believer has access to God in Christ, offers themselves to the Father through Christ and has a share in testifying to the gospel of God's grace.

The priesthood of all believers, however, is not antithetical to differentiation. Within the common priesthood there is a further ordering to facilitate the priestly ministry of the Church as a whole: "in order that the whole people of God may fulfil their calling to be a holy priesthood, serving the world by ministering Christ's reconciling love in the power of the Spirit, some are called to specific ministries of leadership for which they are recognized and enabled through ordination."[27] The purpose of the ordained priesthood is to serve the common priesthood (Eph 4:11–16). This service takes the form of facilitating the common priesthood of the Church in their participation in the reconciling ministry of Christ.[28] For this reason, John Calvin identified the ministry of Church leadership as essential to the unity of Christ and his people.

23. For a superb discussion of the priesthood of all believers from the Roman Catholic perspective, see Küng, *Church*, 370–88. See also Paul VI, "Dogmatic Constitution on the Church (*Lumen Gentium*)," 10, 12, 30–35. See also the ecumenical statement of the same theme, *Nature and Mission of the Church*, 22–23, paras. 82–85.

24. Zizioulas, *Being as Communion*, 215.

25. Gibson, *Berkeley Statement*, 1.

26. Schilbeeckx, *Christ the Sacrament*, 58.

27. Gibson, *Berkeley Statement*, 1.

28. *Nature and Mission of the Church*, 23, para. 86.

[Paul] shows that the ministry of men, which God employs in governing the Church, is a principal bond by which believers are kept together in one body. . . . In this way, the renewal of the saints is accomplished and the body of Christ is edified. . . . Whoever, therefore, studies to abolish this order and kind of government of which we speak, or disparages it as of minor importance, plots the devastation, or rather the ruin and destruction of the Church. For neither are the light and heat of the sun, nor meat and drink so necessary to sustain and cherish the present life, as is the apostolical and pastoral office to preserve a Church on earth.[29]

An iteration of this idea grounded on the sacraments is given by Zizioulas who has pointed out that ordination is the appointment of an ambassador of Christ to his Church, representing Christ as the head and servant of a eucharistic community.[30]

In Israel, the presence of an institutional priesthood was to serve the whole people of Israel who were a nation of priests by merit of being established as such by God. Within that royal priesthood, there was an institutional priesthood who would serve the nation of priests in the temple so to facilitate the entire nation to fulfill its appointment as a nation of priests. The same structure is apparent within the Christian Church. Within the common priesthood, some are set aside to serve the rest of the priesthood. The purpose of this setting aside is so that the whole body may be equipped to participate in Christ's ministry of reconciliation: "Ordained ministers can fulfil their calling only in and for the community."[31] As such, the ordering of the Church into diverse ministries is rooted in the gospel itself. This function of the ordained clergy in relation to the rest of the people of God is the principal reason for which the metaphor of the Church as "mother" is helpful.[32] It is as the mother of believers that the Church teaches, nurtures,

---

29. Calvin, *Inst.* 4.3.2.

30. Zizioulas, *Being as Communion*, 225–36.

31. World Council of Churches, *Baptism, Eucharist and Ministry*, 18.

32. An important concern with this proposal is from the perspective of feminist theology. The place of gender in theology and its relation to dynamics of power is complex. Among others, Rosemary Ruether has argued consistently against that the core gendered symbolism of the Church is patriarchal (Ruether, *Religion and Sexism*; Daly, *Beyond God the Father*; Trible, *God and the Rhetoric of Sexuality*. Closely associated, particularly in Roman Catholic piety, with the typological unity of Mariology and the Church is the notion of motherly virginity and purity. Some suggest this is the imposition of male notions of the ideal woman onto Mary and all women, which as a corollary, holds a punitive function for all other women in comparison to an impossible ideal (Daly, *Beyond God the Father*, 28).

and cares for believers through the ordained ministry of preaching, pastoral care, and celebrating the sacraments.

The Motherhood of the Church

It is possible that the idea of the motherhood of the Church may cause disquiet among some. It may invoke ideas of the Mother Church, a self-perpetuating institution which exists aside from believers. However, this is not what is intended. Instead, what is in view is the Church's maternal function in relation to believers in nourishing, teaching, and caring for believers to enable the body of Christ to take full part in Christ's ministry of reconciliation. The Church is not Mother of Believers in an absolute sense but rather it is mother of believers in a contingent sense, that is, inasmuch as it engages with its maternal role of caring for believers through preaching and sacraments. Cyprian of Carthage described the Church using the metaphor of motherhood in the context of the Decian persecutions and the subsequent Novatian Controversy, which threatened to divide the Church over the question of the re-admittance of the lapsed.

> I entreat you . . . return to the Mother whence you have gone forth . . . for as our unanimity and concord ought by no means to be divided, and because we cannot forsake the Church and go outside her to come to you, we beg and entreat you with what exhortation we can, return to the Church your Mother and to our brotherhood.[33]

This appeal to return to the Church is not purely institutional, but rather was earthed on a conviction that the Church is the means through which God's Fatherly care of his people is extended: "You cannot have God for your Father unless you have the Church as your Mother."[34]

> The Church is one which is spread abroad far and wide into a multitude by an increase of fruitfulness. . . . Her fruitful abundance spreads her branches over the whole world. She broadly expands her rivers, liberally flowing, yet her head is one, her source is one; and she is one mother, plentiful in the results of fruitfulness, from her womb we are born, by her milk we are nourished, by her spirit we are animated.[35]

33. Cyprian, "Epistles," 43.
34. Cyprian, "On the Unity of the Church," 6.
35. Cyprian, "On the Unity of the Church," 5.

Closer to our own time, the document *Lumen Gentium* of the Second Vatican Council draws a strong parallel between the Church and motherhood through the figure of Mary. The document identifies the role of Mary in the economy of salvation not as another mediator,[36] but rather as the one who was obedient to the word of God and so freely cooperating in God's salvific action by her faith and obedience in being the mother of Christ and bringing him to birth.[37] From this understanding of Mary's role in the economy of salvation, the document develops a dense typology in which Mary as the mother of Christ is the type for the Church as the mother of believers.

> By reason of the gift and role of divine maternity, by which she is united with her Son, the Redeemer, and with His singular graces and functions, the Blessed Virgin is also intimately united with the Church. As St. Ambrose taught, the Mother of God is a type of the Church in the order of faith, charity and perfect union with Christ. . . . The Church indeed, contemplating her hidden sanctity, imitating her charity and faithfully fulfilling the Father's will, by receiving the word of God in faith becomes herself a mother. By her preaching she brings forth to a new and immortal life the sons who are born to her in baptism, conceived of the Holy Spirit and born of God. She herself is a virgin, who keeps the faith given to her by her Spouse whole and entire. Imitating the mother of her Lord, and by the power of the Holy Spirit, she keeps with virginal purity an entire faith, a firm hope and a sincere charity.[38]

As mother of Christ, Mary is an exemplar for the Church.[39] Just as Mary received the word of God in faith and so brought Christ to birth, so also the Church receives the word of God in faith and brings new believers to birth in baptism. Just as Mary nourished Jesus physically and spiritually, so also the Church nourishes believers through the Eucharist. The motherhood of the Church follows the type which is the motherhood of Mary. The Church becomes mother of believers in imitating Mary by fulfilling the will

---

36. See especially Paul VI, "Dogmatic Constitution on the Church (*Lumen Gentium*)," 0.

37. Paul VI, "Dogmatic Constitution on the Church (*Lumen Gentium*)," 55–60. See also *Catechism of the Catholic Church*, 9.6.964.

38. Paul VI, "Dogmatic Constitution on the Church (*Lumen Gentium*)," 63–64. See also *Catechism of the Catholic Church*, 9.6.967.

39. For a discussion of the history of the concept of Mary as the mother of the Church in Ambrose and in medieval Mariology, see Neuman, "Mary and the Church," 123–26.

of the Father in obedience to his word and so cooperating in the bringing of the children of God to birth through preaching and baptism.

Within Protestant thought, also, there is a tradition of describing the Church using the metaphor of motherhood. Calvin gives an extended discussion of the motherhood of the Church in Book Four of the *Institutes* in the context of the argument that God provides us with "outward help to beget and increase faith within us and advance toward its goal."[40]

> I shall start, then, with the Church, into whose bosom God is pleased to gather his sons, not only that they may be nourished by her help and ministry as long as they are infants and children, but also that they may be guided by her motherly care until they mature and reach the goal of faith . . . so that for those to whom [God] is Father the Church may also be Mother.[41]

For Calvin, the motherhood of the Church is intrinsically connected to God's accommodation to the capacity of humanity. It is through the maternal care of the Church by its preaching and celebration of the sacraments that God exercises his Fatherly love over his people.[42] This means that the motherhood of the Church is inseparable from its earthly-historical visibility.

> It is now our intention to discuss the visible Church, let us learn even from the simple title "mother" how useful, indeed how necessary it, For there is no other way to enter into life unless this mother conceive us in her womb, give us birth, nourish us at her breast, and lastly, unless she keep us under her care and guidance until, putting off mortal flesh, we become like angels. . . . Our weakness does not allow us to be dismissed from her school until we have been pupils all our lives. Furthermore, away from her bosom one cannot hope for any forgiveness of sins or any salvation.[43]

To be an ordained priest is to be an agent of this care. The institutional priesthood is provided by God to care for believers in the life of the body by "proclaiming and teaching the Word of God, by celebrating the sacraments, and by guiding the life of the community in its worship, its mission and its caring ministry."[44] It is to care for and facilitate the Church in its high calling as the covenant partner of God. In this way, the specific calling to be an ordained

40. Calvin, *Inst.* 4.1.1.

41. Calvin, *Inst.* 4.1.1.

42. Calvin, *Inst.* 4.1.5.

43. Calvin, *Inst.* 4.1.4.

44. World Council of Churches, *Baptism, Eucharist and Ministry*, 19.

priest within the common priesthood of God is a gift to God's people to equip the common priesthood through preaching and sacrament.

The organization of the Church into diverse orders, although an institutional and visible reality of our earthly-historical existence, does not have its rationale along the same lines of other institutions (i.e., for the sake of organizational or pragmatic reasons). Instead, Church orders are established by Christ for the purpose of the unity of Jesus and his Church. The priesthood of the Church cannot be separate from the true priest. This is why the work of the institutional priesthood is precisely to enact the means of grace through which the bond of unity between Christ and his Church is established and maintained in the fellowship of the Spirit. In other words, preaching and the sacraments are the Christological basis of Church order.

Preaching and Sacraments: The Christological Basis of Church Order

The ordering of some for a particular ministry in relation to the rest of the Church for the purpose of being tools of the unity of Christ and his Church takes us to the heart of why the ordering of the Church is rooted in sacraments and preaching. For his part, Barth understood ecclesial organization to have its principal foundation in Christ. Barth wrote that it is Christ "who gives [the Church] not only their faith and confession and prayer and proclamation, but also the form of their life, the law and order of all that they do."[45] By this he meant that the ordering of the Church and its internal legislation did not spring up from within humanity, but it is part of the Church's living relationship with Jesus to be organized in accordance with his Lordship over it. For Barth, then, Church order is not internally justifiable. Its only justification is the living relationship between the Church and her Lord. It is not a replacement for the direct Lordship of Christ by establishing new relations of lordship within a hierarchical framework; it is the very expression of "the lordship of Jesus Christ over his body."[46]

For Barth, this is unpacked as subordination to revelation. By establishing the inner ground of Church order in revelation through which Christ addresses his people and calls them to a form of life together, Barth runs the risk of separating the ethical response of the Church from the vicarious humanity of Jesus Christ. Its *principle* for its organization may well be its devotion to the command of Christ, but this is a different thing to the *presence* of Christ determining the community. This being said,

45. Barth, *Church Dogmatics*, 4.1, 682.
46. Barth, *Church Dogmatics*, 4.1, 713.

Barth's threefold understanding of the word of God means that there can be no simple dualism between the word of God and its perpetuation in the mode of being proclaimed. However, for the order of the Church to be determined by participation in Christ in order for its priestly character to be thoroughly grounded in the true priesthood of Christ, more than this needs to be said. With Barth on the relation between Church order and the Lordship of Christ, but developing beyond the specifics of that relation, the organization of the Church into diverse orders is a function of Christ's presence to it through the proclamation of Scripture and the celebration of the sacraments by which he unites us to himself. This move beyond Barth can be traced out by the approach of Torrance. For Torrance, the purpose of the ordering of priests is to be the means through which the unity of the Church and Jesus Christ is maintained and strengthened in the period before his second coming. In other words, the organization of the Church into diverse orders of ministry is a function of the presence of Jesus with us through sacrament and preaching enabled by the Holy Spirit as various gifts are distributed to the Church.[47]

If the organization of the Church into diverse orders is a function of the relation between the Church and the primary priesthood of Jesus, then Church order is determined precisely by the means of our participation in the true priesthood of Jesus Christ. Therefore, the priestly ministry of the Church cannot be separated from its ministry of preaching the gospel and celebrating the sacraments because it is in these that Jesus continues to come to us and the life of the Church is bound fast to him. The Church has been incorporated into Christ by the Spirit through the preaching of the gospel and baptism so to become his body. This incorporation is nourished through the continued preaching of the gospel and the reception of the sacramental body of Jesus at the Eucharist. These are the means of Christ's continued presence to his Church and so, therefore, constitute the inner rationale for the ordered ministry of the Church. This is the form of Christ the head being present to his body and governing it and structuring its earthly-historical existence: the ordering of the Church by the presence of an institutional priesthood is for the purposes of building up and maintaining the body of Jesus.

The hierarchical ordering of the Church, therefore, is not about some authority that is separate from Christ. Jesus is the Lord and head of the Church. However, the ordination of some within the common priesthood is a gift of Christ to his Church by the power of the Spirit. It is through the ministry of word and sacrament that Jesus orders his community

47. Torrance, *Royal Priesthood*, 65–87.

as its head and is present to it. Of course, the presence of Christ to the Church is not only by the institutional priesthood in their sacramental and proclamatory role. God can be present through Christ and by the Spirit aside from the priestly class. But, within the community of Christ there are established means of grace and this is the stable form of ministry of the Church through which Jesus is present amongst his people. This takes place through preaching and sacraments, and, therefore, it is into these duties that a priest is ordained. The entire purpose of Church orders, therefore, is to facilitate the presence of Christ to his Church through the Eucharist and preaching. To ask why the priest celebrates Eucharist and is responsible for preaching in a parish is like asking why an electrician should do your rewiring: it is what they are for.

Baptism incorporates all believers into the body of Christ and the ministry of his priesthood. Within the common priesthood, the Spirit gives a variety of gifts which shape our role in the ministry of the body. The common priesthood, in other words, is not a homogenous block but is a variegated, multi-skilled organism. Part of this differentiation takes place at the Eucharist, as Torrance has helpfully shown.[48] At the Eucharist, the Church comes under the sovereign presence of the Lord Jesus Christ and assumes an ordered structure in obedience to that presence. The existence of an institutional priesthood is a function of the presence of the risen and ascended Jesus with us at the Eucharist. As such, the order of the Church as an institutional reality is not a matter of the Church organizing its life, but rather is dynamically rooted in the reality of Jesus' presence to us in the Eucharist. In this way, the ordering of the Church is the earthly-historical mark of the headship of Christ over his Church.

Preaching, similarly, is a means of grace through which Jesus is present to the Church through the apostolic witness. It is through the apostolic witness to Jesus that God's revelation in the person of Jesus Christ is mediated to the rest of humanity. The bond between the Spirit-inspired apostolic witness to Jesus and Jesus himself is such that through the Scriptures Jesus himself comes to us. The continued preaching of Scripture is the Church focusing its mind on where Jesus comes to us today and orders our life and belief in accordance with himself through the testimony of the apostles. The authority of Scripture as the apostolic witness to Jesus and means through which Jesus shapes the ongoing life of the Church is closely connected to authority in the Church. The heart of the role of the twelve apostles was to function as a joining point between the self-revelation of God in Jesus Christ and the continued existence of the community gathered around Jesus. It was

48. Torrance, *Royal Priesthood*, 71–73.

the witness of these apostles and not any other which is the proclamation of the truth of God in Jesus Christ. The Church, as the pillar and buttress of truth, protects this apostolic gospel in its own teaching and belief. This is the inner rationale for the ministry of episcopacy. The primary function of the bishop is in continuity with the apostles, which is to maintain conformity to the apostolic gospel.[49] In other words, the ordering of the Church with the ministry of oversight is a function of its task to proclaim the gospel. This does not mean that instantiations of the Church which do not have bishops are not determined by Jesus in their pattern of governance. There are different ways this ministry of oversight can be discharged. All Church expression is contingent, not absolute, and we are looking to pattern ourselves more exactly in accordance with the Lord's means of presence to us. However, it does make the ministry of oversight a necessary condition of apostolicity.[50]

Grounding ecclesial order in the person and work of Jesus means that the relation of faith and order is very closely associated with the Church's apostolicity. The Church orders its life as the servant of the gospel in order to fulfill its mission of being a witness to Jesus Christ. This is the inner essence for the ordering of the Church into diverse ministries, not the creation of a self-perpetuating institution that enforces its power through the creation of arbitrary hierarchies. Take, for example, the notion of apostolic succession. The apostles are the commissioned authoritative witness through whom the complete revelation of God and response of humanity in Jesus pivots off the vertical axis and extends horizontally outwards around the world and throughout time. The power of the apostolic witness is composed purely by the Spirit-inspired conformity to Jesus Christ. Whatever else apostolic succession might mean it cannot be separated from the apostolic function as witnesses to Christ. It would be nonsensical to separate the institutional continuity of the episcopate from the continuity of apostolic teaching because it means submission to the apostolic gospel which itself is in submission to revelation. In this way, the institutional framework of apostolic succession through the ministry of oversight is not a mechanism of departure from the gospel but the very means of subordination to the gospel.

All of this is to say that the visible order of the Church must reflect and serve the basis of its existence as the body of Jesus. The institutional character of the Church as a visible human community is the servant of its charismatic experience of being united to Jesus. As such, to speak of a common priesthood of all believers is not a rationale for an absence of human leadership in the Church but neither is the defence of ordained Christian ministry a

49. Ramsey, *Gospel and the Catholic Church*, 68–85.
50. World Council of Churches, *Baptism, Eucharist and Ministry*, 22.

collapse into arid legalism or institutionalism. Faith and order are the correlate of one another. The order of the Church emerges directly from the gospel. The priestly work of the Church is to bind itself to the great High Priest, Jesus Christ, and share in his worship and his ministry. This provides us the foundation on which to understand the liturgy of the Church.

Liturgy

Liturgy is the human expression of praise in formal, corporate, and public structures of thought. It is the voice of the Church in its freedom as having been given its own distinct existence in the person of Jesus by the grace of God. The liturgy of the Church is not only a human response to the act of God in the same way that the Church itself is not a human society that is formed in response to the act of God. The Church is the body of Christ that shares in Jesus' perfect relation to the Father and in its liturgy the Church's worship is joined to the self-offering of the Son. In this way, the liturgy of the Church has the astounding character of being the body of Christ at voice.

So, as a human body of work, and by the principle of *lex orandi lex credendi* (as we pray so we believe), the liturgy can be abstracted and studied on its own terms as an important insight into the doctrine of the Church as a human institution. However, the liturgy only exists as a free, human voice of praise within its dependence on the act of God in Jesus Christ. The worship of the Church cannot be considered aside from the human life of Jesus Christ who offered himself as a sacrifice of praise to the glory of the Father. For it is Jesus who has offered the true response of praise from faithful humanity to God the Father. In living the life of the Son as one of us and for all of us, Jesus has lived in our humanity a life that glorifies the Father. The liturgy of the Church is our corporate participation in Jesus' self-offering to the Father such that our praise ascends to the Father through the Son in the unity of the Holy Spirit. There is only one life of praise lifted to the Father in love and it is Jesus'. The Church, as the body of Christ, is joined to that life. So, while we worship God with all the integrity and fervor with which we are capable, even this activity is passive in that it is participation in the worship of the true Son of God. At its best, this is the great value of liturgy: it causes us to pray in such a way that is compatible with the inner essence of our worship: the Church corporately shares in Jesus' life of praise and love to the Father. In the Eucharist, for example, the Church takes part in Jesus' self-offering in obedience to the Father. The Church does not offer anything instead of or beyond that which is offered through Jesus Christ. Instead, we can only join ourselves to what has already been offered on our behalf: the

perfect life of human obedience, faith, and love. Christian worship, therefore, is our sharing in all Jesus accomplished as one of us and for all of us in
his life of unbroken prayer and obedience in offering himself to the Father.
This holds implications for what liturgy is understood to be.

The Work of the People and the Work of Christ

The term liturgy is derived from the words *laos* (people) and *ergon* (work).
As with British representative democracy, the work of the people can be
completed by an office holder, who is the *leitorgos*, one who acts on behalf of
the people and accomplishes a given task. In the Letter to the Hebrews, Jesus
is described as a *leitorgos* (Heb 7:28). In the logic of the letter, he is the one
who acts as our priest before God the Father and has gone ahead of us into
the very presence of God. In presenting Jesus in this way, the writer of the
Letter to the Hebrews identified him as the one who accomplishes the work
of the people through his self-offering to the Father.

The primary work of the people is the work of Jesus Christ on our
behalf. The liturgy of the Church is derivative and has the purpose of participating in this primary work. In other words, the worship of the Church
takes its determinative point of start from the fact that Jesus has fulfilled
the priestly role of humanity. All our subsequent priestly activity derives
its power and character from him. The prayer and obedience of Christ
becomes ours; the sacrifice of praise the Son made to the Father on the
cross becomes ours. This is the strength of the liturgy of the Church; it is
participating in the work of Christ to the Father. It is a definitively human
expression of worship. Yet this human expression of worship is inseparable
from the human life and praise of Jesus Christ.

If liturgy is the "work of the people" in worship of God, then the one
who does the work is Jesus Christ and the liturgy of the Church is our participation with that. As Ramsey has said the worship of the Church to God
"is expressed in fixed forms so that it may represent not the topical needs
and moods and feelings of [people], but the changeless and enduring facts
about Christ's work for [us], in history, in heaven and in His one Church."[51]
In our contemporary period which places such a premium on personal experience, liturgy reminds us that prayer and praise is not only about our
active spirituality (although it certainly includes that). The liturgy of the
Church is not simply our response to the saving work of God. It is our recognition that the human response to God's saving work has been made and
we are joining in with what has been done on our behalf.

51. Ramsey, *Gospel and the Catholic Church*, 109.

Theology and Liturgy

The theological academy can, on occasions, appear to be far removed from the Church. Certainly, in his epoch-making study on liturgical theology, Alexander Schmemann described the "rupture between theological study and liturgical experience" as a "chronic disease."[52] The technical, philosophical, and (more recently) analytical language of theologians can be hard to access for people whose experience, training, or expertise are in different areas. However, the separation of the theology of the Church and its worshiping life is harmful and quite unnecessary. Worship and theology are two aspects of the speech of the Church and they must come together. Worship without theology is blind and theology without worship is empty.

With something similar in mind, Aidan Kavanagh delineates a very close relationship between these core aspects of the speech of the Church through a motif of primary and secondary theology.[53] For Kavanagh theology as an academic discipline is theology only in a secondary sense as it follows after and emerges out from the primary theology, which is the experience of the Church in worship. For Kavanagh academic theology as theology in the second sense is the analysis of the primary theology of the Church, which is its worship.[54]

The fundamental thrust of both Schmemann and Kavanagh is very helpful. Theology is the *theology of the Church* and so academic theology makes no sense abstracted from worship. Academic theology is not held in the abstract, as if it could be a purely intellectual exercise disengaged from the central purpose for the renewal of our minds, which is to offer ourselves as living sacrifices to the glory of the Father. Certainly, with Kavanagh, theology needs to be *done* rather than simply assented to. Moreover, the level of intuitive knowledge of God, gathered in the worshiping community, is the irreducible foundation of all theology that is properly theology. The theology of the academy is from the Church and for the Church.

However, there is another point being made here. For Kavanagh, the worship of the Church in its liturgical form is the proper object of theology. The problem, particularly with the way in which Kavanagh's suggestion is constructed, is that rather than overcoming the separation of academic and doxological theology he merely *inverts* the hierarchy. This indicates that, although Kavanagh has rightly identified a symptom, he has misdiagnosed

52. Schmemann, *Introduction to Liturgical Theology*, 10.

53. Kavanagh, *On Liturgical Theology*.

54. Alexander Schmemann employs fundamentally the same definition of liturgical theology as "giving a theological basis to the explanation of worship and the whole liturgical tradition of the Church." Schmemann, *Introduction to Liturgical Theology*, 17.

the problem. Kavanagh casts academic theology as the task of reflecting on the Church's experience of worship. This has the consequence of placing the worshiping life of the Church as the source and norm of all our knowledge of God. This, so far as I can see, is the Achilles Heel of what has become known as liturgical theology in its prioritization of the worship of the community. It can come to a point (although it is not integral to its guiding logic) at which it effectively deploys the liturgy of the Church as the practical (if not theoretical) replacement of Christ as the foundation of our knowledge of God. The problem is not so much a one-upmanship of the academic community over the liturgical community, which can be corrected by inverting that state of affairs. The problem is the decentralizing of Christology from ecclesiology and the separation of the worship of the Church from the person of Jesus Christ, whereby our liturgical formulations can be isolated from their proper ground and analyzed as the ground of theology. This can be addressed by asserting the centrality of the vicarious humanity of Christ and the trinitarian character of worship to what we think of the theology and the worship of the Church.

Building to this point, a better way to delineate the relationship between liturgy and theology is to establish them in a common relationship to a more definitive source. To do this, we can turn to the distinction between God's self-knowledge (*theologia in se* or archetypal theology) and our knowledge of God (*theologia nostra* or ectypal theology). God's own self-knowledge is the primary theology which is the perfect knowledge that God has of himself as Father, Son, and Holy Spirit. This is the ultimate ground of all derivative knowledge of God. Our knowledge of God is the secondary theology which is given to us out of God's gracious self-revelation. Primary theology is not secondary theology for it exists only in the divine life and it is not communicable to us. Secondary theology is that which God has given us to know him. The great importance of this distinction is that it reminds us that God is not trapped in his relations to us for God is quite independent from us and so, therefore, our knowledge of God has a profoundly objective foundation.[55]

Barth employed this fundamental insight in his corresponding distinction between God's self-knowledge and our knowledge of God through his notion of the primary and secondary objectivity of God: God is primarily object to his own knowing and only secondarily and derivatively is he object to our knowing.[56] The terminology of objectivity is helpful because it reminds

---

55. This theme has been explored at length in the superb study by Molnar, *Divine Freedom and the Doctrine of the Immanent Trinity*.

56. Barth, *Church Dogmatics*, 2.1, 16–18.

us that this is still a knowledge in which God is the object but that this has two different modes. There is a primary objectivity in which God is immediately objective to himself and there is a secondary objectivity through which God is truly object to us but through specific mediate objects: "God does not have to be untrue to Himself and deceive us about His real nature in order to become objective to us."[57] We know God revealed in things that are not him, but we do truly know him. Even as God gives himself to be known by us, he remains the Lord of the knowledge of God.

By grace, the primary objectivity of God is lived within the secondary objectivity of humanity through Jesus Christ. God's self-knowledge as the mutual knowing and being known of Son and Father in the joy of the Spirit becomes a human event in Jesus: "All things have been committed to me by my Father. No one knows the Son except the Father, and no one knows the Father except the Son and those to whom the Son chooses to reveal him" (Matt 11:26). Primary theology is the knowledge that the Son has of the Father in the fellowship of the Holy Spirit. In his grace, God makes himself object to us by actualizing this self-knowledge within our human history. What the Church knows and can say about God is given to it by the Son who has actualized the perfect knowledge of God in our human ways of knowing. The voice of the Church in its academic theology and its liturgical worship are given a share in Jesus' knowledge and love of the Father. Neither aspect of the voice of the Church is the source of the other. Both, however, have their source in the knowledge of love of the Father and Son in the unity of the Spirit. This means that, if we are to arrive at a tighter account of the relationship between theology and liturgy, we can only do so by establishing worship upon its proper Christological and trinitarian ground.

The Christological and Trinitarian Ground of Liturgy

Just as the essence and life of the Church is Jesus Christ and his vicarious humanity, so the inner essence of the worship of the Church is the self-offering of Jesus Christ. Torrance has explored this theme in great detail in his seminal essay "The Mind of Christ in Worship: The Problem of Apollinarianism in the Liturgy."[58] Apollinarianism was the fourth-century Christology which held that the divine *Logos* inhabited a human person, effectively displacing the human mind. As such, the divine *Logos* was the center of activity in human flesh. Within Apollinarius's Christology, Jesus did not have a human mind. Instead, God the Son took the outward form

57. Barth, *Church Dogmatics*, 2.1, 16.
58. Torrance, *Theology in Reconciliation*, 139–214.

of humanity as a tool and set aside the human mind. For Apollinarius, the mind is the source of all activity and the human mind has been corrupted by sin, and so if salvation was to take place it would have to be by the replacing of the human mind with the divine *Logos*.

Certainly, such a doctrine would dismantle any substantive view of redemption as the healing penetration of God into the deepest reaches of our humanity. The Apollinarian Jesus is unable to be our representative because he does not share in all we are. It denies Christ a human mind and human agency whereby he is not able to live a human life of love and praise to the Father on our behalf.[59] Torrance argued that such a conception of Jesus Christ lies behind an unsatisfactory understanding of worship. More problematically, the Apollinarian Jesus is not able to actualize within our human minds a real life of worship to the Father.

Torrance traces the implications of Apollinarianism into the liturgy of the Church, in which, he argues, the rug is pulled out from under the feet of ecclesial worship. His concern is with a form of the worship of the Church that does not place at its very center the vicarious self-offering of God the Son as a human as the inner essence of the worship of the Church which we liturgically join ourselves to. A central indication of this, Torrance argues, is when Jesus becomes the *focus* of the praise and worship of the Church to the exclusion of his mediatorial work. Such a focus of worship does not give adequate account to God the Son assuming the totality of our human nature and living from within it a perfect human life of praise which glorifies the Father. The rationale for this as a desire to assert unequivocally the divinity of Jesus is quite understandable but also unnecessary as the Son shares in the glory of the Father.

The problem, though, is that if worship only goes *to* Christ (at the expense of *through* Christ) then it creates a situation in which the vicarious human life of God the Son is pushed further and further into the background. A vacuum is created and the Church rushes in as a substitute to mediate the relationship between humanity and God. In other words, the priesthood of Christ becomes separated from the priesthood of the Church and the worship of the Church becomes orientated to Christ rather than having Christ's worship as its actual content. The connection between the primary priesthood of Jesus and the derivative priesthood of the Church becomes undermined and we are left to rest on ourselves and our own worship. In such a setting, the institutional priesthood ceases to be the means through which the whole body of Christ participate in Jesus' true priesthood and starts instead to be a parallel priesthood. The Church begins to

---

59. Torrance, *Theology in Reconciliation*, 147–48.

get in the way of Jesus Christ rather than being the means through which Jesus unites us with himself and his mediatorial work done for us and as one of us. In this, the fate of the institutional priesthood becomes just like that of the nation of Israel when its liturgical activity became separated from its ground in the act of God. In short, when worship is exclusively offered *to* Jesus rather than *through* Jesus it is a form of prayer that is peculiarly *un-Christian*. Obviously, we worship Jesus Christ as God, but we do so by offering our praise through the Son in the unity of the Spirit to the Father *with* the Son and the Spirit.

For Torrance, we can only have a correct understanding of worship if we take seriously the human mind of Jesus Christ, and so the absolute integrity of the humanity of his self-offering to the Father. Jesus is God as a human acting from the side of God toward humanity and from the side of humanity toward God. This is the inner Christological heart of worship. God the Son became a human just as we are so that he could live the life of perfect faithfulness and self-giving to the Father as one of us and for all of us. Jesus lived the life of God the Son as a human, accomplishing a perfect self-offering to the Father within our humanity by the power of the Spirit. In this way, Jesus Christ does not only fulfill the saving will of God toward humanity, he also fulfills the human response of faithfulness toward God. The prayer and self-offering of Jesus to the Father are a perfect human faithfulness to God actualized in our humanity. However, it is not simply the human response to God, for this is a human response that has as its agent God the Son as a human and from the side of humanity in his perfect faithfulness to the Father. It is this obedience of the Son lived on our behalf once and for all that is the human voice of love and praise which is heard and accepted by the Father.

The fullness of the humanity God the Son assumed into union with himself is crucial. God the Son became just as we are and, from within our human condition, he did not only give us a pattern or example of worship to follow. Instead, he actually accomplished a human worship of the Father on our behalf. If it sounds strange to think of Jesus as God the Son worshiping, then we need to remember that God the Son numbered himself among us and took our side in our relationship to God and accomplished on our behalf all that this entails by his own self-offering to the Father. Just as we are saved through the faithfulness of Jesus, so our worship of the Father is through Jesus' life as the faithful Son. This is what it means to pray through Jesus or in the name of Jesus. Our prayer is heard by the Father through the Son's intercession on our behalf.

Yet, Jesus is also the actual content of our worship. All our worship participates in the real act of worship which was Jesus' offering to the Father through the full course of his life and on the cross. What Jesus offers is his very self in total self-denying love to the glory of the Father. Jesus is the inner essence of all our prayers and worship to God the Father. We come to worship with empty hands, only confessing the self-offering Christ made on our behalf. To join in with Jesus' self-offering is the true charismatic experience of worship. We are baptized into the body of Christ by the Spirit. All Jesus is includes us as his body. So, we share in the human obedience and worship Jesus gave to the Father in the power of the Spirit. As the body of Christ we share together in the Son's priestly and vicarious worship of the Father by the unity of the Holy Spirit. It is by the Spirit that we are united to Jesus and share in all he is and has done toward the Father. We are objectively included in Jesus as his body and share in his worship of the Father as our own. Aside from the unity of the Spirit, we have no share in the vicarious humanity of Jesus and his worship offered on our behalf. However, there is a subjective element to this, also. Jesus is in us by his Spirit enabling us to lift our hearts to the Lord. The Spirit is not only uniting us to Jesus as his body; the Spirit also is Jesus himself come among us such that our lives and activity cannot be clearly differentiated from his (Gal 2:20). The prayer and worship we offer is Christ at work in us by the Spirit causing his own life of self-giving to the Father to echo in us. In other words, our prayer and worship are surrounded from front and back by Jesus Christ in the unity of the Holy Spirit. We are so tightly bound to Jesus as the body of Christ that when we worship, *it is Christ who honors the Father in us.*

In the liturgy, we corporately join our voices in worship that is in accordance with the apostolic gospel. This liturgical worship is not tangential to the Church. Instead, it is where the Church is truly speaking out its very nature as the body of Christ. The reach of liturgy extends far beyond the act of corporate and public prayer. Its true substance is in expressing the Church's true nature as the body of Christ.

> its substance lies in the genuine discovery of worship as the life of the Church, the public act which eternally actualizes the nature of the Church as the body of Christ, an act, moreover, that is not partial, having reference to one function of the Church (her "corporate prayer") or expressing only one of her aspects, but which embraces, expresses, inspires and defines the whole Church, her whole essential nature, her whole life.[60]

The great contribution of Alexander Schmemann was to reverse an improper understanding of the relationship between the Church and its worship. Schmemann observed in his own Orthodox tradition a situation in

---

60. Schmemann, *Introduction to Liturgical Theology*, 14.

which the Church was established as a parallel institution, a "cultic society," that performed worship.[61] The Church, in his view, had come to act as an institution which performed an act of worship, consumed by congregation members as a spiritual experience. This, he argues, emptied the worship of the Church of its true content. Rather than worship being something the Church does, Schmemann argued, worship is integral to what the Church is as the body of Christ. Worship is not a function the Church performs, it is the expression of the real nature of the Church as that which is in union with Christ, participating in his self-offering to the Father.[62] We arrive back where we began with James Torrance: worship is not something the Church does, it is a gift in which the Church is included.

Such a vision of worship, I suggest, cuts across the bows of attitudes to worship in much of the contemporary Protestant Church. We live in a time in the life of the Church where our worship is conducted within an individualistic and experiential mindset. The border between worship services and performances in some Church traditions is becoming ever more blurry. While there is something that is good in this in inspiring the soul and helping us to lift our hearts to the Lord, there is a lot that is problematic, too. Most problematically is that it establishes the Church as an institution which performs an act of worship which is consumed by Churchgoers for their spiritual edification. The Church becomes an *interruption* between Christ and his people rather than the visible manifestation of their invisible union. There is a further level of complication in that the individual becomes complicit in this replacement of Jesus with the cultic society of the Church. With our interiorized concern with spiritual experience, we find that the individual becomes the personal arbiter of their own individual relationship with God. Praise expresses *my* feelings, *my* understanding of the gospel, *my* personal response to God. This generates a solipsist form of worship in which our focus is turned inward and we become concerned with our subjective experience rather than with glorifying God in Christ. The fervor of our spiritual experience becomes the currency by which we can assess the validity of our faith. The problem is that becomes very hard to differentiate agency. We become the personal arbiters of our own personal relationship with God and Jesus, which is not necessarily always orientated to the central fact of the gospel: that Jesus is the one mediator between God and humanity, including at the personal level. Jesus mediates my personal relationship with God as much he mediates the relationship between God and his Church.

61. Schmemann, *Introduction to Liturgical Theology*, 31.
62. Schmemann, *Introduction to Liturgical Theology*, 29.

This does not mean that liturgical worship is a form of panacea which will stop us inserting ourselves between Christ and his Church. After all, Schmemann's principal object of criticism was the liturgical activity of the Church. Certainly, against these excesses, the liturgy of the Church causes us to think and act corporately, the body of Christ giving voice to our praise, united with its head who has offered himself in praise and obedience to the Father. However, it does not do this automatically. The problem comes if we were to follow Kavanagh and accept that theology is the task of analyzing liturgy. If we do that, then the object of our theology becomes the Church itself and we inevitably end up where we came in with the Church inserting itself as an interruption between Christ and his people. If the liturgy of the Church is to serve its purpose, it must be held in a different sort of relationship to theology, in which both are servants of the gospel and help one another in that service.

The task of theology in this connection is to express how in its liturgical worship, the Church is truly being itself.[63] That is to say, the theologian must constantly remind the liturgical community that in its worship it is doing nothing other than speaking as the body of Christ, and this speech is ultimately ascending to the Father through the self-offering of Jesus. Moreover, it is the task of theology, in Karl Barth's sense of the task of dogmatics in relation to the language of the Church,[64] to examine and dialogue with the liturgy of the Church and maintain its substance as the body of Christ at voice. In other words, Schmemann's critique of cultic society and corresponding vision for liturgical theology remind us that the worship of the Church must be integrated with the gospel itself

The Gospel and Liturgy

This whole chapter charts fairly closely to the approach of Michael Ramsey in seeking to establish the visible practices of the Church on the gospel of participation in Christ.[65] With what has been said regarding the worship and thought of the Church grounded in Jesus and the threat of Apollinarianism to what we understand worship to be, the groundwork is in place to articulate a view of liturgy in lock-step with the gospel. Liturgy should be understood as the joining together of the body of Christ with the life of praise and self-offering accomplished by its head.[66]

63. Schmemann, *Introduction to Liturgical Theology*, 17.
64. Barth, *Church Dogmatics*, 1.1, 11–24.
65. Ramsey, *Gospel and the Catholic Church*, 8.
66. See also Jennings, *Liturgy and Theology*, loc. 1159.

Such a view of liturgy is articulated in the document on liturgy emerging from the Second Vatican Council. In a quite remarkable passage, the document gives an account of the liturgy in which Jesus is present in the worship of the Church identifying it with himself and his own self-offering to the Father.

> Christ indeed always associates the Church with Himself in the truly great work of giving perfect praise to God and making [us] holy. The Church is His dearly beloved Bride who calls her Lord, and through Him offers worship to the Eternal Father. Rightly, then, the liturgy is considered as an exercise of the priestly office of Jesus Christ. . . . ; in the liturgy full public worship is performed by the Mystical Body of Jesus Christ, that is, by the Head and His members. From this it follows that every liturgical celebration, because it is an action of Christ the priest and of His Body the Church, is a sacred action surpassing all others.[67]

Liturgy is conceived of as the body of Christ at prayer in unison with its head. The chief agent of liturgical prayer is Jesus himself, and we are joined with him by merit of our incorporation into him and are included in his self-offering to the Father. Gloriously, Christ associates us with him in his priestly work performed as one of us and for all of us. This does not shut us out of the liturgical act. Instead, we see, once again, that there is one offering of praise to the Father and it is the self-offering of Jesus which we participate in via our incorporation into Jesus. This is what it means to offer worship through Jesus. We share in the Son's perfect glorification of the Father. This remarkable vision for liturgical theology so earthed in the vicarious humanity of Jesus Christ and his deep association with us gives a view of the liturgy of the Church in deep complementarity with the gospel.

All of this means that in what we think of liturgy as the Church in its earthly-historical extension at worship needs to be understood with two dimensions: Christological and trinitarian. The actual event that the liturgy of the Church is a participation in is the person and work of Jesus Christ and it is through Jesus that we worship the Father in the unity of the Holy Spirit. In the last chapter we thought about the Church as a sacrament in that it participates in the true sacrament that is Jesus Christ and for this reason it can be an effective sign of God's will to restore all things to union with himself. Liturgy has its place in such an understanding. So far as I can see, this is the only basis upon which ecumenical impasses regarding the liturgy can be resolved. By the respective traditions of the *enhypostatic* aspect of the Church acknowledging their contingence and their anhypostatic

---

67. Paul VI, "Constitution of the Sacred Liturgy (*Sacrosanctum Concilium*)," 141.

dependence on the act of God through Jesus Christ and being willing to be reformed in continuity with Christ.

The core criterion of good liturgy is that it takes seriously the Christological and trinitarian foundations of the worship of the Church. The essence of our worship is Jesus' self-offering to the Father for us and as one of us to which we are joined in the unity of the Holy Spirit. The inestimable value of liturgy is that it reminds us that we participate in Jesus' self-offering to the Father whereby we share in his filial obedience to and glorification of the Father. The worship of the Church should have a clearly discernible trinitarian character. The divine move of grace is from the Father through the Son in the power of the Spirit. Correspondingly, the worship of the Church is through the Son to the Father in the unity of the Holy Spirit. Liturgical prayer should always force us to pray in the format of to the Father through the Son in the unity of the Holy Spirit. Eucharistic liturgy derived from Athanasius: "Jesus Christ our Lord, through whom and with whom, to the Father with the Son himself in the Holy Spirit be honour and power and glory for ever and ever."[68] Here our prayer and worship ascends through and with Jesus' prayer and worship to the Father, but Jesus is also glorified with the Father. This dynamic in which Jesus is both the mediatorial agent through and with whom we worship God the Father in the unity of the Spirit and also the recipient of our worship is a very strong indication of the trinitarian character of liturgical worship. In the worship of the Church we gather together as those united in Christ who also gathers up our worship and prayer and presents it to the Father through his own self-offering. The great strength of liturgical prayer is that it keeps our focus on the Christological and trinitarian ground of the actual event of worship actualized in our humanity through Jesus and does not allow the inner condition of the individual or the mediating role of the Church take center stage.

If the worship of the Church is our participation in Jesus' self-offering then liturgy is powerful because it does not lay the emphasis on us and our subjective spiritual fervor before God. The liturgy of the Church is our corporate participation in Jesus' worship of the Father in which the Church comes before the Father through the self-offering of Jesus and in the power of the Spirit. We offer a sacrifice of praise through the one true sacrifice, which is Jesus Christ. This does not marginalize us as individual worshipers and it does not suggest that our inner states of hearts and minds are of no consequence. Instead, it means that our worship only has its full reality in the worship of Jesus. Our worship is the activity of our passive participation in Jesus. Liturgy enables us to enter into the work of redemption that

68. Athanasius, *On the Incarnation*, 57.

Jesus has won for us. Jesus does not only give us an example for prayer and worship, he gives us its very content. We may well be moved to pray for the sake of Christ or motivated by him and his devotion, and this is all good, but it cannot replace our prayer which self-consciously joins itself to the praise and worship of Jesus. This is the reason for the centrality of liturgical prayer in the life of the Church. It unequivocally corresponds to a distinctively Christian theology of worship as participation in Jesus' vicarious self-offering to the Father.

The Church and the World

The Church has a complex relationship to the world. It is free of the world as its only constitutive relation is its relation to Christ in the power of the Spirit (and so it is not one of the possibilities for creation to bring it into being by its own freedom). However, it is also in the world and it has a unique mission in relation to the world. The Church exists because it is brought into existence by the act of God and it is brought into being with a specific task at its heart, which is to be a witness to the reconciliation of God and his creation through the crucified and risen Christ. As it has been put by a well-known ecumenical document, "the Church is called to proclaim and prefigure the Kingdom of God. It accomplishes this by announcing the gospel to the world and by its very existence as the body of Christ."[69]

Once again, the divine act in bringing the Church into being is the ground of its distinct earthly-historical extension. The Church exists as an act of God which has its own reality as a visible society among other visible societies and it is specifically called to proclaim the gospel of reconciliation to the societies around it. Even though the Church has its life among the other societies, it is apart from them inasmuch as its visible life among other societies is dependent upon an invisible union with Jesus Christ. The Church is both in a necessary relationship to the world and it is free from the world. It is this freedom and necessity that is so important to grasp if we are to see how the Church can be committed to the world in which we have our life without being compromised by it.

Freedom and Necessity

The Church is brought into being by the act of God and is given a distinct existence of its own. The presence of the Church on earth is a result of

69. World Council of Churches, *Baptism, Eucharist and Ministry*, 16.

the miracle of the grace of God. However, that miracle does not make the Church any less part of created reality but is the very condition of its life within the world. At one and the same time, the Church is free from the world, in the sense that it does not depend on the world for its existence (in that the Church did not come into existence through the steady progress of human history), and it is in a necessary relation to the world in that the world is the context in which it lives and that it is inherent to the definition of the Church as apostolic that it is sent out as a witness to the world. As Barth put it, the Church is the "people of God in world-occurrence."[70] The Church has its place as part of world history and has its existence as part of the created cosmos, but it does so as the particular people called out to be the people of God. This curious relationship of freedom and necessity is worth exploring to understand the distinct character of the calling of the Church to be a witness of Christ to the world. The Church is free from the world in a way that no other human society is, but it is inseparable from the world by the context of its existence and the character of its mission. This strange interlocking of freedom and necessity is one reason why the Church is uniquely able to be a compelling voice directed to and shaped in relation to the world in service and love.

Barth introduces this tension as the Church's freedom and dependence. On the side of freedom, the Church did not emerge by the steady progress of human history. The roots of the existence of the Church are not in a human desire for self-transcendence via aesthetics or community, or some other rationale internal to humanity.[71] The Church has been brought into existence in history by an act that came at it from the outside.

> The Christian community exists as it is called into existence, and maintained in existence, by its secret. It exists in this way alone, but in this way truly, indisputably and invincibly. . . . This basis is identical with the will and work of God. Hence it neither needs nor can be established on the part of [humankind] and to this extent it cannot be perceived or explained.[72]

Barth establishes this on the work of Christ in calling and maintaining the Church in existence and the Spirit binding believers to Christ such that the existence of the Church becomes coterminous with the existence of Christ himself,[73] much as was laid out in the previous chapter. The Church, therefore, exists because a new age of God's dealing with the world

70. Barth, *Church Dogmatics*, 4.3.2, 684.

71. Barth, *Church Dogmatics*, 4.3.2, 751.

72. Barth, *Church Dogmatics*, 4.3.2, 752.

73. Barth, *Church Dogmatics*, 4.3.2, 752–62.

has been inaugurated, which looks forward to the fulfillment of what has begun. Both of these elements (its radical contingence and its apocalyptic character) are expressed in the Eucharist. At the Eucharist we strengthen and renew our union with Christ as the body of which he is the head, recognizing that the Church exists because of the act of God in Christ and yet we also recognize that the Eucharist is for this period only. Christ will return and there will not be any need of a sacrament of unity, for the communion of Christ and his body will be perfected. In both having existence by the act of God and its eschatological orientation, the Church is free from the world inasmuch as it does not depend on it for its existence and it does not operate toward the same teleological end.

However, while it is something that has struck human history from the outside and is markedly out of step with the world moving towards a determined end, the Church is also inseparable from the human history into which it has come as an interruption. The first element of this is Christological. Barth's argumentation builds upon his intersection of creation and covenant explored earlier. Barth notes that "in [Christ] the covenant between God and [humankind] has not merely been kept by God and broken by [humankind], but kept by both, so that it is the fulfilled covenant."[74] Jesus is "the new reality of world history";[75] he is the one in whom the rationale for creation as the covenant partner of God is actualized, overcoming the apparent dichotomy between creation and the will of God. The Church, as that which participates in Christ, shares in his reality as the perfect covenant partner of God and so as the new reality of the world, inviting the society around it to share this reality. This thought will be picked up below in contrast to the more polemical vision of John Milbank.

The second element of this is that the Church has the world as the context for its existence. That the Church has its life in world history means that it cannot be considered apart from this relationship. However, the Church has not been brought about by the immanent processes of world history, but by the intervention of God, and so Barth describes the Church's relation to the world as instantly one of freedom and dependence.

> The Christian community, as one people among others and yet also as this people i.e., the people of God, exists in total dependence on its environment and yet also in total freedom in relation to it. Neither its dependence nor its freedom are partial; they are both total. . . . By dependent we mean that for all its freedom it is bound to it, orientated to it, determined and

74. Barth, *Church Dogmatics*, 4.3.2, 712.
75. Barth, *Church Dogmatics*, 4.3.2, 712.

conditioned by it. And by free we mean that for all its dependence it is sovereign in relation to it, having its own law, and
therefore its own will and power.[76]

For Barth, we need to keep both elements of freedom and dependence
in our mind when we are thinking about the relationship between the Church
and the world. However, the notion of "dependence" is a little one-sided in
that it only focuses on the aspect that the Church must have its existence in
the world. Necessity is a better descriptor because it defines the Church as
in a necessary relation to the world, which includes both its dependence on
the world as its context for existence and also the missiological imperative
placed on the Church, to go out to the world as a witness of Christ. The third
element of Barth's delineation of the relationship between the Church and
the world is that the Church is entrusted with being a witness to Christ to
call the whole world to participate in the very reason for its existence, which
is the covenant between God and creation fulfilled in Jesus. One way to put
this tension between freedom and necessity is that the Church does not exist
because of the world (the true ground of the Church's existence is Christ) but
it does exist *in* the world and *for* the world. The interplay of freedom and
necessity means that the Church is defined along two vectors: the act of God
and the ministry that is entrusted to it.

These two vectors converge in the eschatological identity of the
Church. The Church, brought into existence by the direct act of God, is
commissioned to bear the message of the gospel before the inauguration
of the age to come. For this reason, the Church is in a necessary relation to
the world. To use the language of the marks of the Church, its catholicity
(understood as universal relevance) is grounded in its apostolicity, as the
community sent by Christ. As we think about the Church and its relationship to the world, we cannot allow one pole to become separated from the
other. The freedom of the Church cannot be isolated from its necessary
relation to the world because this ignores that the Church has its life in the
world and is called to witness to the world. Likewise, we cannot think of
the necessary relation between the Church and the world in isolation from
the freedom of the Church, for then the Church will become assimilated to
the world in which it lives, come to resemble it in thought and action. Instead, we have to try to hold these two poles in a creative tension. If we can
manage that, the Church will be in the world as a revolutionary, disrupting
the history of human life with a message that strikes the ear, offends the
sensibilities, but which cannot be ignored.

76. Barth, *Church Dogmatics*, 4.3.2, 734–35.

The Church Uncovers the World

The Church only has existence because we have been joined to Christ as his body. This sharing in Christ means a sharing in his mission as his witnesses. This means that the unity of the Church with Jesus is complemented by the necessity of the relation of the Church to the world. The Church is at one and the same time grounded in Jesus and earthed in the world. Our understanding of what the Church is, therefore, must include its outward orientation to the world in which it has its Christ-centered existence.

There are, of course, different formats that this relation to the world might take. On the one hand, there is the antithetical (even *antagonistic*) approach of John Milbank.[77] Milbank's distinctive view on the relationship between the Church and the world is directly related to his broader theological project. For Milbank, creation appears to be divided into two orders of being that are the opposite of one another. On the one hand, there is secularity which is human life that has closed itself off from God and is characterized only by human agency. This is what Milbank describes as a way of being in violence.[78] On the other hand, there is the Church, which is human life that is open to God in which human society is ordered in accordance with God's will. This is what Milbank describes as a way of being in peace.[79] At work here is Milbank's fundamental theological project, which is to contest the validity of the idea of the "secular." For Milbank, nothing in creation can legitimately separate itself from God's purpose. The idea of the secular as a morally and theologically neutral space is an illusion. It is not possible to be in a neutral position in relation to God. You can turn away from God in disobedience but this, Milbank contests, is not morally neutral. If you turn away from the source of goodness, you are turned instead towards the absence of good, toward evil and toward violence. The secular, for Milbank, is, therefore, the world turned away from God and turned inwards in self-love and violence.[80]

From such a foundation, Milbank articulates a view of the Church set over and against the world. The Church is a reconciled community by our common inclusion in the body of Christ.[81] At the heart of this is the Eucharist, for it is in the Eucharist that the Church's participation in the divine

---

77. For a fuller discussion of John Milbank's ecclesiology, see MacDougall, *More than Communion*, 101–40.

78. Milbank, *Theology and Social Theory*, 392.

79. Milbank, *Theology and Social Theory*, 392.

80. Milbank, *Theology and Social Theory*, 393.

81. Milbank, *Being Reconciled*, 103.

communion of love is both expressed and realized. It is in a society that participates in the divine way of being, which is love, that difference can be accommodated into a higher unity of love. For Milbank, then, the Church stands over and against the world as a communion of peace in the context of a society of violence. The Church is a refuge from the world. More than that, the Church for Milbank has an almost imperialistic purpose. Rather than announcing the gospel, pointing away from itself to Jesus, Milbank conceives of the Church as charged with the purpose of being the normative human society which is to bring the world beyond it into accordance with itself: "The point of the Church is the assembly of humanity as such in order that it might govern itself by love. Once one has this 'Church' idea, no other basis for human society can be regarded as fully legitimate."[82] The secular society, therefore, is rendered illegitimate by the Church and to become a true society it must become synonymous with the Church itself.[83]

Barth, on the other hand, offers an approach that is not characterized by antithesis. Certainly, Barth recognizes along with Milbank a tension between the confusion of humankind (*hominum confusione*) and the rule of God (*Dei providentia*).[84] The Church has its place within human history, that is to say, "the confusion continually caused by [humanity]."[85] The Church, therefore, exists as the community ruled by the word of God alongside the confused activity of others around them.

> *Confusio* undoubtedly denotes something very questionable and indeed wholly evil. It opens up a vista of folly and wickedness, of deception and injustice, of blood and tears. But it does not pronounce any absolute sentence of rejection. . . . It simply says . . . that [humanity] make and shape and achieve confusion.[86]

The history of humanity within which the Church has its life is, therefore, "the history of the man who has fallen away from God and fallen out with his neighbour and himself."[87] Premeditating Milbank to some extent, Barth questions whether this necessitates the Church standing in tension against the world.

82. Milbank, *Future of Love*, 273.

83. Milbank, *Future of Love*, xi–xv, 216. On this point, see the criticism of Milbank by Christopher McMahon. McMahon, "Theology and the Redemptive Mission of the Church," 781–94.

84. Barth, *Church Dogmatics*, 4.3.2, 693–700.

85. Barth, *Church Dogmatics*, 4.3.2, 698.

86. Barth, *Church Dogmatics*, 4.3.2, 695.

87. Barth, *Church Dogmatics*, 4.3.2, 698.

The Christian community would then have to accept the fact of being forced to exist, in relation to its environment, in an irrevocable tension or dialectic of faith in God's unconditional overlordship as commanded and authorised by the Word of which underlies it and its knowledge of human confusion which is unavoidable in the light of the same Word. . . . It would have to look to the seriously and definitively certain factor of its goal and meaning on the one side, yet also to all kinds of less certain actualisations of good and better which may perhaps be perceived or deduced here and there in the midst of human confusion. Is it really the case, however, that this must be the existence of the people of God within the world occurrence around it?[88]

Barth articulates a more positive approach in which the people of God in world-occurrence recognizes and attests to the fact that God has turned to the fragile world in redemptive love and so stands "under the gracious address of God."[89] The tension is resolved not through Hegelian synthesis, but through the alteration of the human condition, through assuming it into union with God the Son's own incarnate and redemptive life.[90]

The event indicated by the name of Jesus Christ and identical with His person is that the true Son of God, of one essence with the Father, has in this One assumed humanity and very concretely this humanity, to unity with Himself, that He not only became one with it and adopted its creaturely nature but took to Himself its whole sin as though He had committed it and were its Author, that in His death He bore it away instead, thus achieving in its place the obedience to the Father which the humanity of the first Adam had refused and still refuses. The reconciliation of the world with God, the justification and sanctification of [humankind], of all [humankind] before Him and for Him, the cutting off of human confusion at its root, the restoration of order in world-occurrence, is thus the event in question, the work and Word of Jesus Christ. The Christian community hears this Word, sees this work and knows this person as it hears and sees and knows the One whose call is the basis and meaning of its own existence. Hence what it perceives in this One is not merely an illumination of world history but its correction and reformation.[91]

---

88. Barth, *Church Dogmatics*, 4.3.2, 702.

89. Barth, *Church Dogmatics*, 4.3.2, 709.

90. Barth, *Church Dogmatics*, 4.3.2, 710–11.

91. Barth, *Church Dogmatics*, 4.3.2, 711–12.

As indicated above, Barth parses this in covenantal terms (Christ is the fulfillment of the covenant, both from the side of God and from the side of humanity). Creation, as a reality inseparable from covenant, now is relative to Christ, who is the fulfillment of the rationale of creation: "in Jesus Christ we do really have the new reality of world history."[92]

The Church, therefore, exists in the context of the reconciliation of human confusion and the rule of God in the person of Christ. The Church is the people of God in the world and it has a unique vocation to the world to be a witness to the act of God to reconcile the world to himself through Jesus Christ.[93] Barth is clear, however, that the double aspect of world history as human confusion and the rule of God is not yet ultimately resolved. There is an eschatological character to this resolution; rather what has changed is that to the Christian community, it "loses the appearance of autonomy and finality, the character of irreconcilable contradiction and antithesis, which it always seems to have at first glance."[94] This eschatological resolution is the coming of the Kingdom, for which we pray.[95] Quite unlike Milbank, then, the world and the Church are not conceived of dualistically. Instead, the world is included in the very essence of the Church as sent out to the world to attest to God's redemptive love. This means that the Church is in a necessary relation to the world by merit of its very nature as apostolic. For Barth, then, the Church does not exist over and above the world but it exists *within the world as a servant to the world*. The character of its service is to point beyond itself to Christ in whom the contradiction of human confusion and the rule of God is overcome by a revolution in the human situation, where, in Christ, humanity has accomplished its *telos* as the perfect covenant partner of God.[96]

While the Christological and missiological nature of the Church means that the Church cannot be separated from the world, this does not mean that the Church becomes submerged into the world. Instead, the Church stands as a mirror to the world, *uncovering* it in its contingence. Both the Church and the world share a common relation of dependence upon the act of God. They are different, however, in that the Church knows what it is, articulating it in its gospel message and very structures of being. As the world looks on the Church, like Dorian Grey seeing his portrait, it sees its own mortality and contingence. One reason that the world hates the

---

92. Barth, *Church Dogmatics*, 4.3.2, 712.

93. Barth, *Church Dogmatics*, 4. 3.2, 681–83. This discussion is informed significantly by Bender's work, *Karl Barth's Christological Ecclesiology*, esp. 225–67.

94. Barth, *Church Dogmatics*, 4.3.2, 713.

95. Barth, *Church Dogmatics*, 4.3.2, 715–22.

96. Barth, *Church Dogmatics*, 4.3.2, 719–20.

Church is because the Church reminds the world that it is created and that it is moving towards an end point.

Paul speaks of Jesus as the center of the universe in connection with Jesus as the head of the Church. For Paul, Jesus Christ is the one through whom all things were made, the one in whom all things hold together *and* he is the head of the Church (Col 1:15–18). Christ is both the agent of creation whose agency in relation to creation causes its delicate order to be maintained and he is the Lord of the Church around whom the people of God are gathered and from whom they take their life. There is an equivalence of relationship (formally if not materially) to Christ that is shared by the cosmos in general and the Church in particular. This is the affinity of the Church and the world which binds them together. Both the world and the Church have Jesus their centers, providing each with their existence and their meaning. The difference, however, is that the Church is conscious of that dependence and organizes its life in the light of it. The Church, in short, is positively related to it and to the eschaton. The Church is a sign to the world of its own contingence and dependence on the grace of God in Jesus Christ and it goes to the world bearing the message of God's kindness through the Son. The urgency of the Church's message is that the return of Christ will bring about the separation of humanity at which those not united to Jesus will lose him as that which holds it together. It is at that point that all hell will break loose, demonic flashes of which we have seen in human history.

Even though the Church is in a necessary relation to the world, it knows more explicitly than does creation the mystery of why something exists rather than nothing and the truth of reality disclosed in Jesus Christ. This is at the core of Barth's notion of the Church as that which uncovers the world.

> the true community of Jesus Christ is (1) the fellowship in which it is given to [humanity] to know the world as it is. The world does not know itself. It does not know God, nor [humankind], nor the relationship and covenant between God and [humankind]. Hence it does not know its own origin, state nor goal. . . . It is blind to its own reality. Its existence is a groping in the dark. The community of Jesus Christ exists for and is sent into the world in the first basic sense that it is given to it, in its knowledge of God and [humanity] and the covenant set up between them, to know the world as it is. We may well say that, itself belonging also to the world, is the point in the world where its eyes are opened to itself and an end is put to its ignorance

about itself. It is the point in the world where the world may know itself in truth and reality.[97]

By its way of being, the Church expresses its own inner basis of existence. In celebrating communion and expounding the Scriptures, the Church lives out before the world its knowledge that it exists only by the act of God in the Son in the unity of the Spirit. The Church knows itself to be the covenant partner of God by its inclusion into the Son. In living this out, the Church presents to the world the world's own reason for being and its own status as the covenant partner of the Father, as yet unreconciled. The world exists as that which is made as the counterpart of God to enjoy being the creature of a loving Creator. However, the world does not know that this is what it is. The world is not able to understand itself. The Church, though, is normative over the rest of the created order because the central meaning of the history of the world is Jesus Christ, the true covenant partner of God, and the Church participates in him. The Church offers its witness to Christ and the world must respond to the Church's message if, that is, it is not to suffer the tragedy of not understanding itself.

The Church lives self-consciously by the incarnation, cross, and resurrection through which Jesus united himself to us so that we might be united to him and so is deeply aware of its contingency and dependence on grace. Because of this, the Church is a revolutionary agent in relation to the world. The world in its efforts for self-perpetuation embodies a way of being that is discontinuous with its inner essence as created. The world is as dependent on the grace of God for its existence as the Church, but it does not live self-consciously in that dependence. The Church, though, uncovers the world as contingent and orientated toward an end point. This is why the world hates the Church. Nobody likes the person who shows us where and how we are confused. The Church shows to the world its own contingence and the ambiguity of the dislocation that exists between its basis of existence and its way of existing. In addition to this, the Church is an eschatological community. It waits for the new situation of creation that is real in Christ to replace the human confusion that currently persists.

In this eschatological hope, the Church shows to the world that the proper response of the creature is dependence and gratitude and calls it to repent from the downward call of *sarx* to the covenantal life of *sōma*, the body of Christ. This is utterly unconscionable to the world and so the Church is hated as a sign of contingence, mortality, and creaturehood; a traitor of independent humanity, which would rather define its own *telos*. However, the Church can only serve the world by being the Church. We can only go on confessing and

97. Barth, *Church Dogmatics*, 4.3.2, 769.

celebrating the mystery of God the Creator and Redeemer in word and sacrament and allow our very mode of existence in the world to uncover the world in its own contingence and dependence.

This is why the designation of the body of Christ is so important to the Church's relation to the world. It is *not* that the Church is the earthly-historical form of the existence of Jesus. Instead, it is that as the body of Christ, the Church presents something to the rest of creation of what it is to be a creature. As the body of Christ, the Church has life because of its incorporation into Jesus. It is distinct from Jesus as the body is distinct from the head but cannot have that life in anything other than dependence and gratitude. The Church, therefore, has its life with the logic of creation written deep and clear into it. Moreover, the Church displays in its liturgical and ordered life the human response of dependence on the act of God in Jesus. The visible life of the Church, particularly in the Eucharist and the exposition of Scripture, corresponds to its internal ground of being via inclusion into Jesus.

The body of Christ is also of significance in the question of the relation of the Church and the world because it is by our inclusion into the risen and perfected Jesus Christ that the power of the age to come is operative now in the Church elevating our humanity to an ever more pure expression. In this Milbank's ecclesiology of opposition has something to commend it. As the Church is the body of Christ, the Church is united to the one who is more fully human than anyone who has ever lived. He is the perfect covenant partner of God. In being united to Christ, we become more human, too. Jesus is therefore the humanizing human. Through being joined to Jesus, we are restored to full humanity as we are cleansed from our sins and delivered from the power of sin and death to be restored as the image of God, expressed in our relations with God and with one another. We participate in Christ who ascended to the Father as fully God and fully human. The full humanity of the ascended Lord, Jesus Christ, is a prophylactic against the Church ever being seen as an inhuman institution or an entity in which the final goal is the escape of the human body. We need to be very careful of the Church as a mystical or spiritual society. It is not. It is a human society that should rejoice in the fullness of humanity and be the context in which full human expression and life can have sway. To enter the Church, therefore, is not to depart from humanity. It is instead to engage in the full restoration of our creatureliness which had been impaired by sin. Coming into the Church does not mean that our creaturely nature is moved beyond. Instead, it means that our creaturehood is being fully substantiated as we enter the proper creature-Creator relation. God in his goodness does not overwhelm creation but actually his grace gives it the context to truly and fully exist. At the core of the community that is the Church is the fact that God the Son assumed our humanity. The incarnation does not deny humanity, it is the ultimate affirmation of humanity. In the same way, the Church as the body of Christ must be a joyous affirmation of humanity in which the full fabric of human life is to be celebrated. The artist, the thinker, the musician must all find their capacity for full expression in the Church because the Church is (and should act as) a shout of joy in what it is to be a human being.

The Church *for* the World

That the Church displays to the world its very contingence and tells the world things about itself that the world would know in no other way, this does not mean that the Church relates to the world from a position of supremacy. The Church does not exist over and against the world, but *for* the world. The Church relates to the world in the pattern of Jesus who did not come to be served but to serve. Because the Church is dependent on Jesus for its existence and shares in the mission of Jesus to the world the Church exists for the world *and to be in service to the world*. The Church exists for the world because it has been entrusted a mission by Christ in relation to the world. Just as Christ was sent by the Father in the power of the Spirit to reconcile the world to himself, so Christ sends the Church in the power of the Spirit as the apostolic community giving witness to Christ. The missionary activity of the Church is integral to a definition of the Church, as apostolic and catholic. As the Church engages in the missionary task that has been given to it, it becomes more and more what it is as the body of Christ.

The nature and the mission of the Church (i.e., what the Church is and what the Church does) cannot be separated from one another. The Church is the apostolic community that has been sent out by Christ to the whole world: "the true community of Jesus Christ is the community which God has sent out into the world in and with its foundation. As such it exists for the world."[98] The foundation of the Church's existence for the world is not within itself. Instead, Barth identifies this as a statement of faith, derivative from the self-giving of God to the world through Jesus Christ in the power of the Spirit.[99] To be united in Jesus as his body, therefore, is to be included in his mission to the world: "it would not exist in the reality established by Him if it were not prepared to exist in this commitment to the world."[100] This does not mean that the Church's mission to be for

98. Barth, *Church Dogmatics*, 4.3.2, 768.

99. Barth, *Church Dogmatics*, 4.3.2, 786.

100. Barth, *Church Dogmatics*, 4.3.2, 789.

the world is a response to God's act and nor is it the continuation or the repetition of Christ's work of reconciliation. Instead, the Church is the means through which Christ continues his ministry of reconciliation in the power of the Spirit. The Church, therefore, knows "that its confession of Jesus Christ as the distinctive action for which it is empowered by the Holy Spirit can only be, in all its human and natural spontaneity, a grateful response to the fact that first and supremely Jesus Christ has confessed it, does confess it, and will continually do so."[101] The mission of the Church is derivative and not constitutive. The Church is to give its witness to the reconciling love of God through Jesus Christ, through which Jesus continues to draw people to himself in the fellowship of the Holy Spirit. The mission of the Church to the world is inseparable from the work of Jesus because it has no other content than giving witness to the gospel. Although inseparable, it must not be confused with the work of Jesus. Once again, we have to think of one reality which the Church and Jesus relate to in different ways. There is one work of reconciliation, and Jesus relates to the work of reconciliation as the active agent and the Church relate to it as the passive recipient who act as witnesses to what we have received. This is the centrality of the proclamation of the apostolic gospel to the Church. The Church's responsibility to the world is to point toward the history of God's actions on creation through Christ and in the Spirit by which he has reconciled humanity to himself. In other words, the task of the Church is the proclamation and the explanation of the gospel.[102]

The Church, therefore, is that through which the gospel of reconciliation which is accomplished in Christ is testified to the world. The Church, in this way, is established as sharing in Jesus' ministry of service and itself becomes a servant to the world by proclaiming the gospel. This is the essence of what it means to say that the Church is for the world. The ways in which the Church does this might change over time but the core of what it is doing must not change, if the Church is to be faithful to its mission. Despite the unchanging centrality of the gospel to the mission of the Church the Church cannot ignore the character of the societies it lives alongside. No servant can serve without being cognizant of the needs and wants of the one they serve. As servant, then, the Church is conditioned by the world inasmuch as the world is the context for and the recipient of the Church's witness to Jesus. In other words, the impact of the world on the Church is for the purpose of the Church being a witness to the world. The history of the world has an impact on the history of the Church because the Church must announce the gospel

101. Barth, *Church Dogmatics*, 4.3.2, 790.
102. Barth, *Church Dogmatics*, 4.3.2, 844–46.

to each changing generation. It is precisely because the Church is a servant bearing a message that Küng's balancing act between continuity and change is so effective. The Church must remain permanently established upon its roots and, yet, this apostolic continuity includes within it change whereby the gospel may be proclaimed to each changing generation.[103] The Church only has existence by its origins in Jesus Christ. Likewise, the mission of the Church cannot be separated from the apostolic gospel. The Church as witness does not have the capacity to change or adapt the inner logic of the gospel. We do not confess anything other than the faith we received from the apostles through the Scriptures and the sacraments. However, as a human institution that continues across generations, the Church must be prepared to change in order to truly be a witness of Christ *to the world*. The Church must confess its faith in such a way that the message of the gospel is truly heard by the world to which it is sent. So, we should not speak of returning the Church of the New Testament believers, because this is to reject the very features of apostolicity and catholicity which are so crucial to the mission of the Church: the apostolic gospel must be proclaimed across time and space so that the universal significance of Christ to each person might be recognized. The gospel needs to be retranslated and reapplied to each new generation and each new people group while its inner message remains intact. To return to a first-century mode of Christianity is not only reductive (and quite possibly impossible, within a critically realist perspective); the attempt to do so is antithetical to the mission Christ gave his Church.

The dialectic of freedom and necessity articulated in the terms of catholicity and apostolicity can help us find our way through this. The universal relevance of the Church is not predicated upon whatever new method of evangelism or fresh expression of the Church we might have devised (however well-grounded in the reality of the Church these might be). The universal relevance of the Church is nothing other than the universal relevance of the gospel, which is itself inseparable from Jesus Christ. It would be self-defeating in the extreme to surrender any aspect of the gospel in order to be more conducive to the modes of thought of any given society. The necessity of the Church to the world cannot be engaged with by surrendering its freedom, but rather by the celebration of its freedom. Certainly, the gospel needs to be translated into the modes of thought around us, but it cannot be tempered or accommodated to it. To do that would be to undermine the very thing that the Church can offer to the world and which the world needs to hear: Jesus Christ, incarnate, crucified, and resurrected.

103. Küng, *Church*, 15–24.

There is a need to find a middle road between the Church becoming shaped by the surrounding culture on the one side and retreating from the surrounding culture on the other. On the first way, the Church would become indistinguishable from the other human societies among whom we live and on the second the Church would not be faithful to its mission of proclaiming the gospel *to the world*. There may be any number of ways that the Church presents the gospel and if the Church is to be faithful to its commission to witness to Christ throughout the world then there should be a huge variety of ways the gospel is proclaimed. But while the modes of presentation are contingent upon the condition of the world to which proclamation is made, the gospel itself remains uncompromised. This is the right posture for the Church that stands in solidarity with the world, loves the world, and serves the world in the way we can: "Silver and gold I do not have, but what I do have I give to you. In the name of Jesus Christ of Nazareth, walk."

Bibliography

Afanasiev, Nikolay N. "Una Sancta." In *Tradition Alive: On the Church and the Christian Life in Our Time*, edited by Michael Plekon, 3–30. Lanham, MD: Rowman and Littlefield, 2003.

Anatolios, Khaled. *Retrieving Nicea: The Development and Meaning of Trinitarian Doctrine*. Grand Rapids: Baker Academic, 2011.

Aquinas, Thomas. *The Summa Contra Gentiles*. Translated by the English Dominican Fathers. London: Aeterna, 2014.

———. *Summa Theologiæ*. Vol. 2, *Prima Pars, Q. 65–119: Treatise on the Work of the Six Days; Treatise on Man; Treatise on the Conservation and Government of Creatures*. Michigan: Novantiqua, 2009.

Athanasius. *Four Discourses Against the Arians*. Fig Classic Series. N.p., 2014. Kindle ed.

———. *On the Incarnation of the Word of God*. Translated by A. Robertson. N.p.: Skyros, 2015. Kindle ed.

———. *On the Synods*. Fig Classic Series. N.p., 2013. Kindle ed.

Augustine. *The City of God*. Translated by H. Bettenson. Harmondsworth, UK: Penguin, 1972.

———. *The Confessions of Saint Augustine*. Translated by A. C. Outler. Louisville: Westminster John Knox, 2004.

———. *Letters*. Vol. 1, *Letters 1–82*. Translated by W. Parsons. Washington, DC: Catholic University of America Press, 1951.

———. *The Literal Meaning of Genesis*. Translated by J. H. Taylor. New York: Paulist, 1982.

Avis, Paul. "Baptism and the Journey of Christian Initiation." In *Drenched in Grace: Essays in Baptismal Ecclesiology Inspired by the Work and Ministry of Louis Weil*, edited by L. Larson-Miller and W. Knowles, 50–63. Eugene, OR: Pickwick, 2013.

———. "Is Baptism 'Complete Sacramental Initiation'?" *Theology* 111 (2008) 163–69.

———. "The Revision of the Ordinal in the Church of England 1550–2005." *Ecclesiology* 1 (2005) 95–110.

Badcock, Gary D. *Light of Truth and Love: A Theology of the Holy Spirit*. Grand Rapids: Eerdmans, 1998.

Barth, Karl. *Church Dogmatics*. Translated by T. F. Torrance et al. Edited by Geoffrey W. Bromiley et al. 13 vols. Edinburgh: T. & T. Clark, 1956–75. (German edition: Die kirchliche Dogmatik. 1932–67.)

———. *The Humanity of God*. Translated by T. Wiesler and J. N. Thomas. Richmond: John Knox, 1998.

Basil. "On the Holy Spirit." In *Letters and Select Works: Nicene and Post-Nicene Fathers of the Christian Church*. Translated by P. Schaff and H. Wace. Grand Rapids: Eerdmans, 1983.

Behr, John. "The Trinitarian Being of the Church." In *The Holy Trinity in the Life of the Church*, edited by K. Anatolios, 165–82. Grand Rapids: Baker Academic, 2014.

Bender, Kimlyn J. *Karl Barth's Christological Ecclesiology*. Eugene, OR: Cascade, 2013.

Berkouwer, Gerrit C. *The Church*. Grand Rapids: Eerdmans, 1976.

Berlin, Isaiah. *Four Essays on Liberty*. Oxford: Oxford University Press, 1969.

Billings, J. Todd. *Calvin, Participation, and the Gift: The Activity of Believers in Union with Christ*. Oxford: Oxford University Press, 2008.

Bird, Michael. *Jesus the Eternal Son: Answering Adoptionist Christology*. Grand Rapids: Eerdmans, 2017.

Boff, Leonardo. *Faith on the Edge: Religion and Marginalized Existence*. Translated by R. R. Barr. San Francisco: Harper & Row, 1989.

The Book of Common Prayer and Holy Bible. Cambridge: Cambridge University Press, 2012.

Buber, Martin. *I and Thou*. Translated by R. G. Smith. Edinburgh: T. & T. Clark, 1937.

Calvin, John. *Calvin's Commentaries*. Vol. 17, *Harmony of the Evangelists, Matthew, Mark and Luke and Holy Gospel of Jesus Christ According to John*. Translated by W. Pringle. Grand Rapids: Baker, 2005.

———. *Calvin's Commentaries*. Vol. 21, *Galatians, Ephesians, Philippians, Colossians, Thessalonians, Timothy, Titus, Philemon*. Translated by W. Pringle. Grand Rapids: Baker, 2005.

———. *Calvin's Commentaries*. Vol. 22, *Hebrews, Catholic Epistles*. Translated by W. Pringle. Grand Rapids: Baker, 2005.

———. *Institutes of the Christian Religion*. Edited by J. T. McNeill. Translated by F. L. Battles. Philadelphia: Westminster, 1960.

Canlis, Julie. *Calvin's Ladder: A Spiritual Theology of Ascent*. Grand Rapids: Eerdmans, 2010. Kindle ed.

Catechism of the Catholic Church. London: Chapman, 1994.

"The Church as Communion: Second Anglican-Roman Catholic International Commission." https://www.anglicancommunion.org/media/105242/ARCIC_II_The_Church_as_Communion.pdf.

Coakley, Sarah. "'Persons' in the 'Social' Doctrine of the Trinity: A Critique of Current Analytic Discussion." In *The Trinity: An Interdisciplinary Symposium on the Trinity*, edited by S. T. Davis et al., 123–44. Oxford: Oxford University Press, 1999.

Common Worship: Ordination Services: Study Edition. London: Church House Publishing, 2007.

Cyprian. "Epistles." In *The Writings of Cyprian: The Ante-Nicene Library*, edited by by A. Roberts and J. Donaldson and translated by R. E. Wallis, 8:1–331. Edinburgh: T. & T. Clark, 1868.

———. "On the Unity of the Church." In *The Writings of Cyprian: The Ante-Nicene Library*, edited by by A. Roberts and J. Donaldson and translated by R. E. Wallis, 8:337–97. Edinburgh: T. & T. Clark, 1868.

Cyril. *The Catechetical Lectures of St. Cyril of Jerusalem*. N.p.: Veritatis Splendor, 2014. Kindle ed.

Daly, Mary. *Beyond God the Father: Toward a Philosophy of Women's Liberation*. Boston: Beacon, 1993.

Davison, Andrew. *Why Sacraments?* London: SPCK, 2013.

Dumbrell, William. *The Faith of Israel: A Theological Survey of the Old Testament*. Grand Rapids: Baker Academic, 2002.

Dunn, James D. *Theology of Paul the Apostle*. London: T. & T. Clark, 1998.

Fiddes, Paul S. *Participating in God: A Pastoral Doctrine of the Trinity*. London: Darton, Longman & Todd, 2000.

Florovsky, Georges V. "The Concept of Creation in Saint Athanasius." In *Aspects of Church History*, 39–62. Collected Works of Georges Florovsky 4. Belmont, MA: Nordland, 1972.

———. "Creation and Creaturehood." In *Creation and Redemption*, 43–78. Collected Works of Georges Florovsky 3. Belmont, MA: Nordland, 1976.

Forsyth, Peter T. *The Church and the Sacraments*. 1947. Reprint, Eugene, OR: Wipf & Stock, 1996.

Fretheim, Terrence E. *God and World in the Old Testament: A Relational Theology of Creation*. Nashville: Abingdon, 2005.

Gibson, Paul, ed. *Anglican Ordination Rites: The Berkeley Statement "To Equip the Saints." Findings of the Sixth International Anglican Liturgical Consultation, Berkeley, California, 2001*. Grove Worship Series W 168. Cambridge: Grove, 2002.

Gregory of Nazianzus. "Select Orations." In *Nicene and Post-Nicene Fathers of the Christian Church: St Cyril of Jerusalem and St Gregory Nazianzen*, edited by P. Schaff and H. Wace, 7:203–435. New York: Christian Literature, 1893.

Grenz, Stanley J. *Rediscovering the Triune God: The Trinity in Contemporary Theology*. Minneapolis: Fortress, 2004.

Gunton, Colin E. "The Church on Earth: The Roots of Community." In *On Being the Church*, edited by C. E. Gunton and D. Hardy, 48–80. Edinburgh: T. & T. Clark, 1989.

———. *The One, the Three and the Many: The Bampton Lectures*. Cambridge: Cambridge University Press, 2008.

———. *The Promise of Trinitarian Theology*. Edinburgh: T. & T. Clark, 1991.

———. "The Trinity, Augustine and the Theological Crisis of the West." *Scottish Journal of Theology* 43.1 (1990) 33–58.

———. *The Triune Creator: A Historical and Systematic Study*. Grand Rapids: Eerdmans, 1998.

———. "Two Dogmas Revisited: Edward Irving's Christology." *Scottish Journal of Theology* 41.4 (1988) 359–76.

Hart, Trevor. "Humankind in Christ and Christ in Humankind: Salvation as Participation in our Substitute in the Theology of John Calvin." *Scottish Journal of Theology* 42.1 (1989) 67–84.

Hawking, Stephen W. *A Brief History of Time*. New York: Bantham, 1988.

Heschel, Abraham J. *The Prophets*. New York: Harper & Row, 1982.

Hill, Wesley. *Paul and the Trinity: Persons, Relations, and the Pauline Letters*. Grand Rapids: Eerdmans, 2015.

Holmes, Stephen R. *Listening to the Past: The Place of Tradition in Theology*. Grand Rapids: Baker Academic, 2002.

Hunsinger, George. "The Dimension of Depth: Thomas F. Torrance on the Sacraments of Baptism and the Lord's Supper." *Scottish Journal of Theology* 54.2 (2001) 155–76.

Ignatius of Antioch. *The Epistle of St. Ignatius*. Translated by J. H. Strawley. London: SPCK, 1919.

Irenaeus. *The Ante-Nicene Christian Library: Translations of the Writings of the Fathers Down to A.D. 325*. Vol. 5, *The Writings of Irenaeus, Vol. 1: Against Heresies*, Translated by A. Roberts and W. H. Rambaut. Edinburgh: T. & T. Clark, 1868.

Irving, Alexander J. D. "Baptismal Ecclesiology and the Current Ordination Rites of the Church of England." *The Churchman* 133.3 (2019) 203–24.

———. "Fr Georges Florovsky and T. F. Torrance on the Doctrine of Creation." *St Vladimir's Theological Quarterly* 61 (2017) 301–22.

———. "The Person of Jesus Christ as the Normative Basis for the Doctrine of Creation: Re-Envisioning T. F. Torrance's Christocentric Doctrine of Creation." *Evangelical Quarterly* 88 (2017) 349–66.

Jacob, Edmund. *Theology of the Old Testament*. Translated by A. W. Heathcote and P. J. Allcok. London: Hodder & Stoughton, 1958.

Jennings, Nathan G. *Liturgy and Theology: Economy and Reality*. Eugene, OR: Cascade, 2017. Kindle ed.

Kavanagh, Aiden. *On Liturgical Theology*. Collegeville, MN: Liturgical, 1992.

Kelly, John N. D. *Early Christian Doctrines*. London: Black, 1958.

Kierkegaard, Søren. *Training in Christianity and the Edifying Discourse which "Accompanied" It*. Translated by W. Lowrie. Oxford: Oxford University Press, 1941.

Küng, Hans. *The Church*. Tunbridge Wells: Search Press, 1968.

LaCugna, Catherine M. *God for Us: The Trinity and Christian Life*. San Francisco: HarperSanFrancisco, 1973.

Locke, John. *Essay Concerning Human Understanding*. Indianapolis: Hackett, 1996.

Lubac, Henri de. *Corpus Mysticum: The Eucharist and the Church in the Middle Ages*. Translated by G. Simmonds et al. Notre Dame: University of Notre Dame Press, 2006.

———. *The Mystery of the Supernatural*. Translated by R. Sheed. New York: Herder & Herder, 1967.

MacDougall, Scott. *More than Communion: Imagining an Eschatological Communion*. London: Bloomsbury T. & T. Clark, 2015.

Macmurray, John. *Persons in Relation*. London: Faber & Faber, 1961.

———. *The Self as Agent*. London: Faber & Faber, 1957.

Macquarrie, John. *A Guide to the Sacraments*. London: SCM, 1997.

———. *Principles of Christian Theology*. Rev. ed. London: SCM, 1977.

Maloney, Raymond. "Henri de Lubac on the Church and Eucharist." *Irish Theological Quarterly* 70 (2005) 331–42.

McFadyen, Alistair. *The Call to Personhood: A Christian Theory of the Individual in Social Relations*. Cambridge: Cambridge University Press, 1990.

McFarland, Ian. "Personhood and the Problem of the Other." *Scottish Journal of Theology* 54 (2001) 204–20.

McFarlane, Graham. *Why Do You Believe What You Believe about Jesus?* Carlisle, UK: Paternoster, 2000.

McLaren, Brian D. *The Great Spiritual Migration: How the World's Largest Religion Is Seeking a Better Way to Be a Christian*. New York: Convergent, 2017.

McMahon, Christopher. "Theology and the Redemptive Mission of the Church: A Catholic Response to Milbank's Challenge." *Heythrop Journal* 51 (2010) 781–94.

McPartlan, Paul. "The Body of Christ and the Ecumenical Potential of the Eucharist." *Ecclesiology* 6 (2010) 148–65.

———. *The Eucharist Makes the Church: Henri de Lubac and John Zizioulas in Dialogue.* 2nd ed. Fairfax, VA: Eastern Christian Publications, 2006.

McSwain, Robert, ed. *Scripture, Metaphysics and Poetry: Austin Farrer's "The Glass of Vision" with Critical Commentary.* Farnham, UK: Ashgate, 2013.

Meyers, Ruth A. *Continuing the Reformation: Re-visioning Baptism in the Episcopal Church.* New York: Church Publishing, 1997.

Milbank, John. *Being Reconciled: Ontology and Pardon.* London: Routledge, 2003.

———. *The Future of Love: Essays in Political Theology.* Eugene, OR: Cascade, 2009.

———. *Theology and Social Theory: Beyond Secular Reason.* 2nd ed. Malden, MA: Blackwell, 2006.

Molnar, Paul D. *Divine Freedom and the Doctrine of the Immanent Trinity: In Dialogue with Karl Barth and Contemporary Theology.* 2nd ed. London: Bloomsbury T. & T. Clark, 2017.

Moltmann, Jürgen. *Theology and Joy.* London: SCM, 1973.

———. *The Trinity and the Kingdom of God: The Doctrine of God.* London: SCM, 1980

The Nature and Mission of the Church: A Stage on the Way to a Common Statement. Faith and Order Paper 198. Geneva: World Council of Churches, 2005.

The Nature and Purpose of the Church: A Stage on the Way to a Common Statement. Faith and Order Paper 181. Geneva: World Council of Churches, 1998.

Neuman, Charles W. "Mary and the Church: *Lumen Gentium*, Arts. 60 to 65." *Marian Studies* 37 (1986) 96–142.

Paul VI, Pope. "Constitution of the Sacred Liturgy (*Sacrosanctum Concilium*)." In *The Documents of Vatican Two: All Sixteen Official Texts Promulgated by the Ecumenical Council 1963–1965*, edited by W. M. Abbott, 137–78. London: Chapman, 1963.

———. "Dogmatic Constitution on the Church (*Lumen Gentium*)." In *The Documents of Vatican Two: All Sixteen Official Texts Promulgated by the Ecumenical Council 1963–1965*, edited by W. M. Abbot and translated by J. Gallagher, 14–101. London: Chapman, 1963.

Plantinga, Cornelius, Jr. "Gregory of Nyssa and the Social Analogy of the Trinity." *The Thomist* 50 (1986) 325–52.

Rahner, Karl. *The Trinity.* Translated by J. Doceel. London: Burns & Oates, 1970.

Ramsey, Arthur Michael. *The Gospel and the Catholic Church.* London: Longmans, Green, 1936.

Ratzinger, Joseph. *Church, Ecumenism and Politics.* New York: Crossroad, 1989.

———. *God Is Near Us.* San Francisco: Ignatius, 2003.

———. "Letter to the Bishops of the Catholic Church on Some Aspects of the Church Understood as Communion." http://www.vatican.va/roman_curia/congregations/cfaith/documents/rc_con_cfaith_doc_28051992_communionis-notio_en.html.

———. "The Theological Locus of Ecclesial Movements." *Communio* 25 (1998) 480–504.

Robinson, John A. *The Body: A Study in Pauline Theology.* London: SCM, 1952.

Rohr, Richard. *The Divine Dance: The Trinity and Your Transformation.* New Kensington: Whitaker, 2016.

Root, Andrew. *The Pastor in a Secular Age: Ministry to People Who No Longer Need a God.* Grand Rapids: Baker Academic, 2019.

Ruether, Rosemary Radford. *Religion and Sexism: Images of Women in the Jewish and Christian Traditions*. New York: Simon & Schuster, 1974.

———. *Sexism and God-Talk*. Boston: Beacon, 1993.

Sanders, Ed Parish. *Paul and Palestinian Judaism*. Minneapolis: Fortress, 1977.

Schillebeeckx, Edward C. *Christ the Sacrament of Encounter with God*. London: Sheed & Ward, 1963.

Schmemann, Alexander. *Introduction to Liturgical Theology*. Translated by A. E. Moorehouse. Crestwood, NY: St. Vladimir's Seminary Press, 1966.

Schwöbel, Christoph. "The Creature of the Word: Recovering the Ecclesiology of the Reformers." In *On the Being of the Church. Essays on the Christian Community*, edited by C. E. Gunton and D. W. Hardy, 110–45. Edinburgh: T. & T. Clark, 1989.

———. "God, Creation and the Christian Community: The Dogmatic Basis of a Christian Ethic of Createdness." In *The Doctrine of Creation: Essays in Dogmatics, History and Philosophy*, edited by C. E. Gunton, 149–76. London: T. & T. Clark, 1997.

Slater, Jonathan. "Salvation as Participation in the Humanity of the Mediator in Calvin's *Institutes of the Christian Religion*: A Reply to Carl Mosser." *Scottish Journal of Theology* 58 (2005) 39–58.

Smail, Thomas A. *The Giving Gift: The Holy Spirit in Person*. London: Hodder & Stoughton, 1988.

Suchocki, Marjorie H. "Introduction." In *Trinity in Process: A Relational Theology of God*, edited J. A. Bracken and M. H. Suchocki, vii–xiii. New York: Continuum, 1997.

Tanner, Kathryn. *God and Creation in Christian Theology: Tyranny or Empowerment?* Minneapolis: Fortress, 1988.

Thielicke, Helmut. *The Evangelical Faith*. Vol. 1, *Prolegomena: The Relation of Theology to Modern Thought-Forms*. Translated by G. W. Bromiley. Edinburgh: T. & T. Clark, 1997.

Thornton, Lionel S. *The Common Life in the Body of Christ*. London: Dacre, 1941.

Torrance, Alan. *Persons in Communion: An Essay on Trinitarian Description and Human Participation with Special Reference to Volume One of Karl Barth's "Church Dogmatics."* Edinburgh: T. & T. Clark, 1996.

Torrance, James. *Worship, Community and the Triune God of Grace*. Downers Grove, IL: IVP Academic, 1996.

Torrance, Thomas F. *Atonement: The Person and Work of Christ*. Edited by R. Walker. Downers Grove, IL: IVP Academic, 2009.

———. *The Christian Doctrine of God: One Being Three Persons*. London: Bloomsbury T. & T. Clark, 2016.

———. *Conflict and Agreement in the Church*. Vol. 1, *Order and Disorder*. London: Lutterworth, 1959.

———. *Divine and Contingent Order*. Edinburgh: T. & T. Clark, 1981.

———. *Incarnation: The Person and Life of Christ*. Edited by R. Walker. Downers Grove, IL: IVP Academic, 2008.

———. *The Mediation of Christ*. Colorado Springs: Helmers & Howard, 1992.

———. *Royal Priesthood*. Edinburgh: Oliver & Boyd, 1955.

———. *Theological Science*. Edinburgh: T. & T. Clark, 1996.

———. *Theology in Reconciliation: Essays towards Evangelical and Catholic Unity in East and West*. London: Chapman, 1975.

————. *Theology in Reconstruction*. London: SCM, 1965.

————. *The Trinitarian Faith: The Evangelical Theology of the Ancient Church.* Edinburgh: T. & T. Clark, 1988.

Towards a Common Understanding of the Church: Reformed/Roman Catholic International Dialogue: Second Phase, 1984–1990. Geneva: World Alliance of Reformed Churches, 1991.

Trible, Phyllis. *God and the Rhetoric of Sexuality*. Minneapolis: Fortress, 1978.

Vogel, Walter. *God's Universal Covenant: A Biblical Study*. Ottawa: University of Ottawa Press, 1979.

Volf, Miroslav. *After Our Likeness: The Church as the Image of the Trinity*. Grand Rapids: Eerdmans, 1998.

Vorgrimler, Herbert. *Sacramental Theology*. Translated by L. M. Maloney. Collegeville, MN: Liturgical, 1992.

Webster, John. *Barth*. London: Continuum, 2000.

————. "Trinity and Creation." *International Journal of Systematic Theology* 12 (2010) 4–19.

Wells, Samuel. *A Future That's Bigger than the Past: Catalysing Kingdom Communities.* Norwich, UK: Canterbury, 2019.

Williams, Rowan D. *Christ: The Heart of Creation*. London: Bloomsbury, 2018.

————. "The Church as Sacrament." *International Journal for the Study of the Christian Church* 11 (2011) 116–22.

————. *Eucharistic Sacrifice: The Roots of a Metaphor*. Cambridge: Grove, 1982.

————. "Foreword." In *Communion and Otherness: Further Studies in Personhood and the Church*, edited by P. McPartlan, xi–xii. Crestwood, NY: St. Vladimir's Seminary Press, 1985.

————. "On Being Creatures." In *On Christian Theology*, 63–78. Oxford: Blackwell, 2000.

————. *Resurrection: Interpreting the Easter Gospel*. London: Darton, Longman & Todd, 2003.

————. "Sacraments of the New Society." In *On Christian Theology*, 209–21. Oxford: Blackwell, 2000.

World Council of Churches. *Baptism, Eucharist and Ministry*. Faith and Order Paper 149. Geneva: World Council of Churches, 1982.

Wright, Christopher. *Old Testament Ethics for the People of God*. Nottingham, UK: InterVarsity, 2004.

Wright, Nicholas T. *What Saint Paul Really Said*. London: Lion, 1997.

Yocum, John. *Ecclesial Mediation in Karl Barth*. Aldershot, UK: Ashgate, 2004.

Young, Frances. *God's Presence: A Contemporary Recapitulation of Early Christianity*. Cambridge: Cambridge University Press, 2013.

Zizioulas, John. *Being as Communion: Studies in Personhood and the Church*. London: Darton, Longman & Todd, 1985.

————. "The Church as Communion." *Saint Vladimir's Theological Quarterly* 38 (1994) 7–19.

————. *The One and the Many: Studies on God, Man, the Church, and the World Today.* Alhambra: Sebastian, 2010.

Index

Made in the USA
Las Vegas, NV
28 February 2022

44772574R00146